ENVIRONMENTAL CRIME

The Criminal
Justice
System's
Role in
Protecting the
Environment

Yingyi Situ

David Emmons

Sage Publications, Inc.
International Educational and Professional Publisher
Thousand Oaks ■ London ■ New Delhi

For information:

Sage Publications, Inc.
2455 Teller Road
Thousand Oaks, California 91320
E-mail: order@sagepub.com

Sage Publications Ltd.
6 Bonhill Street
London EC2A 4PU
United Kingdom

Sage Publications India Pvt. Ltd.
M-32 Market
Greater Kailash I
New Delhi 110 048 India

Printed in the United States of America

Library of Congress Cataloging-in-Publication Data

Situ, Yingyi.
  Environmental crime: The criminal justice system's role in protecting the environment / by Yingyi Situ and David Emmons.
      p. cm.
  Includes bibliographical references and index.
  ISBN 0-7619-0036-5 (cloth: acid-free paper)
  ISBN 0-7619-0037-3 (pbk.: acid-free paper)
  1. Environmental law—United States—Criminal provisions.
 2. Offenses against the environment—United States.
 I. Emmons, David, 1940- II. Title.
  KF3775 .S549 2000
  345.73′0242—dc21   99-6583

00   01   02   03   04   05   7   6   5   4   3   2   1

Acquiring Editor:	Kassie Gavrilis
Editorial Assistant:	Anna Howland
Production Editor:	Denise Santoyo
Editorial Assistant:	Karen Wiley
Typesetter/Designer:	Marion Warren

For Peter, Charles, and Justin

and

Molly

Contents

Preface   xiii

1. INTRODUCTION   1

Approaches to Defining Crime   1
A Definition of Environmental Crime   3
The Extent of the Environmental Crisis   4
    Toxic Waste   5
    Pollution Violators   5
    Water Quality   6
    Air Pollution   6
Impacts of the Environmental Crisis   7
    Human Impact   7
    Economic Impact   8
    Social and Psychological Impact   9
Public Opinion and the Environmental Crisis   9
Criminal Justice and the Environmental Crisis   11
    Congress   11
    The Executive Branch   12
    Courts   13
    State Governments   14
    Summary   15
Emerging Legal Issues   15
    The Erosion of Mens Rea   15
    Prosecutorial Discretion   16
    Search and Seizure   16

Preview   17
Review Questions   17

2. CRIMINAL LAW AND THE ENVIRONMENT   19

Understanding Criminal Law   19
   Social Control   20
   Social Engineering   20
   The Differences Between Civil and Criminal Law   21
The Development of Environmental Law   22
An Overview of Key Environmental Criminal Laws   24
   Resource Conservation and Recovery Act   24
   Clean Air Act   25
   Toxic Substances Control Act   25
   Federal Water Pollution Control Act and Amendments   26
   Safe Drinking Water Act   27
   Federal Insecticide, Fungicide, and Rodenticide Act   27
   Comprehensive Environmental Response,
      Compensation, and Liability Act   28
   Refuse Act   29
   Summary   30
Liability in Environmental Crime   30
   Knowing Offenses   31
   Negligent Violations   32
   Endangerment   33
   Noncompliance With Permits, Self-Reporting,
      Inspection, and Fees   34
   Summary   37
Civil and Other Criminal Sanctions   38
Environmental Criminal Law at the State Level   39
   The Role of the States   39
   State Variations   41
Key Legal Issues: Is Justice Strained?   43
Review Questions   44

3. CORPORATE ENVIRONMENTAL CRIME   45

Corporate Environmental Crime Defined   45
An Overview of Industrial Pollution   47

Toxic Dumping as a Corporate Way of Life:
    The Hooker Chemical Case 50
Hazards in the Workplace 53
Environmental Pollution in the Developing World 55
Explaining Corporate Environmental Crime 59
  Motivation 60
  Opportunity 62
  Law Enforcement 65
Conclusion 67
Review Questions 68

4. ORGANIZED CRIME AGAINST
THE ENVIRONMENT *69*

Organized Crime Defined 69
Organized Crime and Hazardous Waste 70
Hazardous Waste Offenses as Group Crime 74
  Group Crime 75
  Interfirm Connections 76
  Organized Crime in New Jersey 77
Explaining Organized Environmental Crime 78
  Anomie 78
  Differential Association 78
  Cultural Transmission 79
  Social Control 80
Review Questions 82

5. ENVIRONMENTAL CRIME
BY THE GOVERNMENT *83*

Governmental Crime Against the Environment Defined 83
Crimes of Commission 86
  Nuclear Testing by the Atomic Energy Commission 86
  Disposal of Hazardous Waste by the Military 87
  Environmental Damage During Wartime Military
    Operations 89
  The U.S. Department of Energy and Federal Weapons
    Production Facilities 91
  Deforestation by the U.S. Forest Service 94

Crimes of Omission	96
The Departments of Energy and Defense at Weapons Production Facilities and Military Bases	97
The Environmental Protection Agency	99
The Government's Role in the Love Canal Disaster	103
Explaining Environmental Crime by the Government	105
Goal Attainment	106
Legal Doctrine	107
Institutional Capability to Enforce the Law	109
Review Questions	112

6. PERSONAL ENVIRONMENTAL CRIME	**113**
Personal Environmental Crime Defined	113
Key Characteristics	113
Types of Personal Environmental Crime	114
The Criminological Heritage	115
Personal Environmental Crime in New Jersey	116
Methodology	116
Types of Environmental Offenses	117
Prosecution of Personal Environmental Offenses	117
The Offenders	118
Explanations of Personal Environmental Crime	118
Review Questions	120

7. COMBATING ENVIRONMENTAL CRIME: ENFORCEMENT	**123**
Environmental Law Enforcement at the Federal Level	124
Environmental Law Enforcement at the State Level	126
Jurisdiction	127
Perceived Roles	127
Personnel	127
Facilities and Equipment	128
Training	128
Levels of Activity	128
Environmental Law Enforcement at the Local Level	129
Approaches to Investigation	130
Reactive Investigation	130
Proactive Investigation	132

Training for Law Enforcement 134
Methods of Obtaining Evidence 136
Regulatory Agencies and Enforcement Issues 140
The Importance of Interagency Cooperation 140
Obstacles to Interagency Cooperation 142
Approaches to Interagency Cooperation 143
Review Questions 145

8. *COMBATING ENVIRONMENTAL CRIME. PROSECUTION* 147

Criminal Prosecution at the Federal Level 147
Criminal Prosecution at the State Level 150
Criminal Prosecution at the Local Level 152
Environmental Criminal Liability 154
The Scope of Corporate Criminal Liability 154
The Scope of Individual Criminal Liability 157
Prosecutorial Discretion: Civil Versus Criminal Charging 161
Introduction 161
The Lack of a Central Review System 163
The Absence of Clear Guidelines 163
Weak Culpability 166
Attitudinal Obstacles 168
The Problem of Parallel Proceedings 169
Criminal Sanctions and Their Effects 171
Criminal Sanctions and Their Problems 171
Sentencing Guidelines and Their Impacts 172
Preventing Environmental Crime 174
Review Questions 175

9. *THE GLOBAL ENVIRONMENTAL CRISIS* 177

Features of the Global Environmental Crisis 178
Global Warming 178
Air Pollution 178
Water Pollution 179
Acid Rain 180
Toxic Waste Dumping 181
International Environmental Law 182
A Brief History of International Environmental Law 182

The Nature and Problems of International
    Environmental Law   183
Environmental Control Around the Globe   184
    The European Community   184
    Air Quality   185
    Marine Protection   185
    Reducing Acid Rain   186
    Control of Waste Trading   186
A Realistic View of Protecting the Global Environment   186
Fighting Environmental Crime in Other Nations   187
    Great Britain   187
    Australia   188
    China   189
Conclusion   191
Review Questions   192

References   193
    Court Cases   208
    Statutes   209

Index   210

About the Authors   218

Preface

This book is both a text and a reference work for the emerging field of environmental crime—violations of environmental law which are subject to criminal prosecution and punishment. Most environmental offenses are processed by regulatory agencies and corrected by civil and administrative remedies. But the most important environmental legislation, enacted during the first bloom of the environmental movement in the 1970s, always contained some criminal sanctions for the worst offenses. The "criminalization" of environmental wrongs grew in the 1980s and 1990s, a trend we believe will continue. This book charts the new mission of criminal justice in controlling the environment. It examines the nature and causes of four types of environmental crime and reviews the criminal justice system's role in combating them.

This book fills an empty space at the boundaries between criminal justice, criminology, law, and environmental studies. We are both faculty members in the criminal justice program at Richard Stockton College of New Jersey. In 1992, Dr. Emmons designed an undergraduate curricular track in environmental crime. Dr. Situ joined the program to supervise the track and teach its core course on environmental crime. She quickly discovered there were no texts in the field, although other institutions were beginning to offer similar courses. So she proposed we write this book. Our motto has been: If you don't find the book you want, make the book you need. Our hope is that we have "made" a useful and enduring text for a wider audience.

We wish to extend our thanks to our many faculty colleagues, to Dr. David Carr, Vice President for Academic Affairs, and to Dr. Vera King Farris, President of Richard Stockton College of New Jersey, whose encouragement and support were instrumental to the success of this project. A special thanks goes to the college committees for Distinguished Faculty Fellowships and for Research and Professional Development. Their support to Dr. Situ helped make this book possible. Dr. Situ wishes to express her love for her parents, who gave her the confidence and ability to accomplish this project. Dr. Emmons wishes to express his love for his parents, whose continuing support and example have been an inspiration. Finally, we appreciate the constructive comments of three anonymous reviewers. By adopting most of their suggestions, we have written a better book.

YINGYI SITU
DAVID EMMONS

CHAPTER 1

Introduction

We and our environment are at risk. Air, water, and soil pollution; hazardous waste disposal; global warming; acid rain; and reduction of the ozone layer threaten the natural environment and endanger people's health.

Researchers have documented these disturbing trends with accelerating alarm, at least since the publication in 1962 of Rachel Carson's *Silent Spring*. Government and industry heeded the environmental movement's call in the early 1970s and began with uncertain commitment and only partial success to slow further damage to the environment and to repair the worst damage already done. Administrative regulations and technology have been the chief weapons in these efforts.

Since the late 1980s, however, the procedures and perspectives of criminal justice have been applied to the environmental crisis. Environmental violations have been defined as crimes, and violators viewed as criminals; criminal prosecution of the accused and criminal sanctions against the convicted have accelerated. We are witnessing for the first time the criminalization of environmental wrongdoing. This book examines this new development.

Approaches to Defining Crime

The human assault on the natural environment reaches back to prehistory when our predecessors first burned wood for food, warmth, and light. But the first serious human threat to the environment and public health arose from the Industrial Revolution. Industry began to consume enormous quantities of hydrocarbon fuels and manufacture a vast array of products from raw materials, leaving in their wake hazardous waste and pollution. Although the Industrial Revolution created modern civilization, it became capable of destroying that civilization (Gore, 1993).

Until the 1970s, in the United States, the prevailing view held that the environmental harm from industrial production was the unavoidable price for economic progress. As this view was challenged with increasing frequency in the 1970s and 1980s, the perception grew that damages to the environment and individuals were not inevitable costs but punishable crimes. If pollution and hazardous waste were controllable, then corporations and persons could be held responsible for their offending behavior—and some of this misbehavior could be considered crime. If disasters were not natural "acts of God" but human catastrophes, then the persons who make them may be committing crimes. The enormity of such highly publicized man-made catastrophes as Love Canal has only deepened this view.

This shift in perspective illustrates the key assertion of labeling theory: that an act is not criminal by virtue of its inherent quality but by virtue of definitions assigned to it by culture and society. These definitions can change over time, as the government's shifting view of drug use demonstrates. Opium, morphine, and other mind-altering drugs were legally available in the early 1900s to consumers. Growing concern about addiction led in 1914 to passage of the Harrison Act, designed to regulate the domestic use, sale, and transfer of opium and coca products. The Marijuana Tax Act of 1937 placed a prohibitive tax of $100 an ounce on the drug. Not until the 1970s, however, did a law—the Drug Abuse Prevention, Treatment, and Rehabilitation Act (1972)—define drug abuse as a crime and prescribe criminal sanctions.

Although all societies have a concept of murder, few share the same one. The killing of a spouse's lover by her enraged husband is murder in some societies but not even an indictable offense in others. Killing in a war may be celebrated as heroism, whereas the same killing at home may be condemned as mass murder. The question of what constitutes crime, then, does not yield straightforward answers. Criminologists are divided into two schools on this question: the strict legalist perspective and the social legalist perspective.

The strict legalist perspective emphasizes that crime is whatever the criminal code says it is. Many works in criminology define crime as behavior that is prohibited by the criminal code and criminals as persons who have behaved in some way prohibited by the criminal law (Schmalleger, 1995). Thus, crime is self-evident in the sense that the criminal code defines it. The strict legalist perspective on crime can be traced to a fundamental principle of English common law of the 12th century: *nullum crime sine lege, nulla poena sine lege* (no crime without law, no punishment without law).

The social legalist perspective argues that some acts, especially by corporations, may not violate the criminal law yet are so violent in their expression or harmful in their effects to merit definition as crimes. This view originates with Edwin Sutherland, a leading theorist of modern criminology, and is shared by many contemporary advocates (Clinard & Yeager, 1980; Frank & Lynch, 1992; Lynch, 1990; Reiman, 1979). Sutherland (1940) observed in his classic study on white-collar crime that the harmful acts of large U.S. corporations were often treated as mere regulatory violations or civil offenses. They carried neither criminal stigma nor the typical sanction of imprisonment. Sutherland attributed this exemption to the ability of the corporate elite and their powerful allies to turn the spotlight of criminal law away from their misdeeds. He advocated a much stronger role for criminal justice in the adjudication of corporate wrongdoing.

These perspectives are more complementary than conflicting. The social legalist approach focuses on the construction of crime definitions by various segments of society and the political process by which some gain ascendancy, becoming embodied in the law. The strict legalist approach, without denying this dynamic, emphasizes these final legal definitions of crime as the starting point of any analysis because they bind and guide the justice system in its work. This book adopts the strict legalist approach, for the most part, because our chief interest is in analyzing the growing number of environmental offenses that are being defined as crimes by the legal system and in assessing the effectiveness of criminal justice techniques in environmental protection.

A Definition of Environmental Crime

We adopt the following definition in this book: An environmental crime is an unauthorized act or omission that violates the law and is therefore subject to criminal prosecution and criminal sanctions. This offense harms or endangers people's physical safety or health as well as the environment itself. It serves the interests of either organizations—typically corporations—or individuals. This definition stresses three features of environmental crime.

First, environmental crime violates existing environmental laws. Behavior, however egregious or offensive, that does not violate the law is not crime. Environmental crime, in other words, is the creation of environmental law. For instance, hazardous waste dumping was not prohibited until enactment of the federal Resource Conservation and Recovery Act of 1976. This environmental law defined the act of hazardous waste dumping as a felony, subject to a maximum fine of $50,000 and/or 5 years of imprisonment.

Second, environmental crime has two real victims—people and the environment—whereas the victims of street crime are usually persons. Moreover, when one street crime occurs, generally one victim at that moment is produced. An environmental crime, in contrast, typically has many victims—sometimes the population of an entire region. Their victimization may also be gradual and silent, going undetected for years. The environment that is victim is often public property (e.g., a state park) or resources on which there is no private claim (e.g., the air), whereas the property that street crime harms is usually private.

Third, although corporations are the chief environmental offenders, other organizations (e.g., criminal combines or government agencies) as well as individuals can also commit environmental crimes. For example, organized crime has infiltrated the waste disposal industry and illegally dumped hazardous contaminants. Local governments have shipped solid waste to prohibited sites. Individuals have contributed to the destruction of protected forests and wildlife. Vendors have sold contaminated meat and seafood to the public.

The Extent of the Environmental Crisis

Criminal justice's role in environmental regulation expands as the environmental crisis grows. The crisis is both the context and stimulus for heightened interest in criminal justice remedies. Consequently, the scope of the crisis merits review before examining how the criminal justice system may—or may not—help abate the crisis.

Charting the extent of the crisis is not easy. The illegal disposal of hazardous waste illustrates the difficulties. Estimates of the number of hazardous waste sites range from 4,000 to 50,000 (Day, 1989; Rosenbaum, 1991). Consensus is also lacking on the amount of hazardous waste generated annually. Although several widely cited studies from the mid-1980s claim that the United States produces 245 to 275 million metric tons per year, these figures are subject to dispute (Gourlay, 1992; McCarthy & Reisch, 1987). No single definition of hazardous waste prevails. Problems persist in identifying the universe of hazardous waste generators and treatment, storage, and disposal facilities (McCarthy & Reisch, 1987). Although the crisis cannot be quantified with precision, its broad dimensions can be sketched. We focus here on selected indicators that point to a surge in environmental crime.

Toxic Waste

Toxic emissions by U.S. industry, largely unchecked, pose the most serious current threat to the environment. Underreporting and the absence of data from small firms make official estimates suspect. The reported level of 10 million tons per year may be underestimated by a factor of 20 (Commoner, 1990).

Pollution Violators

The U.S. Environmental Protection Agency, Office of Solid Waste and Emergency Response, reported in 1990 that 211,000 industrial generators of hazardous waste were in violation of the Resource Conservation and Recovery Act, a ninefold increase over the number in 1980. Most of this noncompliance, several studies suggest, may lie with small-quantity generators (SQGs). As many as half of New Jersey SQGs, for example, have failed to use required hazardous waste manifests, whereas in the San Francisco Bay area, 57% of SQGs illegally disposed of at least some of their hazardous waste (Russell & Meiorin, 1985). A survey of SQGs in 42 Florida counties revealed that they illegally disposed of approximately half their waste (Schwartz et al., 1987). Thus, although precise national figures on the extent of illegal handling and disposal of hazardous waste are unknown, surveys of scattered sites suggest that illegal practices are not unusual. Indeed, according to one estimate, one of every seven firms generating toxic wastes may have illegally dumped during the first half of the 1980s, to cite one period (Meier, 1985).

Water Quality

About half of the U.S. population (97% in rural areas) relies on underground sources of water—groundwater—for drinking and other personal uses. Today, landfill and chemical storage leaks, hazardous waste, and fertilizer runoff are contaminating underground aquifers. For example, a 1982 U.S. Environmental Protection Agency (EPA) survey found 45% of large public water systems supplied by underground aquifers to be contaminated with organic chemicals. In New Jersey, every major aquifer is compromised by chemical pollutants. In California, pesticides contaminate the drinking water of more than 1 million residents. Underground aquifers near almost all the nation's nuclear fuel plants have been contaminated by radioactivity (Null, 1990). According to one estimate, it would take 3,000 years, starting tomorrow, for pollutants to bleed out of Long Island's water table, the region's only source of freshwater (Day, 1989). Day comments, "As New York has some of the strongest legislation in America to control water pollution, it is frightening to imagine what the water pollution rate must be in less well-protected industrial areas" (p. 239).

Air Pollution

Air pollution has become a growing threat to the nation's health and welfare because of the ever increasing emission of contaminants into the atmosphere. Nationwide emissions of carbon monoxide reached 109 million tons in 1992 (Erickson, 1992). In the 1970s, in contrast, cleaner air seemed one of the few, albeit partial, victories in the war to save the environment. The decade began with passage of the Clean Air Act (1970). Other, tougher standards on particulate emissions were enacted at the state and local levels. Emission control devices became standard issue on cars and smokestacks across America. But 60% of the U.S. population lived in areas in which air quality failed the standards set by the Clean Air Act, and the air inversions of the summer of 1988 reminded the nation that "the air has been so bad that it again needs a warning label: caution, breathing may be hazardous to your health," as one science writer put it (Begley, 1988, p. 47). She notes,

Seventy-six cities registered ozone readings at least 25 percent above EPA's limit of 120 parts per billion. Atlanta has topped the standard 21 times, New

York 27 times. In July, 1988, Chicago suffered its first "yellow alert" in a decade: Illinois EPA asked 34 industries to shut down some operations for the day to keep the air breathable. New England's ozone levels are almost triple those of 1986. . . . Seventy-five million urbanites live where ozone regularly exceeds federal limits and 41.4 million live where carbon monoxide (CO) is too high. (p. 48)

Impacts of the Environmental Crisis

Human Impact

The environmental crisis causes substantially more illness, injury, and death than street crime does. Polluted water is the single greatest cause of human illness and death through disease (Day, 1989). Almost half of Americans regularly consume tainted drinking water. Countless toxic agents threaten water safety. Many specialize in their victims. Lead, a common and highly toxic pollutant, is especially dangerous to children and pregnant women; it can delay growth in babies and cause mental impairment in children. Lead also poses risks of nerve system damage, hearing loss, anemia, and kidney damage. The U.S. Centers for Disease Control and Prevention estimate that 10.4 million children have been exposed to excess amounts of lead in their drinking water (Null, 1990). Pollutants in water have also been linked to cancer. The Council on Environmental Quality (1981) concludes that the widespread practice of chlorinating public drinking water appears to have increased the risk of gastrointestinal cancer through an individual's lifetime by 50% to 100%.

In the United States, approximately 53,000 persons a year die prematurely of lung ailments brought on by air pollution. Air pollution caused by toxic agents in the workplace annually kills about 100,000 workers and results in 400,000 cases of disease (Nelkin & Brown, 1984). A somewhat overlapping estimate is that particulate emissions kill 100,000 persons annually, about one and a quarter times the number of U.S. soldiers killed in battle in each year of World War II (DiSilvestro, 1991). Cancer death rates are highest in areas close to petrochemical plants, steel mills, and metal refineries (Berry, 1988; Whelan, 1985). New Jersey, to cite the worst example, harbors the country's highest mortality rates from cancer—up to two and a half times above normal in the counties with the heaviest levels of petro-chemical waste (Morton, 1990).

Solid waste dumps pose threats of miscarriage, birth defects, cancer, chromosome damage, skin rashes, headaches, nervous disorders, and other ailments to residents who live in their vicinity. These dangers were etched on public consciousness by the environmental catastrophe at Love Canal in Niagara Falls, New York, where Hooker Chemical and Plastics Company had disposed of 27,000 tons of toxic waste. The dump site and surrounding area were developed into suburban tract housing in the 1950s. By 1976, residents had endured a variety of calamities. After several years of unusually heavy rains, the water table rose, leaving house foundations awash with chemical waste. Gardens withered, pets died, and children suffered severe chemical burns on their hands and feet. High rates of birth defects, miscarriage, cancer, and blood disorders, along with other maladies, were detected. When only 2 of 17 pregnant women in Love Canal gave birth to healthy babies, authorities judged the area in grave and imminent peril. Surveys indicated pollution several hundred times above safe levels. The local school was closed, more than 200 houses were demolished, and more than 1,000 families were evacuated. Cleanup and liability costs from the disaster exceed $200 million (Albanese, 1984; Newton & Dillingham, 1994). Love Canal is only the most notorious of more than 50,000 hazardous waste sites across the nation, a monument to the widespread negligence and environmental indifference over chemical dumping by U.S. industry (Rosenbaum, 1991).

Economic Impact

Although comprehensive data on the cost of pollution and the price of cleaning up the environment are not available, selective figures reveal the enormous financial burden on society. Between passage of the Clean Water Act in 1972 and 1990, more than $100 billion was spent on improving water quality (Commoner, 1990). Compliance with the Clean Air Act and acid rain legislation has cost more than $26.5 billion (Starheim & Steen, 1989). Since 1980, EPA's Superfund has spent more than $16 billion on cleaning up hazardous waste sites. To complete the job will take, by conservative esti-mates, an additional $80 billion (Orme, 1992).

The human cost of pollution is equally high. The American Lung Association estimates that air pollution from motor vehicles, power plants, and industrial fuel combustion costs the United States $40 billion annually in health care and lost productivity (Renner, 1980). The cost of treating employees with diseases contracted from toxic agents in the workplace ranges from $30 billion to $50 billion annually, according to a U.S. Department of Labor study (Green & Berry, 1985).

Social and Psychological Impact

The victims of natural disasters experience stress because their way of life is disrupted, and what they lost cannot easily be restored (Barton, 1969). Man-made disasters to the environment compound this stress because victims' anger about human error cannot be assuaged by stoicism (Couch & Kroll-Smith, 1985; Erickson, 1976; Janis, 1971). A study of Jackson Township, New Jersey, reveals the persisting human effects of environmental disasters (Edelstein, 1988). In the 1950s, Jackson gained a reputation for genteel country living, as a haven for the American dream. This status was tarnished in the 1960s when a landfill for a paint manufacturer opened in the township. Noise, litter, dust, and mosquitoes beset the community. Most upsetting to the residents was the decline in water quality. When the board of health declared residential well water contaminated and trucked in supplies from outside sources, homeowners reacted with surprise, anger, and antagonism. Despite the hookup to city water in 1980, their feelings of anxiety, resentment, and vulnerability persisted. Their image of the rural suburb as protected haven had already dimmed. Loss of trust in government and a diminished sense of personal control endured. Because environmental health problems would take some time to become manifest, questions about illness, life span, and genetic damage persisted well into the future. This change in "lifescope"—an individual's cognition and perception about self, others, and the larger world—is a more significant impact from catastrophic toxic exposure, according to Edelstein, than any material change in lifestyle.

Public Opinion and the Environmental Crisis

In a democracy, public opinion helps define social problems, place issues on the public agenda, and shape public policy. Public opinion has played these roles in environmental affairs. The criminalization of environmental regulation—in law and administrative practice—partly reflects a shift in public attitudes toward environmental wrongs as crimes.

The late 1960s evidenced an awakening of public concern about the environment. Pollution and pesticide control became causes for the Sierra Club and other traditional advocates of conservation. In addition, as people became more affluent, their interests shifted from questions of basic survival to quality-of-life issues such as the environment. The first Earth Day in 1970, celebrated by 20 million people, elevated the environment to a top spot on the public agenda (Dunlap, 1989). From 1965 to 1970, public support for governmental action against pollution more than doubled to 53%, according to Gallup polls (Mitchell, 1980). At the same time, the perception of pollution as a serious problem spread from 28% to 69% of the people.

Public interest in environmental problems declined during the 1970s: Support for more spending on pollution control dropped by more than half, from 78% to 32% (Dunlap & Dillman, 1976). The public had come to believe that new laws, such as the National Environmental Policy Act of 1969, and the new EPA, established in 1970, were doing the job. Moreover, the energy crisis of 1973 to 1974 let fuel consumption trump pollution control as a public issue.

During the 1980s, public support for environmental protection grew, partly in reaction to President Reagan's downsizing of federal efforts and partly in reaction to the dire news of environmental disasters (Dunlap, 1989). Reagan dismantled the Council on Environmental Quality, sought smaller budgets for the EPA, and pressed for environmental deregulation in general. Environmentalists responded angrily, and the broader public renewed its earlier concerns for protecting the environment.

In the early 1980s, 67% of the public supported existing environmental law even at the cost of some economic growth (Rosenbaum, 1991). Almost half the public—more than three times the level a decade earlier—favored greater regulation of the environment (Gillroy & Shapiro, 1986). This tough mood followed the disasters of toxic waste at Love Canal, acid rain in the Northeast, and reports of holes in the ozone layer of the atmosphere.

The 1990s ushered in an even tougher perception of environmental protection. More than 70% of the American public in 1990 favored the use of jail terms when firms are guilty of purposely violating pollution laws (Ladd & Bowman, 1995). The following year, 84% of Americans believed that damaging the environment is a serious crime, and 75% favored holding corporate officials personally responsible for environmental offenses by their firms (Arthur D. Little, Inc., 1991).

Criminal Justice and the Environmental Crisis

The heightened public sensitivity about the environment is, from the broadest perspective, the inevitable response to the worldwide technological revolution of this century (Thornburgh, 1991). More specifically, the first postwar upsurge in environmental regulation in the United States coincided in the late 1960s and early 1970s with the onset of the environmental movement.

For the most part, regulation had been considered a civil matter by courts and legislatures. Fines had been the penalties of choice against violators. Monetary sanctions were rarely effective, however. This cost of violating environmental laws was calculated by polluters to be a small enough price to pay compared with the cost of compliance. Nominal civil fines often became viewed by corporations as an acceptable cost of doing business, rather than as a deterring penalty (Wilson, 1986).

The disaster of Love Canal exposed the failure of civil remedies and fueled public demands for tougher penalties (Kuruc, 1985). As a result, criminal liability became an important tool in environmental enforcement as all three branches of the federal government—as well as state and local authorities—began to adopt a tougher posture toward environmental violators. Marzulla and Kappel (1991) provide the following summary of this new development.

Congress

Throughout the 1980s, Congress systematically amended major environmental statutes to strengthen the criminal penalties available to punish environmental violators. Congress amended the Resource Conservation and Recovery Act of 1976 in 1980, making it a felony for any person knowingly to treat, store, or dispose of hazardous waste without a permit. This marks

Congress's first approval of felony sanctions for breaking a federal environmental law (Marzulla & Kappel, 1991). Just 4 years later, Congress revisited the act and doubled the maximum allowable prison term to 5 years for the same class of violations.

Congress reauthorized the Comprehensive Environmental Response, Compensation, and Liability Act (Superfund) in 1986 and elevated the knowing failure to report the release of a hazardous substance from a misdemeanor to a felony. Meanwhile, Congress also amended the Clean Water Act, upgrading many violations to felonies.

In 1989, Congress completely reworked the provisions for criminal penalties in the Clean Air Act. For instance, knowing violations of Clean Air Act permits are now punishable by a prison term of up to 5 years. The knowing failure to comply with any of the act's reporting requirements can result in 2 years in prison. Finally, any person who knowingly releases a hazardous air pollutant and who knows that such a release will place another person in imminent danger of death or serious bodily injury can be imprisoned for up to 15 years.

Apart from the amendments to existing laws, two other developments of significance occurred in the mid-1980s. First, Congress enacted the Criminal Fine Improvements Act of 1987, which doubled to $200,000 per misdemeanor the criminal fine that may be imposed on an organization. More significantly, Congress enacted the Sentencing Reform Act of 1984, whose aim is to eliminate unwarranted disparity in sentencing while still maintaining flexibility when appropriate. One effect has been the imposition of tougher sanctions on first-time offenders, including pollution violators.

The Executive Branch

In the early 1980s, the Department of Justice (DOJ), the EPA, and the Federal Bureau of Investigation (FBI) launched a coordinated, nationwide effort to prosecute vigorously corporations and their officers for environmental crimes (Marzulla & Kappel, 1991). In 1980, the DOJ created a new Environmental Enforcement Section in its Land and Natural Resources Division, whose first priority was criminal enforcement. A year later, an Environmental Crime Unit was established within the Environmental Enforcement Section. Staffed by attorneys with both criminal and environmental law experience, the unit together with the EPA has investigated and prosecuted federal environmental crime. In addition, an Environmental Enforcement Council has been created to coordinate efforts in this area between state governments and federal agencies.

Federal resources committed to these efforts have increased. The number of attorneys working on criminal enforcement increased from 5 in 1983 to 25 in 1991. Moreover, the DOJ's budget for enforcing environmental crime expanded more than 10-fold from $257,000 in 1983 to $3 million in 1989. By 1993, the budget was $44.5 million (U.S. Department of Justice [DOJ], 1993).

As the DOJ moved on environmental crime, the EPA did not sit idly by. It opened an Office of Criminal Enforcement in 1981; a year later, it hired its first criminal investigators, with the authority to carry firearms and execute search and arrest warrants. The Pollution Prevention Act of 1990 directed EPA to hire additional criminal investigators annually for the next 5 years. By October 1995, the EPA's Office of Criminal Enforcement had a staff of at least 200 investigators.

A 1992 memorandum of understanding with the EPA brought the FBI into environmental enforcement for the first time (EPA, 1992). Under the agreement, environmental crimes became a special priority of the FBI. In support of that effort, the FBI had fielded approximately 65 agents by 1996.

Clearly, criminal enforcement has moved beyond the experimental stage. Efforts have been institutionalized within the DOJ and EPA. Clear criteria and procedures have been promulgated for case selection and prosecution (McMurray & Ramsey, 1986). The payoff for 1990 was 134 criminal indictments, the highest number in DOJ history (EPA, 1990).

Courts

In the past decade, two actions by the federal courts have made it easier to convict corporate executives of environmental crimes. First, the courts have loosened the requirement for *mens rea* (intent) in the prosecution of environmental offenders. Mens rea is a defining element of crime. To be culpable of a crime, a defendant's action must reflect his or her mental state. Usually, a person is not guilty of a criminal offense unless he or she committed the forbidden act with purpose, foreknowledge of its nature, recklessness, or negligence. Recently, however, federal courts have allowed juries to infer intent based on an executive officer's position in the corporation (Weidel, Mayo, & Zachara, 1991). This eroding of mens rea has prompted steady growth in the conviction of middle- and upper-level managers for environmental offenses. Second, the courts have carried out tougher sentencing guidelines, which impose harsh sentences for environmental crime. Probation, once the standard punishment for environmental criminals, is severely restricted under the guidelines (Marzulla & Kappel, 1991).

State Governments

The states have passed a variety of environmental statutes of their own and devoted considerable resources to pollution deterrence and abatement. During the past decade, they have also resorted to criminal sanctions. Indeed, some states merely do not satisfy the minimum requirements required by federal environmental law but have developed more comprehensive and aggressive statutory schemes for punishing environmental violators.

An Illinois statute, for example, imposes a $500,000 per day criminal fine, up to 7 years in prison, or both for the knowing criminal disposal of hazardous waste, whereas the federal Resource Conservation and Recovery Act sets only a $50,000 fine and/or 5 years in prison for the same offense. New Jersey has exceeded the criminal sanctions minimally required by the EPA to comply with the Resource Conservation and Recovery Act.

Many states have built networks for environmental enforcement, with a variety of agencies cooperating on enforcement tasks. State departments of environmental protection and public health, which normally have responsibility for permits, inspections, and administrative enforcement, have been given prominent roles in the criminal investigation of environmental offenses. Many states have added environmental crime units to their divisions of criminal justice. Not surprisingly, agencies of state government carry out the lion's share of environmental inspections and enforcement actions, which may lead to criminal indictments (EPA, 1990).

In many states, county prosecutors have mounted environmental task forces to investigate environmental crime at the local level. The city police, county sheriff, fire department, and state highway patrol also actively serve as the watchdogs of the community to detect environmental crime (Epstein & Hammett, 1995).

Summary

In sum, the three branches of federal government are beginning to convey a clear message that environmental crime does not pay. Criminal sanctions for environmental offenses are a higher national priority than in the past (Strock, 1991; Thornburgh, 1991). Violation of an increasing number of environmental laws is subject to criminal liability. Corporations may save money in the short run by violating these laws, but their managers may go to jail as a consequence (Stewart, 1991).

Emerging Legal Issues

Although the soil of criminal law has nurtured new solutions to the environmental crisis, it has also produced a thicket of procedural and theoretical issues that must be cut through.

The Erosion of Mens Rea

Judicial interpretation has eroded the common-law definition of mens rea in environmental prosecution. The criteria of purpose, willfulness, and knowledge that underlay the concept of intent have been challenged by new principles: the responsible corporate officer doctrine, strict liability, the willful blindness or deliberate ignorance doctrine, and the collective knowledge doctrine (Weidel et al., 1991). Although these departures from the tradition of English common law have made the conviction of environmental offenders easier, they raise serious questions about justice and fairness in environmental prosecution.

Prosecutorial Discretion

The dilution of mens rea has given greater license to the prosecutor in deciding whether to file a criminal charge against an environmental violator. In the past, criminal intent was the critical element to justify a criminal charge. Now, according to the principle of strict liability, judge and jury can sustain a criminal conviction without proof of criminal intent. Thus, the substantial difference between civil and criminal cases is obliterated.

As a result, the consequences of prosecutorial discretion are more ominous. In a conventional criminal case, the prosecutor's discretion on how to charge and prosecute will result only in the guilty defendant's receiving a lighter or harsher criminal sentence. In an environmental case, the prosecutor's discretion on how to charge and prosecute can result in the guilty defendant's experiencing one of two dramatically different outcomes: a highly stigmatizing criminal sentence of incarceration or a lighter and stigma-free civil sanction. The question is whether discretion of this magnitude serves justice and fairness.

Search and Seizure

Although the constitutional protections for search and seizure in conventional criminal cases still apply to environmental cases, there may be creative alternatives for inspecting sites. For example, statutorily authorized inspections of environmental sites can be treated as warrantless searches. In a routine authorized inspection, without a warrant, the illegal storage of hazardous waste or other environmental violations can be disclosed. Such evidence can be used against the offender in court. Moreover, an administrative inspection warrant, obtainable with less than a showing of criminal probable cause, is available for environmental cases. Finally, warrantless search under a voluntary written consent is more likely in environmental cases because owners often believe they have nothing to hide. Owners may also believe that denying permission to search will incur unwanted antagonism or suspicion from the investigator (Hammett & Epstein, 1993a).

Thus, although the exclusionary rule is still theoretically applicable to all environmental crime cases, in practice it may not be invoked because a warrantless search and seizure can almost always be conducted. The central question is whether the normal protections against unwarranted search and seizure can too easily be avoided in environmental cases.

Preview

This book examines the nature, causes, investigation, prosecution, and prevention of environmental crime. In this chapter, we have defined environmental crime and reviewed theoretical approaches to studying it. We have described the environmental crisis, the broader context for environmental crime. Special emphasis has been placed on the human, economic, social, and psychological impacts of the crisis. We have charted the shifts in public attitudes toward the crisis. Finally, we have discussed the criminalization of environmental violations and pointed to some of the vexing legal issues it raises.

Chapter 2 analyzes the criminal components of environmental law at federal and state levels in more detail. The constitutional issues they raise are more fully explored. Varieties of environmental crime are discussed in the next four chapters. Corporate environmental crime is examined in Chapter 3, followed by treatments of environmental crime by criminal organizations (Chapter 4), the government (Chapter 5), and individuals (Chapter 6).

Chapters 7 and 8 focus on the processing of environmental crime with discussions on prevention techniques, investigation and prosecution procedures, and sentencing decisions. Chapter 9 examines environmental crime from an international perspective. Global environmental problems and the barriers to international environmental law are addressed. Promising approaches by other nations in fighting environmental crime are reviewed.

Review Questions

1. What are the chief differences between the strict legalist and social legalist perspectives on crime?
2. What are the key features of the text's definition of environmental crime?
3. What changes have occurred from the 1960s onward with respect to public opinion about the environmental crisis?

4. What developments by the federal government, the courts, and state governments reflect the growth of criminal enforcement and prosecution of environmental offenses? (Discuss at least three examples.)

5. How has the erosion of mens rea affected prosecutorial discretion in environmental cases?

CHAPTER 2

Criminal Law and the Environment

An environmental crime is an unauthorized act or omission that violates the law and is therefore subject to criminal prosecution and sanctions. Not all flagrant disregard of the environment is criminal, however; it must be specified as crime by the law. As discussed in Chapter 1, the Latin dictum *nullum crimen, nulla poena sine lege*—there can be no crime and no punishment except as the law prescribes—applies here. Environmental criminal law defines environmental crime.

Understanding Criminal Law

There are two types of criminal law: substantive and procedural. Substantive criminal law, typically embodied in state criminal codes, defines the "wrongful" behavior of citizens and stipulates corresponding punishments. Crimes are committed not only against individuals but at the same time against society as a whole. As the guardian of society's interests, government, not the harmed individual, takes legal action against the offender.

Procedural criminal law, which finds its strongest grounding in the Bill of Rights, provides a host of legal protections for the accused and sets forth the rules of conduct that government officers must follow in enforcement, adjudication, and corrections. Both types of law are closely linked in practice. Criminal justice workers must fight crime, which is defined by substantive criminal law, in a manner established by procedural criminal law.

Social Control

In a variety of cultures, jurisdictions, and eras, criminal law has served as an agent of social control and an instrument of social change. Criminal law is intended to control the offensive behavior of people through punishment. In a traditional, homogeneous society, behavioral conformity is ensured by self-control, which is shaped by socialization, mores, and folkways and refined by informal practices such as gossip, ridicule, humiliation, and ostracism from the family, clan, village, or tribe.

In a modern, heterogeneous society, however, formal social control through the law becomes essential. The great diversity of the population, the growing conflict among groups with different interests, and the elaborate division of labor discourage deeply held, uniform, socially acceptable values and standards from forming. As a result, law, as a written statement of rules to which people must conform, comes to play an indispensable role. By punishing or isolating criminal offenders, law performs its social control function.

In a similar manner, environmental criminal law serves as an agent of social control in today's complex society. By defining what is illegal in people's use of the environment and setting punishments for infractions, environmental criminal law is intended to control and deter illicit acts and omissions.

Social Engineering

Criminal law is also a proactive and reactive instrument of social change. On the one hand, it promotes planned social change by the government (Aron, 1989; Grossman & Grossman, 1971; Vago, 1994). By defining the boundaries between legal and illegal behavior, criminal law guides people to act in the direction that political authority desires. On the other hand, criminal law sometimes codifies social change already accomplished by society. It reflects changes already made, rather than creating the changes themselves. For example, the legalization of gambling and, in a few places, prostitution reflected shifting social conditions and public attitudes. The history of environmental criminal law reflects changing public opinions and concerns about the quality of the environment during the past several decades (Kuruc, 1985). Environmental criminal law is also an instrument of change, shaping new attitudes and action toward the environment (Falk, 1988; Glick, 1988; Jacob, 1984).

The Differences Between Civil and Criminal Law

Criminal law differs in key respects from civil law. Criminal law's domain for the most part is offenses that victimize both individuals and society as a whole. Crimes are public wrongs that by their harm or bad example threaten the social order. Consequently, the state claims a special interest in prosecuting the criminal wrongdoer. The guilty are subjected to punishment, typically incarceration, which fulfills society's need for retribution and deterrence. In contrast, civil law regulates commercial and social relationships. Violations of civil law are private wrongs. The harmed person (human or corporate), not the state, takes legal action, typically filing a civil suit against the accused offender. The goal of adjudication is to rectify the wrong or compensate the victim.

Criminal law and civil law also differ in their requirements for conviction. Under criminal law, an act must have been done with intent—mens rea—to be a crime. A killing is not a murder if the killer did not mean to do it. Under civil law, an act is a wrongdoing without mens rea. The wrongdoer must simply be deemed objectively responsible—*strictly liable*—for committing the illegal act. Under this standard of strict liability, conviction is easier to achieve because the offender's intent need not be established.

Finally, the stigmas of criminal and civil sanctions vary. Crimes generally entail immoral behavior. Appropriately, the criminal law exacts punishments—from incarceration to the death penalty—that reflect society's moral outrage and stigmatize the offender. In contrast, civil law seeks mainly to redress wrongs and compensate injured victims under less morally charged circumstances, in which social shame is not a likely outcome. As a consequence, criminal law draws on the stigma of its punishments to strengthen deterrence, whereas civil law, for the most part, cannot. The stigma of criminal conviction and punishment is one of the attractions of applying criminal law to environmental misconduct.

The Development of Environmental Law

Criminal penalties against pollution can be traced to as early as the 14th century. To reduce the pall of noxious smoke blanketing the London sky, King Edward I issued a royal proclamation on smoke abatement. Violators of the new law could be put to death (Albanese & Pursley, 1993).

In the United States, the Refuse Act of 1899 was the first environmental law to contain criminal sanctions. The act prohibited the discharge of "any refuse matter of any kind or description whatever" into the country's navigable waters. Violation was a misdemeanor punishable by a fine of up to $2,500, imprisonment of 1 year, or both. The most notable legal impact of the Refuse Act was to introduce the principle of strict liability into environmental criminal law. Under strict liability, the defendant's guilt does not rest on establishing any degree of intent (mens rea). Instead, *actus reus* (the criminal act itself) suffices; the polluter is guilty merely by dumping refuse in the water, whether or not intended. Intent is not ignored but provides an additional grounds for charges: "knowingly" [to] aid, abet, authorize, or instigate a violation." The act was generally ignored by both polluters and enforcers (Albanese & Pursley, 1993, p. 72). In any case, it stood for much of this century as the lone instance of environmental criminal law. Most environmental law until the 1970s focused on conservation and the efficient use of natural resources (Schoenbaum & Rosenberg, 1991).

The environmental movement took root in the American political landscape of the late 1960s as public awareness of environmental crises grew and concerns about the quality of life deepened (Carson, 1962; Dunlap & Van Liere, 1978). The movement drew vision and technical expertise from the science of ecology, which stresses the interdependence between living creatures, their habitats, and the larger world. By the 1970s, the environmental movement had become a powerful political force. By the end of the decade, it had prompted a major shift in national policy (Kraft & Vig, 1990).

The 1970s took title as the environmental decade, witnessing passage of a flood of environmental legislation (Yeager, 1992). Among notable laws were the Clean Air Act Amendments of 1970; the Resource Recovery Act of

1970; the Coastal Zone Management Act of 1972; the Federal Environmental Pesticide Control Act of 1972; the Federal Water Pollution Control Act and Amendments of 1972; the Marine Protection, Research, and Sanctuaries Act of 1972; the Endangered Species Act of 1973; the Safe Drinking Water Act of 1974; the National Forest Management Act of 1976; the Resource Conservation and Recovery Act of 1976; the Toxic Substances Control Act of 1976; the Federal Land Policy and Management Act of 1976; the Surface Mining Control and Reclamation Act of 1977; the Public Utility Regulatory Policies Act of 1978; and, in 1980, the Comprehensive Environmental Response, Compensation, and Liability Act. The passage of this environmental legislation made these years the most innovative environmental era in a century. "No other domestic policy challenge of recent times," noted the Commission for a National Agenda for the Eighties, "has been addressed as forcefully and quickly" (Rosenbaum, 1991, p. 89).

Such a remarkable increase in federal legislation reflected an optimistic faith in law as a mechanism for environmental protection and an abiding belief in government's responsibility to control big business. New developments in the 1980s, however, challenged this vision. The environmental legislation of the 1970s attacked the most obvious villains such as sulfur oxide emissions, photochemical smog, and dissolved organic chemicals, but later research uncovered new and more damaging threats to the environment: air pollution by arsenic, benzene, and radionuclides; water pollution in nonpoint sources, especially farmland and septic tank systems; more than 2,000 known toxic waste sites across the country; and the greenhouse effect (Rosenbaum, 1991). At the same time, public alarm about pollution was heightened by environmental disasters such as Love Canal (Kuruc, 1985). Through most of the decade, the public concluded that the overall quality of the environment had worsened (Rapp, 1990).

Scientific discoveries and public awareness of a deepening environmental crisis justified greater vigilance by the government, however, just as the ineffectiveness of environmental law was becoming more apparent. Polls during the 1980s found a public disillusioned that important antipollution laws had not lived up to their advance billing (Rosenbaum, 1991). A major source of failure was the civil character of federal enforcement actions. Their chief sanction was fines, which many corporations took in stride as a cost of doing business (Box, 1983; Fromm, 1990; Green, 1972; Kadish, 1968; Thornburgh, 1991). Fines were set too low to carry any deterrent punch. The corporation stood to profit more from committing an offense than it lost financially if convicted (Conklin, 1977). Faced with new scientific knowledge about pollutants, an alarmed public, an impatient environmental movement, and the failure of civil penalties, Congress in the 1980s turned to the criminal law for solutions to the environmental crisis (Cartusciello & Hutchins, 1994).

An Overview of Key Environmental Criminal Laws

Environmental law, in its broadest sense, is "all of the laws in our legal system to minimize, prevent, punish or remedy the consequences of actions which damage or threaten the environment, public health and safety" (Sullivan, 1993, p. 1). It applies an array of penalties against wrongdoers ranging from "traffic tickets"—modest administrative fines, for example—to incarceration (Epstein & Hammett, 1995). Environmental criminal law, however, covers narrower ground. Its core consists of the criminal provisions of eight federal statutes, passed mainly in the 1970s and amended in the last two decades. A review of these laws follows.

Resource Conservation and Recovery Act

Enacted in 1976 and significantly amended in 1984, the Resource Conservation and Recovery Act is designed to control waste from "cradle to grave" by regulating its generation, treatment, storage, transportation, and disposal. The U.S. system of hazardous waste regulation is widely viewed as the most innovative and comprehensive in the world (Case, 1993). The Resource Conservation and Recovery Act is the cornerstone of this system.

Solid waste is hazardous, according to the act, if it is ignitable, corrosive, reactive, or toxic or has otherwise been cited on the EPA's hazardous waste lists. A waste manager must notify the EPA of his or her hazardous waste actions, whereas a waste producer must have a permit for disposal and a manifest to track the shipment of waste to treatment, recycling, or disposal facilities. No hazardous waste can be exported to a foreign country without notifying the EPA at least 4 weeks before the shipment and without a manifest signed by the foreign accepter. A transporter of hazardous waste must first obtain an EPA permit. He or she must identify the waste properly, store it in proper containers, and respond to spills. A transporter can accept only waste that is accompanied by a signed manifest from the producer, which he or she too signs and dates. Any violation of these regulations can be subject to criminal penalties.

Clean Air Act

The Clean Air Act grew out of general guidelines in the mid-1960s for antipollution efforts by the states. Enacted in 1970, the law was amended in 1977, 1989, and 1990, becoming in the process a strong instrument of federal enforcement, administered by the states (Brownell, 1993).

Central to the Clean Air Act are the National Ambient Air Quality Standards (NAAQS) for air pollutants such as sulfur dioxide, nitrogen oxide, carbon monoxide, ozone, and lead. Each state designs a state implementation plan for bringing its air quality into compliance with the NAAQS. States must monitor their implementation plans by maintaining complete records, issuing permits, and reporting permit violations. By setting up the NAAQS and requiring each state to implement them, the Clean Air Act became the centerpiece of the ambitious environmental program begun in the 1970s. Although few states achieved air quality standards by the original, or even extended, deadlines, the total volume of regulated air pollution has diminished significantly since 1974 (Switzer, 1994).

Toxic Substances Control Act

The Toxic Substances Control Act of 1976 aims to eliminate the unreasonable risk of injury to public health or the environment from introducing toxic substances into the market. Manufacturers maintain records and submit reports on their chemical manufacturing, importing, and processing and provide data on the environmental health effects of the toxic chemicals they produce or handle. The EPA has comprehensive authority to regulate the testing of high-risk chemicals; review new chemical substances prior to their commercial production and sale; and limit, delay, or prohibit the manufacture of a chemical substance by exercising a significant New Use Rule, which gives EPA 90 days to make such decisions.

Violations of the act include failing to establish, maintain, and submit required information showing the effects of chemical products; failing to report the commercial manufacture, import, or processing of a chemical substance; failing to submit a significant New Use Notice before distribution of a chemical substance; failing or refusing to permit EPA inspection; and failing or refusing to comply with other rules, orders, or requirements of the act.

Federal Water Pollution Control Act and Amendments

Water pollution control law is composed of many federal water quality acts, passed during the last hundred years. The Refuse Act of 1899, which focuses on the protection of navigation, is the oldest of these laws. Serious concern about the quality of water in streams and lakes, however, did not begin until the late 1940s when waste treatment plants were established across the country with federal support. Prior to 1970, however, weak enforcement by the states and the federal government left surface water largely unprotected from pollution (Arbuckle, 1993b).

Then, in late 1972, Congress passed the Federal Water Pollution Control Act, a comprehensive, modern water pollution statute that establishes national effluent limitations, water quality standards, permit programs, special provisions for oil spills and toxic substances, and a grant program for constructing publicly owned treatment works (Arbuckle, 1993b). The act was amended by the Clean Water Act in 1977 and 1978. The Clean Water Act is dedicated to national water quality that will ensure an abundance of fish and wildlife while promoting aquatic recreation and eliminating the pollution of surface water. The act pursues these goals by setting discharge standards for certain pollution sources, establishing a permit program, registering and monitoring pollution facilities, funding municipal sewage treatment plants, and imposing substantial criminal penalties on violations of some provisions. In addition, the Clean Water Act requires the owner or operator of any vehicle, vessel, or facility from which there is a discharge of oil or a reportable quantity of a hazardous pollutant to notify the National Response Center. By tightening control of toxic discharges, establishing toxic-oriented water quality standards, and strengthening the enforcement mechanisms, the Clean Water Act attempts to meet the need for comprehensive water quality control in a modern era.

Safe Drinking Water Act

The Safe Drinking Water Act of 1974 is the first federal attempt to control harmful contaminants in public water systems and to regulate underground drinking water. The act ensures the drinking safety of tap water by requiring the provider to meet national drinking water standards, and it combats the contamination of groundwater through underground injection control programs. The Safe Drinking Water Act requires the EPA to set national drinking water standards, implement a permit scheme for underground injection, and impose traditional sanctions to force compliance where necessary.

Under the Safe Drinking Water Act, the states have primary enforcement responsibility for protecting drinking water supplies and implementing EPA regulations. A state program must meet or exceed minimum federal requirements. The EPA, however, may limit or revoke a state's primary enforcement authority or act on its own against contamination that endangers public health. In 1986 and 1988, programs were added to the Safe Drinking Water Act to protect the areas around wellheads from contamination and to prevent lead pollution in drinking water coolers.

The Safe Drinking Water Act has accelerated the development of national water quality standards. Implementing some provisions of the act at state and local levels, however, has proved difficult. State and local governments need more discretion and initiative in assessing environmental risk and combating drinking water contamination.

Federal Insecticide, Fungicide, and Rodenticide Act

Pesticides threaten the safety of the food supply and farmers' health. Their regulation has long been central to environmental protection. Responding to growing public concern, Congress in 1910 passed the Insecticide Act, which protected consumers against ineffective insecticides or their deceptive labeling. In 1947, Congress enacted the Federal Insecticide, Fungicide, and Rodenticide Act (FIFRA), which requires interstate distributors of pesticides to register with the government. Since 1970, Congress has amended the FIFRA five times—in 1972, 1975, 1978, 1980, and 1988. These amendments have

Toughened FIFRA's enforcement powers

Downplayed an earlier legal emphasis on labeling and efficacy while placing health and the environment at the center of the act's concerns

Broadened discretion in dealing with dangerous chemicals

Expanded federal law to govern interstate registrations and specific uses of a pesticide

Simplified the appeals process (Miller, 1993)

Under FIFRA, all new pesticides must first be registered with the EPA. Producers must submit the pesticide's complete formula, a proposed label, and a complete description of tests and their results on which claims are based. The EPA may restrict the availability or use of pesticides. Most significant, the agency may cancel production or remove from the market a substance suspected of posing an unreasonable adverse effect on humans or the environment (Miller, 1993).

The federal control of pesticides reflects concern by Congress, environmentalists, and the public about the potentially harmful impact of these chemicals on humans and the balance of nature. Because pesticides benefit agriculture and scientific uncertainty about their effects persists, however, FIFRA is continuously under attack, and the government's ability to regulate and control pesticides is greatly hampered.

Comprehensive Environmental Response, Compensation, and Liability Act

Congress enacted the Comprehensive Environmental Response, Compensation, and Liability Act (CERCLA) in direct response to the catastrophe in the late 1970s at Love Canal, where leaks from an inactive hazardous waste site contaminated a neighborhood and school in upstate New York with powerful toxic chemicals. The act provides a broad spectrum of responses to the problems posed by abandoned and inactive hazardous waste disposal sites. As such, it supplements the Resource Conservation and Recovery Act of 1976, which regulates hazardous waste generation, handling, and disposal.

In the face of a threatened or actual release of hazardous substances into the environment, the EPA may, under the act, conduct a *removal action* to diminish the toxic dangers in a site or a *remedial action* to eliminate permanently any site's threat. The act also requires the EPA to investigate the threat from a release, identify hazardous sites, and evaluate all site information that is necessary to determine a response action.

Most important, CERCLA created a hazardous substance Superfund, bankrolled by special taxes on the petroleum and chemical industries as well as by an environmental tax on corporations in general. The Superfund also has recourse to general tax revenue. The fund may be used to pay EPA's cleanup and enforcement costs, certain natural resource damages, and the claims of some private parties.

CERCLA does not target private industry exclusively but also addresses the environmental harm posed by many federal facilities such as the massive military-industrial complexes that processed the materials and built the weapons of World War II and the Cold War. The act waives the government's sovereign immunity, allowing individuals at the state level to bring lawsuits against federal facilities. This provision has prompted many long-term cleanup plans by both the U.S. Department of Defense and the Department of Energy.

Private industry has criticized CERCLA as a

> draconian system which hinders its economic growth and penalizes individual companies by requiring them to perform extensive and costly cleanups without regard to where the original disposal took place or the fact that a company may have exercised due care in handling hazardous material. (Lee, 1993, p. 267)

These challenges to CERCLA, like those to other environmental statutes, will continue until a balance between the costs to the market and the benefits to the environment can be achieved.

Refuse Act

The Refuse Act of 1899 was the first environmental statute that imposed criminal penalties on discharges from any ship or shore installation into navigable or tributary waters. Because the act, now a hundred years old, was not drafted as a comprehensive water pollution control statute, it has left many problems unsolved in the modern era (Arbuckle, 1993b). For instance, the act provided no standards for the grant or denial of discharge permits from the Army Corp of Engineers, nor any procedure for establishing them. Moreover, penalties under the act have been considered inadequate by many.

Significantly, however, the Refuse Act did break precedent by abandoning mens rea—the showing of bad intent—in favor of strict liability for criminal prosecution of violators. As a result, hundreds of criminal cases were prosecuted under the act.

Summary

The eight environmental statutes reviewed here are not criminal laws as such. They empower government agencies to regulate the use of the environment and stipulate a broad spectrum of sanctions that include criminal penalties against violators. They generate most of the criminal prosecutions against environmental offenders, but they offer a variety of noncriminal remedies as well. Because these laws govern almost all parts of the environment—from air and water to landfills—and regulate all stages of toxic chemical production—from generation to handling and disposal—they nonetheless greatly expand the opportunities to use criminal sanctions. In addition, the amendments to these laws in the 1980s and 1990s reveal a trend toward the increased use of criminal, rather than civil, sanctions to punish and deter environmental law violators.

Liability in Environmental Crime

An environmental lawbreaker may have to suffer administrative or civil penalties, undertake a remedial cleanup or other corrective action, or provide compensation. But only the criminally liable violator can be subject to criminal punishments. What does environmental law define as crimes, and what liabilities are imposed by committing them? The following discussion examines these issues.

Knowing Offenses

Under the eight principal environmental criminal laws, a *knowing* offense or failure to comply with requirements is a crime. The Clean Air Act, for example, imposes criminal liability on any person who knowingly violates the statute. A *person* includes both individuals and corporations or partnerships. Felony offenses include tampering with EPA monitoring devices, violating a state implementation plan, defying a compliance order or emissions standards, ignoring ozone research and production provisions, and failing to pay noncompliance penalties. The 1990 amendments to the Clean Air Act have increased criminal fines for individuals to $250,000 per day of violation and up to 5 years in prison per incident. Corporations are subject to even bigger fines—up to $500,000 per day of violation—and up to 3 years of imprisonment per day of violation.

For *knowing violations,* the Federal Water Pollution Control Act calls for fines of not less than $5,000 nor more than $50,000 per day of violation and up to 3 years of imprisonment per day of violation. Penalties double for a second offense. The Resource Conservation and Recovery Act imposes criminal penalties of up to $50,000, 2 years of imprisonment, or both, on persons—including generators, transporters, and treatment, storage, and disposal facility operators—who knowingly violate provisions discussed earlier. Under the Toxic Substances Control Act, it is a misdemeanor punishable by up to 1 year of imprisonment and up to $25,000 for each day of violation for any person "knowingly or willfully" to violate some provisions of the act. According to the Safe Drinking Water Act of 1974, willful violation of underground injection regulations carries a prison term of up to 3 years, a criminal fine of $25,000 for each day, or both. The Federal Insecticide, Fungicide, and Rodenticide Act authorizes criminal penalties for both commercial and private applicators, wholesalers, dealers, retailers, and other distributors who knowingly violate the act. Such criminal penalties include a maximum fine of $25,000, imprisonment of up to 1 year, or both.

The knowledge requirement in an environmental crime case differs markedly from the requirement for a showing of bad intent (mens rea) in street crime. The defendant in a street crime case is guilty if he or she meant to commit the prohibited act. In contrast, the defendant in an environmental crime case is guilty if he or she should have known that his or her action violated an environmental statute. Courts have held, for example, that companies working in the highly regulated field of hazardous waste should know—and are legally responsible for knowing—regulations and rules for the industry. Indeed, corporate executives have been held criminally liable although they lacked personal knowledge of wrongdoing.

Negligent Violations

Negligence is "the omission to do something which a reasonable man, guided by those ordinary considerations which ordinarily regulate human affairs, would do, or the doing of something which a reasonable and prudent man would not do" (*Black's Law Dictionary,* 1990, p. 1032). It is, simply put, the failure to exercise due care. Intent is not a defining characteristic of negligence. A violator of environmental regulations is not negligent by virtue of meaning to break the law or to cause harm. Rather, his or her negligence is failing to comply with environmental regulations with the due care that would be exercised by a reasonable person under the same circumstances. Negligence is considered a crime here—in the absence of intent—because the consequences could be so devastating. For instance, flagrantly disregarding reasonable safeguards for storing liquid toxins is, in general, criminal negligence because it poses the serious risk of a harmful spill or discharge. The criminalization of negligence demands effective compliance procedures and the clear designation of who is responsible for carrying them out (Brownell, 1993).

Many of the environmental criminal statutes make exercise of due care a substantial burden and negligent violation a crime. Violations of the Federal Water Pollution Control Act, for example, are criminally liable, with fines of not less than $2,500 or more than $25,000 per day of violation, as well as up to 1 year of imprisonment. Fines and length of imprisonment are doubled for a second offense. Under the Clean Air Act, a person can be criminally liable for negligently releasing illegal amounts of contaminants into ambient air. The penalties can be a fine of up to $100,000 and up to 1 year in jail for individuals. Companies may be fined up to $200,000. A subsequent violation is classified as a felony, subject to 2 years in prison, $250,000 for an individual or $500,000 for a corporation, or twice the gain received from or the loss caused by the violation, whichever is greater. The negligent failure to apply in a timely fashion for a permit or to report a pollution incident are made subject to criminal sanctions under some environmental criminal laws.

Endangerment

Endangerment is the crime of knowingly or negligently placing another person in imminent danger of death or serious bodily injury. All the environmental criminal statutes classify endangerment as a felony and impose the most severe penalties. In general, the crime of endangerment has two elements under the environmental statutes: The defendant must have committed a prohibited offense that endangers others, and the defendant must have known at the time that he or she was causing imminent danger of death or serious bodily injury to another person. Thus, endangerment in environmental criminal law is, for the most part, knowing endangerment. The Clean Air Act provides one exception, however: Endangerment is extended from knowing to negligent release of air toxins that place another in imminent danger of death or seriously bodily harm. In this instance, the requirement of knowing is completely eliminated.

The EPA has construed *imminent danger* to mean posing a risk of harm or potential harm as opposed to actual harm. In other words, injury or death need not actually occur to sustain a conviction of endangerment. Rather, the placing of another person in imminent or potential danger suffices.

The evidence required to prove imminent danger varies somewhat from statute to statute. Under the Resource Conservation and Recovery Act, the government need show only that the defendant was aware of the illegal nature of his or her conduct. The Federal Water Pollution Control Act, however, insists on proof of actual awareness or belief, which may be shown by circumstantial evidence, including evidence that the defendant took affirmative steps to shield him- or herself from relevant information.

The Resource Conservation and Recovery Act (1976) creates a crime of

> knowing endangerment attached to the generators who knowingly allow hazardous waste to be transported to an unpermitted facility, the operators who knowingly violate federal interim status standards as counterpart state requirements, and the transporters who knowingly transport hazardous waste without a manifest. (Sec. 6902, pp. 214-215)

All such violations place another person in imminent danger of death or serious bodily injury. An individual, convicted under the act, may receive a fine of up to $250,000, imprisonment of up to 15 years, or both. A corporate defendant faces a fine of $1 million or twice the gain or loss, whichever is greater. Under the Federal Water Pollution Control Act, knowing endangerment consists of knowingly obstructing, or dumping refuse in, navigable waters; introducing a pollutant or hazardous substance into sewer systems; breaking a permit condition or limitation; or disregarding federal or state pretreatment programs. Knowing endangerment has also occurred if the offender knows that these actions place others in imminent danger of death or serious bodily injury. Criminal penalties under the act are imprisonment of up to 15 years and a fine of up to $250,000 for individuals and a fine of not more than $1 million for organizations. Penalties are doubled for a second offense.

Crimes of knowing endangerment occur under the Clean Air Act when a person or corporation knowingly releases hazardous air pollutants or extremely hazardous substances into ambient air and thereby knowingly places others in imminent danger of death or serious bodily injury. Penalties for individuals include a fine of up to $250,000 per day and up to 15 years of imprisonment. Corporations may be fined up to $1 million per day. Under the Clean Water Act, if oil is knowingly discharged with the knowledge that another person is placed in imminent danger of death or serious bodily harm, a maximum criminal fine of $250,000 and 15 years of imprisonment are imposed. For an organization, knowing endangerment carries a maximum fine of $1 million.

Noncompliance With Permits, Self-Reporting, Inspection, and Fees

Although criminal law prohibits harmful acts, it also requires adherence to rules of safe procedure to prevent dangerous outcomes. Environmental criminal law establishes three special requirements for safe procedure; violators are subject to criminal penalties.

Permits

The first requirement is to obtain a permit for operating a regulated facility, producing or selling a new pesticide product, disposing and transporting hazardous waste, or discharging certain amounts of pollutants into the water or air.

A permit sets forth the conditions under which these activities can be conducted. For example, it might specify that the

> permittee is authorized to discharge from outfall number 001 "x" pounds per day of pollutant "y" subject to the condition that the discharge be monitored in accordance with the specific protocols and that periodic reports be provided. (Sullivan, 1993, p. 17)

A permit is a useful tool for assessing compliance with environmental laws.

The criminal penalties for failing to obtain a permit are severe. Under the Resource Conservation and Recovery Act, felonies include knowingly transporting hazardous waste—or causing it to be transported—to a treatment facility that lacks a permit and treating, storing, or disposing of hazardous waste without a permit or in knowing violation of the permit's terms. They carry a maximum of 5 years of imprisonment and a fine of up to $250,000 for an individual or $500,000 for a corporation. A subsequent violation doubles the penalties.

The Federal Water Pollution Control Act designates as misdemeanors the negligent violation of any permit conditions for ocean dumping and discharging of pollutants into surface water. Penalties are set at a maximum of 1 year of imprisonment and a fine of up to $100,000 for an individual and $200,000 for a corporation. A subsequent negligent violation is upgraded to a felony, with penalties doubling.

Under the Clean Air Act, each permit must declare applicable emission limitations and standards, monitoring and reporting requirements, and a guarantee for the timely payment of source fees. Penalties for a knowing violation of the permit include 5 years of imprisonment and a $250,000 fine for individuals and a $500,000 fine for corporations. Penalties are doubled for a subsequent violation. Penalties for a negligent violation of the permit are identical to those set by the Federal Water Pollution Control Act.

Self-Reporting

The second special requirement is self-reporting, or giving notice to the appropriate regulatory agency of certain violations. Most environmental laws, like the Internal Revenue Code, depend on self-reporting as the first line of enforcement (Sullivan, 1993). Environmental law enforcement would be impossible without such voluntary disclosure because business activity is so enormous, far-flung, and often hidden from public scrutiny. Self-reporting also speeds up the response time of regulators to contain the damage from polluting releases or spills. For example, without a self-report, an oil discharge by a vessel at sea could go undetected until millions of fish and other species had died or hundreds of miles of shoreline had been contaminated.

Making false statements and failing altogether to report polluting discharges or releases are criminal offenses. The Clean Air Act specifically requires permit holders to report the violation of any permit conditions. Falsifying, or failing to submit, reports can result in a jail term of 1 or 2 years and fines of up to $250,000 for individuals. Corporations face fines of up to $500,000. The Federal Water Pollution Control Act requires the owner or operator of any point source to report periodically the results of self-monitoring to the permit-issuing authority. Failure to report properly is a violation of the permit, and any person who knowingly falsifies monitoring records or reports or compliance or noncompliance notification is subject on felony conviction to 2 years of imprisonment and a fine of up to $250,000. Corporations may be fined up to $500,000. Double penalties are imposed for a second violation. If a vessel operator fails to notify the National Response Center of a hazardous spill, he or she commits a felony subject to 3 years of imprisonment and a fine of up to $250,000. The corporate owners may be fined up to $500,000. A subsequent violation is subject to 5 years of imprisonment and a doubling of fines.

The Oil Pollution Act of 1990 increases the criminal penalties for failure to notify authorities, such as a Coast Guard Strike Team or National Response Unit, of a threatening oil spill from $10,000 and 1 year of imprisonment to a maximum of $250,000 and 5 years of imprisonment for individuals and a maximum fine of $500,000 for organizations. Under the Toxic Substance Control Act of 1976, companies must maintain records and submit reports on their chemical manufacturing, importing, processing, storing, and disposing activities. Failure to submit this material is a misdemeanor subject to a maximum of 1 year of imprisonment and a $100,000 fine for individuals, or a $200,000 fine for corporations. The Superfund Act (CERCLA, 1986) requires notice of the release of a reportable quantity of hazardous substances. Reportable amounts are approximately 1 pound, if not specifically set by the EPA. Failure to report can result in a criminal penalty of 3 years in prison for a first offense and 5 years for a second one.

Inspection

The third special requirement is inspection, for which many statutes grant regulatory agencies wide latitude. Environmental enforcers may, for example, enter the premises of pollutant dischargers at any reasonable time, inspect required records, and take test samples. Under the Toxic Substances Control Act, an EPA agent may inspect any establishment in which chemical substances or mixtures are manufactured, processed, stored, or held before or after distribution in commerce. The agent may also examine any conveyance that transports these materials for sale. To refuse entry or inspection is a misdemeanor, subject to 1 year of imprisonment and a $100,000 fine ($250,000 if death results) for individuals. Corporations may receive a $200,000 fine ($500,000 if death results). Breaking the requirement for inspection under the Clean Air Act is a felony. A sentence of 5 years of imprisonment and a fine of up to $250,000 may be imposed on individuals. Corporations are subject to fines of up to $500,000. The penalties double for the subsequent violation. A negligent violation of the inspection requirement under the Federal Water Pollution Act is a misdemeanor. Criminal penalties for an individual include 1 year of imprisonment and a $100,000 fine, $200,000 for a corporation. A subsequent violation is subject to double penalties.

Fees

The Clean Air Act also requires states to establish a fee schedule, revenue from which will cover permit program costs. Schedules are to be set for emission application and service-based fees as well as for other types of fees. Knowing failure to pay any of these fees is a criminal act and is subject to criminal fines of up to $250,000 and 1 year in jail for individuals and fines of up to $500,000 for corporations. Penalties are doubled for repeat offenses.

Summary

The major environmental laws apply criminal liability to knowing and negligent violation; endangerment; and noncompliance with permits, reporting, inspection, and fee submission. Although infractions are crimes, they vary in status from misdemeanor to felony and in the severity of punishment for committing them. Imprisonment ranges from 1 to 15 years; fines range from $2,500 per incident to $1 million per day of violation. Nevertheless, these criminal environmental laws share four features in common. First, they generally define *persons* to include both individuals and corporations; both may be subject to criminal penalties for violations. Second, these laws call for the same types of punishment: imprisonment and fines. Third, they often invoke strict liability instead of mens rea as a criterion of guilt. Thus, a crime has occurred if the violator of an environmental statute can be presumed to have knowledge of the law, whether he or she actual does. Finally, these statutes view endangerment as the most serious environmental crime.

Civil and Other Criminal Sanctions

Although the environmental statutes now bristle with criminal sanctions, they still mostly reflect the traditions and principles of civil and administrative law. All environmental statutes entail the application of regulatory law by administrative agencies such as the EPA. As a result, civil penalties are most typically involved as the legal remedy against environmental wrongdoers. Criminal penalties are usually invoked only when environmental statutes have been willfully or knowingly broken (Frank & Lynch, 1992). As a result, the imposition of civil and administrative penalties continues to be the keystone of environmental enforcement. The range of civil options is illustrated in the following three environmental laws.

First, the Resource Conservation and Recovery Act (1976) empowers the EPA to initiate administrative orders and civil sanctions against wrongdoers. A person who violates any regulation or permit requirement is liable for a civil penalty of up to $25,000 for each day of violation. In addition, the EPA can issue an order requiring compliance without delay or by a specific deadline. The Resource Conservation and Recovery Act also authorizes civil actions by citizens against any alleged violators of its regulations. Second, the 1990 amendments to the Clean Air Act authorize the EPA to take direct administrative action against violators directly without filing a charge in court. These actions range from issuing an environmental "traffic ticket" of $5,000 to exacting a fine of $200,000 or more. Violators may request a hearing or simply pay the fine. Private citizens are also authorized to seek civil penalties for violation of the Clean Air Act. Finally, infractions of the Marine Protection, Research, and Sanctuaries Act (1972), which is part of the Federal Water Pollution Control Act (1972), are subject to an administrative penalty of up to $50,000 per day of violation, injunctive relief in court, a citizen suit, and a seizure of the offending vessel.

The range of choices in prosecuting environmental cases extends in another direction as well. Traditional crimes not specified in the environmental statutes themselves may nonetheless be committed during environmental violations. They include conspiracy, making false statements, fraud, bribery, deception, corrupt practices, racketeering, and even the Part I offenses of murder and manslaughter. Thus, prosecutors often have a choice of charging offenders with either or both nonenvironmental and environmental crimes. In practice, charges "are never lonely—they always travel in packs" (Arbuckle, 1993a, p. 50). A false statement about an oil spill violates not only the Water Control Act but also the criminal statutes penalizing the falsification, destruction, or concealment of public records. If two or more corporate executives conspire to discharge polluted water into public sewers, they can also be criminally charged with violation of the conspiracy statutes.

This arsenal of both environmental and nonenvironmental criminal charges strengthens environmental law enforcement in two ways. First, it may disabuse companies and governments of the traditional view that polluting is a routine part of doing business. Environmental infractions belong to the world of traditional crime and carry its labels and stigmas. Second, it offers a sometimes simpler avenue of prosecution. Failing to disclose hazardous waste dumping, for instance, may be prosecuted as a traditional crime long before the environmental crime of endangering the public health can be demonstrated to have occurred. Juries may understand a charge of false reporting much more easily than an environmental criminal charge concerning the evaporation of toxic emissions. In addition, a report containing false data may often be introduced in court without recourse to expert testimony or opinion (Mustokoff, 1981).

Environmental Criminal Law at the State Level

The Role of the States

The role of the states in environmental criminal law has become increasingly important during the last 20 years. First, the amount of state environmental legislation has grown dramatically. Between 1967 and 1983, for example, environmental laws and amendments increased from 375 to 1,330 (Speer & Bullanowski, 1984). Their diversity has expanded as well from air and water pollution and illegal dumping to citizen action, facility siting, business confidentiality, operation of publicly owned treatment plants and landfills, and the right to know. As this list indicates, state law often focuses on more specialized issues than those addressed in federal law.

Second, although federal environmental law sets general goals, standards, and guidelines, its implementation and enforcement take place mostly at the state level. For instance, under the Resource Conservation and Recovery Act, the states plan hazardous waste programs in accordance with EPA guidelines and administer them with EPA approval. State enforcement activities—including monitoring emission effluent, inspecting facilities, issuing notices of violation, administering permit programs, and invoking civil and criminal penalties—exceed those by the EPA (Lowry, 1992; Wood, 1991).

Third, although the states may choose to adopt the federal government's minimum criteria and to achieve its regulatory objectives, they have some discretion to set up their own standards for environmental quality and to design their own innovative programs. Under the rule of preemption, the states are preempted from legislating more lenient environmental standards than those that the Congress has mandated (Nixon, 1992). Thus, less stringent pollution standards legislated by a state would be void and preempted by federal environmental statutes. Many states had taken advantage of the opportunity to exceed federal pollution standards and sanctions. For example, 11 northeastern states adopted California's strict standards for new car emissions, which are more stringent than those required by the federal government (Ringquist, 1993). Although the federal Clean Air Act imposes 1 year of imprisonment for a knowing violation, a violator is subject to up to 10 years of imprisonment under Louisiana air pollution control laws. Some states also design pollution control laws or programs to fill gaps in the federal environmental statutes or to exceed federal protections of the environment. New York, for example, passed the nation's first law to control acid rain (Ringquist, 1993). California requires extraordinary efforts to publicize the health consequences of environmental risks. New Jersey requires extensive investigations and cleanup of contaminated sites before they are sold or transferred (Sullivan, 1993). Wisconsin created a comprehensive toxic pollution control program to deal with the problems not covered by federal legislation (Lowry, 1992).

These important developments during the last 20 years have enhanced the role of states in environmental policy. States have become not only the "administrative arms of the federal government" but also the "laboratories of democracy, expanding their political vitality and increasing the number and the quality of their policy experiments" (Ringquist, 1993, p. 78).

State Variations

Not surprisingly, as the number and complexity of criminal provisions in state environmental law have expanded, their variation has increased as well (Allan, 1987; DeCicco & Bonanno, 1988). Some states, for example, have enacted comprehensive laws with strict criminal penalties to control hazardous waste, whereas other states have adopted only the minimum federal requirements for its transportation, storage, and disposal.

New Jersey has passed the most comprehensive and aggressive statute. It stipulates a wide variety of environmental crimes including three levels of knowing violations. A knowing infraction can be a crime regardless of harm, with the risk of widespread harm, or with actual widespread harm. The New Jersey penal code also criminalizes the spill of hazardous wastes and hazardous substances not enumerated in the Resource Conservation and Recovery Act. The state's penalties for environmental crimes are more severe than those prescribed by federal law. For example, although knowingly treating, storing, or disposing of hazardous waste without a permit is subject to a maximum fine of $50,000 and 5 years of imprisonment under the Resource Conservation and Recovery Act, New Jersey law specifies a $100,000 fine and up to 10 years of imprisonment. In contrast, such states as Montana, Utah, and Oklahoma merely meet the minimum requirements set by the EPA (DeCicco & Bonanno, 1988).

Seventeen jurisdictions (Arizona, Colorado, Connecticut, District of Columbia, Georgia, Hawaii, Illinois, Iowa, Kansas, Maryland, Missouri, Nevada, New Mexico, South Dakota, Texas, West Virginia, and Wisconsin) have not established any criminal sanctions for air pollution control (Allan, 1987; DeCicco & Bonanno, 1988). Among those states that do, disparities are significant. For example, in Rhode Island, violating the governor's order during an air pollution emergency is subject to a fine of not more than $500, 90 days in jail, or both. The same offense in New Jersey is punishable by a fine of up to $100,000 and imprisonment for up to 10 years (Allan, 1987). Criminal enforcement of water pollution by the states displays even greater variety because many states make no efforts on their own in this area (DeCicco & Bonanno, 1988). Lack of uniformity in state laws hinders the overall battle against pollution. Inconsistency encourages businesses and governments to exploit lax states as dumping grounds for water. Some businesses may also favor relocating to a state that does not aggressively prosecute polluters.

Although a full explanation is lacking, variations in state environmental criminal law are influenced by the level of pollution, economic resources, and the enforcement discretion granted by the federal government (Lowry, 1992). Ringquist (1993) has identified a more complex process of policy influences on state regulations for pollution control. In the case of air quality, states with greater wealth, more liberal voters, and more professional legislatures pass tougher regulations. For water quality, however, both state wealth and the strength of political institutions are less important than they are for air quality regulation. Instead, interest group politics plays a stronger role. States are less able to resist pressures from mining industries than from other heavily polluting industries. As a result,

> States with strong mining industries respond to these political pressures by developing weaker water pollution control regulations. On the other hand, states with serious pollution dangers react to political pressure from strong agricultural and environmental interest groups by strengthening their water pollution control programs. (Ringquist, 1993, p. 93)

Nevertheless, Ringquist points out that although organized interest groups are central to policy making, they do not create public policy on their own. Government institutions shape the policy for air and water pollution control. Additional factors impinging on aggressive prosecution of air pollution cases include the unclear guidelines for criminal enforcement provided by the EPA, the long approval process for implementing state plans, the lack of financial resources for criminal enforcement of pollution control, multistate pollution sources, and the difficulty of establishing proof in criminal pollution cases (DeCicco & Bonanno, 1988).

Key Legal Issues: Is Justice Strained?

Although criminal environmental enforcement has strong advocates (Strock, 1991; Thornburgh, 1991), a debate about its efficacy and effects has emerged in the 1990s. The main concern is whether environmental regulation is becoming overcriminalized. If the critics are right, one danger may be making the criminal label commonplace, thus diminishing the moral stigma of criminalization (Cohen, 1992a). Criminal sanctions may also pose a threat to individual rights and move the nation a dangerous step closer to a bureaucratic, authoritarian state (Hedman, 1991).

Critics have also expressed alarm about the diminishing status of mens rea. Although environmental law requires some knowledge of a prohibited act for a crime to exist, the traditional concept of mens rea or "guilty mind" has been significantly eroded. A polluter can be convicted if he or she should have known the law. *Actual* knowing is not a requirement for criminal prosecution. The ascendancy of strict liability has been criticized for dangerously expanding the prosecutor's discretion. Little effort is given to define thresholds at which a defendant's conduct justifies adding the criminal sanctions to civil penalties (Lazarus, 1994). In a conventional criminal case, the prosecutor's discretion over how to charge and prosecute will affect only the guilty defendant's length of criminal sentence. In an environmental case, these decisions can determine the guilty defendant's mode of punishment: a highly stigmatizing prison sentence or a lighter and stigma-free civil sanction. Thus, discretion in prosecuting environmental offenders raises more serious questions about justice and fairness than it normally does in prosecuting conventional criminals. Some believe that criminal sanctions should be reserved for the most culpable subset of environmental offenses and not used more widely to assuage the public yearning for dramatic action or to deter potential violators.

The criminalization of environmental law raises more practical concerns as well. For example, trials and incarceration make criminal sanctions more costly than administrative sanctions (Tietenberg, 1992). Imprisoning of the corporate environmental violator is also problematic. Corporations are common offenders in environmental cases. Although top executives must take ultimate responsibility for the corporation's infractions (Frank & Lynch, 1992), they may have lacked personal knowledge of their firm's violations and may not have personally participated in illegal behavior. Many environmental cases, in practice, resist the logical apportionment of blame. It may prove difficult to divide responsibility among different corporate defendants in a complex case (Albanese & Pursley, 1993).

Finally, some argue that using criminal sanctions to promote environmental protection hardly seems the most promising way to deal with ecological problems in a democratic society. The criminal sanction is one of the most coercive tools at the disposal of the state. We should not use such tools unless the entire array of less coercive options has been tested and rejected (Hedman, 1991). The impact of recent alternatives such as license revocation, divestiture for persistent offenders, and a ban on government contracting remains to be documented.

Despite these concerns, criminal enforcement of environmental law is likely to gain momentum in the future so long as environmental problems continue and the public demands remedies. In coming years, the U.S. Department of Justice is likely to treat more environmental violations as crimes and impose harsher sanctions on violators (Thornburgh, 1991).

Review Questions

1. What are the chief differences between civil and criminal law?
2. What are the key federal environmental laws, their chief areas of concern, and their criminal provisions?
3. What are the chief differences between a knowing environmental offense, a negligent violation, and endangerment?
4. How do permits, self-reporting, and inspections help ensure safe procedures in the handling and disposal of toxic wastes and other pollutants?
5. What roles have the states played in environmental criminal law during the past 20 years?
6. What concerns have been raised about overcriminalizing environmental regulation?

CHAPTER 3

Corporate Environmental Crime

Although all environmental crimes share a common target, they exhibit important differences. They differ principally in the perpetrators who commit them, the criminal action they entail, the victims they harm, and the laws and enforcement agencies that govern them. The most useful basis for comparison is who commits environmental crimes. On this basis, four types of environmental crime can be distinguished: corporate, organized, state, and personal. Each variety has its own type of offenders with their special characteristics. Each entails different levels of risk to public health and the environment. And each is illuminated by a different mix of criminological theories. In this chapter, we discuss corporate environmental crime. Subsequent chapters will review organized, state, and personal environmental crime.

Corporate Environmental Crime Defined

Corporate environmental crime is a major variety of corporate crime, which, in turn, constitutes a substantial part of white-collar crime (Clinard & Yeager, 1980). Criminologist Edwin Sutherland (1940) coined the term *white-collar crime,* defining it as "a crime committed by a person of respectability and high social status in the course of his occupation" (p. 7). Sutherland's pioneering research on upper-class crime helped reorient criminological theory and empirical inquiry on this new topic (Volk, 1977). Sutherland emphasized that people of high status are able to commit crimes because of the opportunities offered by the prestigious occupational positions they hold. Yet his empirical argument drew mainly on data about the violations of law by the 70 largest American corporations. As a consequence, the differences between individual and corporate white-collar crime were not sharply drawn (Frank & Lynch, 1992). More recently, researchers have disentangled the two, and the distinction between occupational and corporate white-collar crime is widely accepted (Clinard & Quinney, 1973; Clinard & Yeager, 1978, 1979, 1980; Geis & Meier, 1977; Nader, 1965, 1973). Occupational crime refers to personal violations that take place for self-benefit during work in a legitimate occupation, whereas corporate crime is committed by employees on the job, not principally for personal gain but on behalf of their corporation or business (Clinard & Yeager, 1980; Coleman, 1994; Farrell & Swigert, 1985; Frank, 1987).

Corporate crime is "enacted by collectives or aggregates of discrete individuals. It is hardly comparable to the action of a lone individual" (Shapiro, 1976, p. 14). Thus, it emphasizes corporate gain, not individual benefits. Individual employees do not directly profit from breaking the law. Therefore, illegal corporate activity can continue despite personnel changes; the exiting employee leaves behind the illegal behavior for others to carry on (Braithwaite & Fisse, 1990; Cressy, 1989; Sutherland, 1949). *Corporate crime* is a convenient term, but it should be cautioned, "something of an oxymoron: organizations do not 'act' or 'commit' at all" (Jamieson, 1994, p. 3). People within the organization, not the corporation as such, engage in corporate crime. These individuals are not, for the most part, low-level employees. Instead, they are corporate executives who have the power and authority to obey the law—and secure the obedience of others—but fail to do so. The corporation is characterized by the decisions and behaviors of these officers.

Corporate environmental crimes are a subset of corporate crimes. They harm the environment or endanger public health while benefiting the corporation. They are embedded in the practices of organizations, not the preferences of single individuals. They are committed in the course of doing business by employees, often at the highest levels, mainly to further corporate goals rather than personal interests.

An Overview of Industrial Pollution

Pollution is any undesirable change in the physical, chemical, or biological characteristics of the air, water, or land. Pollution threatens or harms the health, survival, or activities of humans or other living organisms. Most pollutants are created when industrial facilities release harmful by-products or waste into the environment.

Damage to the environment did not originate in the industrial age. Deforestation and overhunting, for example, were practiced by preindustrial societies. But premodern people tended to manage their interaction with the environment in more harmonious and sustainable ways than members of industrialized society have (Stretton, 1976). The most serious environmental problems, especially pollution, have accompanied the Industrial Revolution, which began in the mid-1700s.

The original culprit of the English Industrial Revolution was coal, which became the principal energy source by the mid-1700s as wood steadily disappeared. Coal-powered engines made the diverse and widespread use of machines possible. New machines, powered by coal and later by oil and natural gas, were a keystone to transition in human society from the small-scale, scattered, and manual production of goods to large-scale, centralized, and automatic production. Thus, the Industrial Revolution greatly increased the production, as well as consumption, of goods by altering and shaping the earth to meet society's needs and wants.

Nevertheless, the Industrial Revolution also had devastating effects on public health and the quality of the environment. It prompted a shift in energy sources from renewable and environmentally harmless wood and running water to nonrenewable and more toxic fossil fuels. Coal burning was respon-sible for most of the air pollution in the 18th and 19th centuries. In 1880, New York City housed 287 foundries and machine shops. At the same time, the Pittsburgh area's Monongahela Valley contained hundreds of iron and steel plants with approximately 14,000 chimneys dotting the landscape. Chicago was home to the stockyards, eight major railroads, a busy port, and heavy industry (Petulla, 1987). The smog from these industries darkened the cities with a foul-smelling, disease-causing shroud. By the early 1900s, smoke abatement leagues and ladies' health clubs had proliferated in cities in reaction against the pollution crisis.

By providing fossil fuels for farm machinery and commercial fertilizers that greatly increased agricultural productivity, the Industrial Revolution pushed many farmers off the land and into the city where new industrial jobs beckoned. The urban population grew rapidly in the 19th century. Immigrants, for instance, accounted for at least 70% of the populations of New York, Boston, Buffalo, Detroit, and Chicago (Bailes, 1985). Coal mines, metal-working factories, and textile mills, which were filled with many risks to health and safety, also developed rapidly. Because factories and people were concentrated increasingly in cities, industrial and human waste also accumulated there as well. City residents found an environment of hazards: thick smog from factories; foul-smelling, unsanitary streets pocked with excrement, kitchen slop, dead animals, and horse manure; and drinking water contaminated by industrial wastes such as oils, benzene, tars, and acids. The sewage treatment systems in industrial cities were of poor quality. For example, in the 1840s, Manchester, England, had available only one indoor toilet for every 212 residents (Schnaiberg & Gould, 1994). Not surprisingly, workers of the Industrial Revolution suffered from occupational as well as environmental diseases, including byssinosis, caused by inhaling cotton, flax, or hemp dust, and a variety of infections from soot and other airborne contaminants. In 1840, workers could expect on average to survive only 17 years in the mines around Manchester, compared with 34 years for other workers in surrounding rural areas.

By the early 20th century, the automobile had emerged as a new source of air pollution. Although the auto spurred the economy, altered housing patterns, and revolutionized social relations and lifestyles, it also became the leading contributor to air pollution in modern industrialized society. Motor vehicles are the main source of air pollution in the United States in the 1990s. They account for about half the hydrocarbon and nitrogen oxide emissions that together form the smog in most U.S. cities. They emit up to 90% of the carbon monoxide and more than half of other toxic pollutants in the air—all despite the most stringent emissions control program for motor vehicles in the world (Curtis & Walsh, 1991). General Motors, the nation's largest automaker, has been named California's largest producer of ozone-depleting chemicals (Crawford, 1994).

During the peacetime economy after World War II, a variety of new products and materials, such as detergents, synthetic fibers, plastics, and pesticides, enriched life while threatening the environment. The chemical plants that manufacture these items from petroleum, natural gas, or coal tar generate excess heat, toxic gases, and hazardous waste as typical by-products. Workers and downwind neighbors suffer from some of the highest cancer rates in the nation. Chlorofluorocarbons (CFCs) have depleted the atmosphere's ozone layer, which filters out harmful ultraviolet radiation from the sun. As a consequence, the incidence of skin cancer and cataracts will increase, and human immune systems' defenses against many diseases will be weakened. Despite efforts to develop CFC substitutes, DuPont Corporation remains the world's largest producer of ozone-depleting substances. In 1989, General Electric Company allowed CFC-laden coolant from 300,000 defective refrigerators to escape into the atmosphere (Crawford, 1994). Industrial countries, led by the United States and followed by western European countries and Japan, account for 84% of CFC production.

Industrial production also contributes to acid rain, which depletes animal and plant life, especially forests, and contaminates drinking water (Howells, 1990; Kemp, 1990; Park, 1987). About 5% of the pollutants in acid rain come from processes in nature; the rest are generated by industrial activity. For example, 90% of the sulfur dioxide in acid rain derives from burning coal or petroleum for heat and electricity; 10% comes from smelting metallic ores and other industrial processes (Karplus, 1992). Not surprisingly, the most active constituents of rain are acid sulfates and acid nitrates in the most industrialized regions of the world, such as eastern North America, Western Europe, and Japan. The average concentration of sulfates in rain was 60 to 100 microequivalents per liter in these areas, compared with less than 2 microequivalents per liter in Antarctica and Greenland. Rainfall in upstate New York contains nearly 10 times as much acidity, sulfates, and nitrites as rain in Oregon (Gould, 1985).

Although agricultural sources are the leading cause of water quality impairment—contributing to 60% of impaired stream miles and 57% of impaired lake acres in the nation (Curtis & Walsh, 1991)—industrial discharge also adds to the problem in local areas. General Electric Company, for example, discharged about 500,000 pounds of polychlorinated diphenyls into the Hudson River during a 30-year period. General Motors Corporation was alleged to have caused groundwater contamination by emitting large quantities of toxic polychlorinated biphenyls (PCBs) near Michigan's Rogue River. State regulators sought more than $32 million in penalties. The EPA estimates that at least 1 million of the estimated 6 million underground tanks used to store petroleum, gasoline, solvents, and other hazardous chemicals throughout the United States are leaking their contents into groundwater. The estimated amount of gasoline and other solvents leaking from these under-ground tanks each year equals the volume of oil from the *Exxon Valdez* tanker's Alaskan coastline spill (Miller, 1992).

Along with its endless supplies of goods and wealth, industry has produced many environmental problems. Although the Industrial Revolution of the 19th century grew in defiance of any environmental constraints, the late 20th century is more sensitive to these limits (Schnaiberg & Gould, 1994). Our civilization, according to U.S. Vice President Al Gore (1993), has been addicted to the consumption of the earth itself. This addictive relation-ship not only distracts us from the pain of our losses but also makes us believe that the environmental problems of industrialization are the inevitable price that must be paid for the unquestionable advantages of industrial society (Mumford, 1963).

Toxic Dumping as a Corporate Way of Life: The Hooker Chemical Case

More than two decades ago, public opinion polls on environmental issues revealed that most people were worried about air pollution, especially smog (Commoner, 1990). Since the disaster in Love Canal was disclosed in 1977, public concern has switched to a new environmental threat—toxic chemicals. Toxic by-products are typical of the new, unexpected hazards created by the massive production of man-made chemicals, which have been rapidly developed and marketed since World War II. By 1965, the American Chemical Society had registered more than 4 million chemicals. The devel-opment of new chemicals has been accelerating in recent years so that the list of distinct chemical compounds grows at a rate of more than 5,000 new substances weekly (Rosenbaum, 1991). The extensive use of this expanding number of chemicals results in a massive problem of toxic wastes. According to the EPA, about 240 million metric tons of federally defined hazardous waste are emitted by U.S. industry each year. The American Chemical Society estimates the true amount is 2 to 10 times the EPA figure (Miller, 1992).

There are five methods to treat hazardous wastes. They may be deposited in a deep well, pond, pit, landfill, or the ocean; burned in an incinerator; detoxified; recycled; or reused. A preventive strategy is to ensure that they are not produced in the first place. Because land disposal is simple, cheap, invisible, and less strictly regulated, it has been the most popular means of disposing of hazardous waste in the United States. At the present time, more than 68% of hazardous waste is handled by disposal. In contrast, 22% is discharged into streams and sewers, 5% is burned, and the remaining 5% is recycled (Miller, 1992).

The legacy of hazardous waste disposal by industry is more than 50,000 abandoned dumping sites across the country. Of this total, 1,235 are believed to pose a serious risk to human health and have consequently been singled out for the National Priorities List of the federal government's Superfund program (EPA, 1982). In addition, as many as 3,500 of the 5,100 active hazardous waste sites are required to conduct extensive cleanups under the 1976 Resource Conservation and Recovery Act. Leaky and corroded underground storage tanks at another 295,000 locations allow hazardous wastes to seep into the surrounding ground where they contaminate groundwater (Hoyle, 1993). In California's Silicon Valley, solvents used in the manufacture of computer chips have leaked from buried storage tanks into the water supplies of several communities. A New Jersey landfill that contained 9 million gallons of hazardous waste contaminated the local aquifer and forced the shutdown of deep water wells that supplied Atlantic City. In Florida alone, 6,000 lagoons and ponds are filled with toxic waste, and contaminants found in the groundwater forced the shutdown of more than 1,000 wells.

In addition, corporations dump approximately 8 million tons of toxic wastes into rivers and coastal waters each year (Erickson, 1992). The long list of toxic substances that end up in the ocean includes nonbiodegradable carcinogens and mutagens, which persist in the environment for extremely long periods. These substances contaminate marine life, some species of which are widely eaten seafood.

The chemical, petroleum-refining, and metal-processing industries have amassed the worst records for toxic chemical dumping. A study of *Fortune* 500 law violators found that the oil industry accounted for half of all—and a third of serious—environmental violations (Clinard & Yeager, 1980). DuPont Corporation released more than a million pounds a day of toxic wastes, mostly into deep wells. General Electric Company is potentially responsible for hazardous waste contamination at about 200 Superfund sites. The EPA found that Rockwell International Corporation's facility for manufacturing nuclear weapons at Rocky Flats, Colorado, may be the nation's most polluted site: 166 hazardous waste dumps were documented there.

USX, Inc., the parent corporation of U.S. Steel and Marathon Oil, has paid more than $34 million in EPA fines for its illegal dumping (Crawford, 1994).

The Hooker Chemical and Plastics Company may provide the most infamous example of illegal corporate dumping. Between 1942 and 1953, the company dumped almost 27,000 tons of toxic and cancer-causing chemical waste into Love Canal, an unused canal excavation in western New York state. Years later, the chemicals began leaking from badly corroded steel drums into storm sewers, gardens, basements, and a playground, contaminating 949 homes and an elementary school built in the 10-square block residential area of Love Canal (Brown, 1981; Gibbs, 1982). The neighborhood was declared a federal disaster area by President Jimmy Carter in 1979. Love Canal, however, is not the "only place where Hooker left its dirty footprints" (Tallmer, 1987, p. 113).

In Bloody Run Creek, a small town not far from Love Canal, Hooker dumped more than 80,000 tons of chemical wastes into a ditch on the bank of a creek. Company officers took few precautions to cover their handiwork. As a result, large quantities of chemicals leached off the site, contaminating the creek and the surrounding area (Tallmer, 1987). In Hicksville, Long Island, just 6 miles east of New York City, Hooker operated a plastics manufacturing plant. Plastic's main component, polyvinyl chloride, is toxic, causing liver cancer, degenerative diseases of the bones, and inflammation of the lungs. From 1946 until 1968, Hooker shipped solid waste in drums from the Hicksville plant to an old municipal landfill in the nearby town of Syosset. After the dump was shut down, the waste was shipped to another municipal dump in Bethpage. These drums contained 478,300 pounds of what Hooker memos called "major current environmental pollution" (Tallmer, 1987, p. 116). In 1973, after the operators of the Bethpage dump refused to take any more drums from Hooker, the company shipped the waste to a landfill in Brentwood. The waste contaminated the wells at Grumman Aerospace Corporation's huge plant adjacent to the landfill. Many Grumman workers had been drinking contaminated water for years.

In White Lake, Michigan, Hooker dumped more than 20,000 barrels of toxic waste on vacant company property behind its plant. Increased rates of birth defects, cancer, sterility, heart attacks, convulsions, and nerve damage among area residents have been attributed to leaks from the barrels, whose storage Hooker kept hidden for more than 20 years. Starting in 1953, Hooker began burning waste DDT and other deadly pesticides on its property in Lathrop, California, after earlier dumping the material. Such burning contaminated several area wells, poisoned animals, and may have threatened human life. Illegal dumping activities by Hooker have been documented in California, Florida, Louisiana, Michigan, New Jersey, New York, and Ohio. Chemical dumping has been Hooker's way of life (Tallmer, 1987).

Hooker exemplifies corporate disregard of the environment at its worst during an era when there were few restrictions on chemical dumping. When tough regulations were enacted in the 1980s, however, hazardous waste violations by major U.S. corporations continued at still alarming rates. One indicator is provided by the country's chemical junkyards, many of which are illegal; they grew in volume by 3% to 10% annually during this period (Rosenbaum, 1991). Although laws such as the Resource Conservation and Recovery Act more strictly regulate the disposal of hazardous waste, they may have heightened the corporate impulse to dump illegally. The expanded ban on dumping confronted companies with the increased costs and technical complexities of treating hazardous waste legally. As a result, illegal dumping became an inviting alternative for companies producing toxic waste—perhaps as many as one of seven (Meier, 1985). Moreover, the Resource Conservation and Recovery Act may have increased the temptation to dump illegally by failing to focus attention on the generation of waste. Instead of curtailing waste production or requiring new technology to control it, the act relies on a compliance system of permits, licenses, manifests, inspections, and ultimately the good faith of waste generators. As a consequence of this arrangement, ruthless or insensitive generators may exploit the need for trust by casting a blind eye on practices of dumpers who dispose of their toxic waste (Scarpitti & Block, 1987).

Hazards in the Workplace

Although the long-term effects of corporate pollution on public health are often disputed or uncertain, the illness and death associated with hazards in the workplace are well documented. Thousands of workers have risked their health from exposure at the workplace to chemical toxins, nuclear radiation, coal dust, asbestos fibers, and other substances. Studies by the National Institute of Occupational Safety and Health in the early 1980s reveal that 1.7 million of the 38 million manufacturing workers are exposed to a carcinogen each year and that on-the-job exposure to chemicals causes 20%

to 40% of all cancers (Claybrook, 1984). Because the production and use of synthetic chemicals by industry have increased in recent years, the workplace dangers to employees in these related industries are growing. The federal government estimates that 15 to 20 million jobs in the United States expose workers to chemicals that might cause reproductive injury. Ninety million workers are exposed to radio frequency or microwave radiation, which causes embryonic death and impaired fertility in animals. At least half a million workers are exposed to glycol ethers, known to cause testicular atrophy and birth defects in animals. Some 200,000 hospital and industrial employees work with anesthetic gases and ethylene oxide, both linked to miscarriages in humans (Marshal, 1987).

Corporate disregard of health and safety in the workplace takes a variety of forms. Some companies ignore the workplace dangers to the health and safety of workers to reduce costs or enhance profits. Film Recovery Systems, Inc., a Chicago-area firm involved in recycling silver from used photographic plates, presents one dramatic example. Because the cyanide solution in plates is highly poisonous if swallowed, inhaled, or absorbed through the skin, workers must be protected with rubber gloves, boots, and aprons, respirators, and effective ventilation. To save money, however, the firm provided workers only paper face masks and cloth gloves. Ventilation was so poor inside the plant that the air was thick with the odor of cyanide. Workers frequently became ill, retreating outside the plant to vomit. Finally, in early 1985, a worker exposed to these conditions died from cyanide poisoning. At the close of the trial, five executives were convicted of murder and sentenced to 25 years in prison. The verdicts were later overturned on technical grounds. Two others were found guilty of involuntary manslaughter (Frank, 1987).

Allied Chemical Corporation, a major producer of pesticides, also placed profits ahead of worker safety (Stone, 1987). The company knew from its own research that its pesticide Kepone was linked to a variety of cancers, deteriorative conditions, and other illnesses. Nevertheless, the company continued producing the deadly substance. Eventually, hundreds of workers were disabled by Kepone traces in their blood. Some lost the ability to walk or stand; others showed signs of sterility.

Some corporations violate environmental laws and then deceive workers about the jeopardy in which they have been placed. Companies may falsify, understate, or deny workplace dangers to their workers. They may submit fraudulent samples, file false reports, or alter health records. Heavy fines were imposed on the Chrysler Corporation, for example, for failing to notify employees about the presence of toxic chemicals at its assembly plants. General Motors Corporation, Union Carbide Corporation, and USX, Inc., were among the firms fined for failing to keep adequate records about occupational health and safety incidents (Clinard, 1990).

Occupational hazards may be a necessary evil in modern industrial societies, but corporate subterfuge in unnecessarily exposing workers to such threats is not (Hagan, 1994). When corporations willingly ignore evidence about occupational illness, continue dangerous manufacturing processes, remain silent about the extreme hazards of dangerous chemicals or the precautions necessary for safely working with them, or falsify reports to escape inspection or penalties, then workers sometimes die, and their employees are in some sense killers.

Environmental Pollution in the Developing World

On August 31, 1986, the *Khian Sea,* a ship of Bahamian registry, sailed from Philadelphia with 13,476 tons of toxic ash from a waste haulage firm, Paolina and Sons. The ash, which contained alarming concentrations of deadly dioxin, presented a significant risk to human health and the environment (Greenpeace International, 1988). When the Bahamian government barred the ship from docking, an endless search for a dumping place began. Rejected by Bermuda, Honduras, Guinea-Bissau, and the Dominican Republic, the ship's cargo was finally accepted by Haiti after an almost 14-month journey. But after only about 3,000 tons of ash were unloaded, the Haitian government suddenly ordered the ship from its waters, citing a constitutional prohibition against importing foreign waste. The *Khian Sea* was forced back to Delaware Bay with about 11,000 tons of ash still on board. In August 1988, the ship appeared in Yugoslav waters but found no way to discharge its cargo there—or at other ports in Europe. Finally, in April 1990, after 18 continuous months at sea, the ship secretly dumped the remaining ash in Bangladesh Bay.

This is not an isolated incident. Many vessels laden with hazardous wastes from the industrialized West make their way from one developing country to another in search of a dumping port (Greenpeace International, 1988). Corporations in the West are anxious to dispose of their toxic waste at the lowest possible price, and developing countries, which are often impelled by poverty and debt to risk their health and environment for money, become the most inviting dumping grounds.

Typically, Western corporations contract with developing countries in Africa, Asia, and South America to dump hazardous wastes. For example, Intercontract, an Italian corporation, contracted with the Department of Natural Resources and Industry of Guinea-Bissau to dispose of at least 50,000 tons of its toxic waste a year for 5 years. Guinea-Bissau was paid $40 per ton of toxic waste and applied the proceeds against its foreign debt of $400 million (Gourlay, 1992). Waste Export Management, Inc., a New Jersey firm, negotiated a contract with the Republic of the Congo to dump up to 6 million tons of chemical waste at the rate of 15,000 tons a week. Sesco Ltd., a British firm, arranged a contract with Benin to store 5 million tons of waste within the country at the ridiculously low price of $2.50 per ton.

Faced with growing public concern about the dangers of plastics to health and the environment, American plastics manufacturers began exporting their waste to less industrialized countries (Gourlay, 1992). In 1991 alone, more than 200 million pounds of plastic waste were exported from the United States to more than 25 countries, including such far-flung locations as China, Ghana, Guatemala, India, Indonesia, Russia, and Trinidad and Tobago (Leonard, 1994). Workers handling plastic powder—the most common form of the waste—contracted illnesses and skin rashes that they avoided when processing locally produced plastic waste. Corporations claimed that their plastic waste was being recycled at foreign sites, but an investigation by Greenpeace, the environmental advocate, questioned this assertion. Its study of recycling facilities in Asia revealed that much of the imported plastic waste was stored in landfills or dumped at random locations (Leonard, 1994).

The U.S.- and other foreign-owned *maquiladoras,* factories just inside Mexico, have also found it more profitable to pollute Mexican terrain than to dispose properly of their waste in the United States. They "have poured chemical wastes down the drains, dumped them in irrigation ditches, left them in the desert, burned them in city dumps and turned them over to Mexican recycling plants that are not qualified to handle toxic waste" (Brook, 1994, p. 81). According to Brook, environmentalists have estimated that cleanup costs from pollution by *maquiladoras* could exceed $50 billion—significantly more than the total earnings of the industry.

Some corporations also relocated production facilities to developing countries to take advantage of their low safety standards and to avoid U.S.

regulations. A case in the furniture industry illustrates this phenomenon. Until 1968,

> Los Angeles was the second largest site for furniture manufacturers in the United States. This $1.3 billion industry employed 63,000. In that year, the South Coast Air Quality Management District mandated the use of spray chambers in all furniture manufacturing plants within its jurisdiction. Shortly thereafter, over 40 firms, constituting the bulk of the industry, announced their plans to relocate in northern Mexico, where the requirements for spray chambers are not enforced. The U.S. General Accounting Office reported that 78 percent of the furniture manufacturers cited environmental regulations as a major reason for moving to Mexico. (Brook, 1994, p. 83)

Clinard (1990) found that the sulfur dioxide limit in Indian chemical plants is six times the limit allowed in U.S. facilities and four times the permissible U.S. limit in battery manufacturing plants. The Indian ammonia limit is seven times greater than the allowed limit in U.S. fertilizer plants. Moreover, in many developing countries, the quality of government inspections of industrial plants is badly compromised by lower safety and health standards, understaffing, and/or inadequate funding. In the 1980s, for instance, Mexico had only about 230 safety inspectors for a workforce of more than 20 million. Indonesia fielded about 300 labor inspectors for its 110,000 companies. India mounted a federal environmental protection staff of only some 150 (Clinard, 1990). Thus, these countries offer Western corporations tempting sites for escaping their homelands' stricter regulation and inspection.

Nuclear power technology branded as hazardous by the United States is being dumped on energy-starved nations such as the Philippines and India (Dowie & Mother Jones, 1987). Since 1975, asbestos use has declined 90% in the United States, and in 1989, the EPA announced a ban on almost all remaining uses of the insulation material by 1997. Nevertheless, products now abound in developing countries as American asbestos manufacturers have relocated operations there. Arsenic trioxide, a mainstay in herbicides, has been strictly regulated in this county to protect workers from the risk of cancer. Asarco, the sole producer of this carcinogen in the United States, has largely shifted its production to the less regulated developing world. In 1990, Asarco owned a 34% interest in Mexico's largest mining company, which produces more than 5,500 tons of arsenic trioxide annually (Rebhan, 1980).

Corporations do not fully insulate themselves from penalty by shifting facilities to locations in the developing world with more lax regulations. When foreign plants operate without the same safety devices or standards present in their U.S. counterparts, their owners are more likely to be held accountable for accidents and negligence. Discrepancies in operations may strengthen findings of liability, especially in high-profile disasters. The gas leak at a Union Carbide plant in Bhopal, India, illustrates this outcome. Union Carbide is one of the 50 largest U.S. industrial corporations; it operates 700 facilities in 35 countries around the world. The Bhopal plant has produced the deadly gas methyl isocyanate since 1980. On December 2, 1984, more than 50,000 pounds of the poisonous gas seeped from a chemical tank and quickly spread airborne across a densely populated city. Between 2,000 and 8,000 persons died, and 200,000 were injured—40,000 of them seriously (Kurzman, 1987; Weir, 1987). The accident has been labeled by the media as the worst environmental disaster in history (Everest, 1988). The disaster occurred when water washed into a methyl isocyanate storage tank and sparked a chemical chain reaction that spewed thousands of pounds of deadly toxins into the atmosphere over Bhopal.

Inadequate safety precautions contributed enormously to the disaster. The amount of deadly methyl isocyanate stored at the Bhopal facility was dangerously large. The plant's safety systems were not designed to cope with enormous releases of gases. Safety equipment to combat accidents was insufficient. Normal maintenance, training, staffing, and company safety procedures were ignored under the pressure of cost cutting (Everest, 1988). Indeed, 2 years prior to the tragedy, a team of American experts detected deficiencies and problems in the plant's equipment and maintenance procedures. The team's warning that the plant posed a serious risk for sizable releases of toxic materials went unheeded.

The export to developing countries of pesticides, especially those prohibited in the United States, is another corporate scandal (Hornblower, 1980). In 1987, nearly 40% of the 1.6 billion pounds of pesticides sold annually by U.S. firms went to foreign buyers. A full 15% of the foreign export is never registered, licensed, tested, or otherwise reviewed by the EPA (Dowie & Mother Jones, 1987). A teaspoon of DDT spilled on the skin can be fatal, yet this toxin is used extensively around the world, particularly in South America (Asinoff, 1986). A number of American chemical companies, including American Cyanamid, Monsanto, Dow, and Hooker, supply the foreign market (Silverman, Lee, & Lydecker, 1982).

Dumping pesticides such as DDT on the developing world has not been without dangerous consequences. Ignorance by developing world residents about the proper use of pesticides has resulted in injury and even death. Many agricultural workers in Latin America, for example, cannot read the instructions and warning labels printed in English or Spanish on pesticide containers (Weir & Schapiro, 1981). Consequently, they often pour excessive amounts of poison on crops or are sprayed while working in the fields, with or without their consent, by crop duster planes. Rural inhabitants use pesticide drums as water collectors and plastic pesticide liners as raincoats. In Indonesia, leptophos, a nerve-damaging pesticide, was sold "alongside the potatoes and rice. . . . People just collect it in sugar sacks, milk cartons, Coke bottles" (Dowie & Mother Jones, 1987, p. 53). In Central America, the pesticide aldrin has been detected at almost 2,000 times the level permitted on food products in the United States (Dowie & Mother Jones, 1987). According to the Oxford Committee on Famine Relief, pesticide poisoning has reached epidemic proportions in developing countries—an estimated 22,000 people die each year (Asinoff, 1986). The World Health Organization found that about half a million people are poisoned by pesticides yearly. Some die immediately, but the long-term effects of exposure on those who live are unknown (Dowie & Mother Jones, 1987).

The American public, caught up in a "circle of poison," suffers as well (Weir & Schapiro, 1981, p. 28). In many developing countries, imported pesticides are not generally used for domestic production. Instead, some 70% of the pesticides are used to increase the production of large-scale export cash crops such as cotton, coffee, tomatoes, and bananas (Clinard, 1990). The Food and Drug Administration found that approximately 10% of the food imported to the United States is contaminated with illegal levels of pesticides (Clinard, 1990). Thus, U.S. residents have become indirect victims of corporations' pesticide dumping overseas.

Explaining Corporate Environmental Crime

Corporate environmental crime is best understood as one type of corporate crime. Theories that illuminate corporate crime in general also shed light on corporate environmental crime in particular. The best explanations are *integrative,* to borrow the term of Frank and Lynch (1992); they analyze different levels of the problem, assess a variety of factors, and accommodate a wide array of facts.

Frank and Lynch (1992) argue that no single theory is able to explain the causes of corporate crime and that a full understanding of the problem requires a more sophisticated strategy. For them, a "good" theory of crime should be integrative in nature, examining both the micro- and macrolevels of causation and addressing the key issues of motivation, opportunity, and law enforcement and social control. This integrative approach has been used widely by researchers on corporate crime. Shover and Bryant (1993), for example, explain corporate crime by reference to the level of the individual firm and the aggregate level of its industry and beyond. The supply of criminal opportunities and the number of firms predisposed to offend at the aggregate level determine the rate of corporate crime. Performance pressure, the estimated certainty and severity of punishment, and the crime-facilitative culture at the level of the individual firm contribute to the probability of criminal participation. Snider (1993) adopts a three-tiered model of explanation. At the psychological level, particular personality characteristics facilitate or inhibit lawbreaking. At the organizational level, certain corporate goals and structure are more susceptible to criminal behaviors. At the social-cultural level, some political and economic systems produce more criminogenic pressures on corporations than do others. In their explanation, Clinard and Yeager (1980) combine characteristics from the individual firm, its industry, and corporate life in general. They argue,

> The immensity, the diffusion of responsibility, and the hierarchical structure of large corporations foster conditions conducive to organizational deviance. In addition, the nature of corporate goals may promote marginal and illegal behavior, as may the characteristics and the social climate of the industries in which firms operate. (p. 43)

Adopting Frank and Lynch's (1992) integrative approach to understanding corporate crime, we propose an explanation of corporate environmental crime that focuses on motivation, opportunity, and law enforcement.

Motivation

Merton (1938) argued that criminal behavior may be a response to the disjuncture (structural strain, as he called it), quite dramatic in American society, between the cultural goal of material success and the available legitimate means to attain it. The ambitious individual may adopt illegal means to become successful, especially if law-abiding norms are weak or ambiguous. Merton's anomie theory offers a macrolevel explanation for corporate crime as well.

The marketplace is highly competitive, and corporations face enormous pressures to outperform rival firms. Confronted by a gap between their goal of financial success and their access to the legitimate resources for achieving it, some corporations commit crimes. They embrace illegitimate means to accomplish their legitimate organizational goal. The extent of strain confronting a corporation—and thus the pressure on executives to commit crimes—is affected by a host of factors, including whether excess competition marks the industry, government controls add to production costs, and bans or delays on marketing products exist (Frank & Lynch, 1992). Thus, a number of chemical firms, for example, succumbed to selling pesticides that are prohibited in the U.S. market to developing countries.

Corporations, however, are legal fictions, not real persons. They cannot carry out action as such. Their middle- and upper-level managers act on their behalf and in their name. So the macrolevel effect of strain—the discrepancy between aim and legitimate means—plays itself out through the behavior of executives. To conform, keep their jobs, or advance their careers, corporate executives commit crimes that benefit corporate success. The goal of corporate success, to which executives may contribute through crime, takes a variety of forms.

The most common version of the goal is increasing profits or reducing costs. Cost containment lies behind much illegal dumping of hazardous waste, for example. The cost of disposing of hazardous waste rose from $10 per ton before the Love Canal catastrophe to $500 per ton by 1988 (Hirschhorn, 1988). As the cost of legal dumping rose, the incidence of illegal dumping grew to scandalous proportions in some parts of the country. The high cost of safety equipment and well-trained workers may prompt manufacturers to get by with dangerous working conditions or unstandardized operations. For example, Allied Chemical Corporation attempted to save money by neglecting safety measure in the production of the pesticide Kepone. As a consequence, many workers experienced liver and brain damage, chest ·pains, personality changes, diminished ability to walk, or sterility (Stone, 1987; Tallmer, 1987).

The goal of corporate success, however, does not always focus on maximizing profits or cutting costs. Companies may seek instead to increase their market share, sustain rapid growth, reduce uncertainty in the market-place, or enhance their prestige. Ciba-Geigy Corporation, a major chemical manufacturer, falsified reports about the nature and amounts of its hazardous waste dumping during a period of rapid growth (Sloan, 1993).

At the microlevel, the fear of failing, losing a coveted assignment or promotion, or being dismissed may push an executive closer to corporate crime. In the *China Syndrome,* the film about meltdown at a nuclear power plant, the general manager and supervisor ignored fatal defects in the gener-ating equipment from fear of losing their jobs. Criminal behavior may also be a virtual job requirement far down the corporate ladder. In the solid waste disposal industry, haulers and yard workers who resist criminal directives may be fired (Rebovich, 1992). Clearly, in the social world of the modern corporation, dedication to the company and conformity to the wishes of one's superiors are seen as essential to success or moving up the ladder (Coleman, 1994).

Psychological factors may also drive some corporate officials to commit environmental crime. Frank and Lynch (1992) report that egocentricity, recklessness, cunning, and the willingness to take self-aggrandizing chances stand out among elite criminals. Rebovich (1992) found that treatment, storage, and disposal facilities for solid waste intentionally select employees who are careless, tolerant, and naive in the hopes of promoting systematic criminality at the workplace.

The factors we have discussed thus far in no way guarantee that envi-ronmental crime will be committed. Executives may have character traits conducive to crime. They may labor in circumstances that invite crime. But they do not all drive their companies into illegitimacy (Frank & Lynch, 1992). In a major study of corporate lawbreaking, Clinard and Yeager (1980) found that approximately 40% of 582 large corporations and 477 manufac-turing firms in the study were not charged with any violations by 25 federal agencies in 1975 and 1976. Illegal behavior is not a necessary condition for business success (Clinard & Yeager, 1980). What else, then, leads corpora-tions down the road of environmental crime?

Opportunity

Motivation combines with opportunity to make corporate criminality more likely (Frank & Lynch, 1992). The opportunity to commit crime has both subjective (or psychological) and objective (or physical) dimensions (Snider, 1993). The subjective opportunity is provided by a company's crime-facilitative culture (Shover & Bryant, 1993). Objective opportunity arises from physical access to a special type and size of corporation (Clinard & Yeager, 1980) or special positions within the firm (Rebovich, 1992).

In a corporate culture that facilitates crime, certain indicative practices are present. They include amoral calculation, organizational incompetence (Shover & Bryant, 1993), ignorance of others' illegal acts, lack of individual initiative to police others (Frank & Lynch, 1992), and a sense of obligation to cover up friends' mistakes (Jackall, 1988). A crime-facilitative culture, however, may also be conceived as a setting that promotes techniques of neutralization—rationalizations for committing crime. Although these techniques were originally discerned in the discourse of juvenile delinquents (Sykes & Matza, 1957), almost identical versions are often espoused by corporate officials to justify violating environmental laws. These techniques consist of denying responsibility for a crime, denying injury to any parties, denying the existence of victims altogether, condemning the condemners, and appealing to higher loyalties. These linguistic devices, when invoked by corporate managers, effectively blunt the moral force of the law, justify the illegal acts, and neutralize any feeling of guilt generated by criminal participation. When these rationalizations dominate a corporate culture, executives are more likely to embrace them and thereby create the subjective opportunity to commit corporate crimes.

When defending the company's pesticide dumping in developing countries, for example, a Velsicol Chemical Company executive argued, "We see nothing wrong with helping the hungry world eat" (Dowie & Mother Jones, 1987, p. 53). West Point-Pepperell Company denied knowing that cotton dust had lethal effects on its textile workers, although thousands of them contracted a variety of diseases, especially brown lung. Kepone, produced by Allied Chemical Corporation, poisoned most plant workers and contaminated the historic James River in Virginia. The chief chemical engineers and plant managers denied that they were Kepone experts and complained that the company failed to give them adequate warning of the pesticide's dangers (Kelly, 1981). Hooker Chemical and Plastics Company denied its responsibility for the Love Canal tragedy by claiming that the potential hazardous risk from their dumping had been documented in local property deeds. Consequently, the school board that bought the site caused the disaster by building a school there (Zuesse, 1981). Where the dumping of toxic chemicals has been considered a common industry practice, many companies have invoked the rationalization, "Everyone does it, so why can't we?" They also blame new environmental laws that they believe interfere with corporate enterprise and disrupt normal productivity (Box, 1983). By condemning laws, they transform themselves in their own eyes from offenders of environmental crime to the victims of government.

Once psychological opportunity is present, access to physical opportunity becomes important (Snider, 1993). An executive, armed with a powerful rationalization, still cannot commit corporate environmental crime unless two other conditions also exist. First, the executive must, in most cases, work in a large company whose business can cause environmental harm. Second, the executive must occupy a management position with the authority to make decisions on behalf of the corporation. Clinard and Yeager (1980) found that the type and size of a company are two important independent variables associated with corporate violation. Although large corporations committed a significantly disproportionate share of the violations, the leading types of violators were the oil, motor vehicle, and pharmaceutical industries. The first two of these industries can cause significant damage to the environment.

The structural characteristics of the large company—more than those of the small firm—favor illegal behavior. In general, as an organization grows in size, its specialization and decentralization also increase (Blau, 1970; Hall, 1982; Pugh, 1984; Scott, 1975). Organizational differentiation and delegation of authority in a large firm foster a climate that allows corporate executives and managers to abdicate decision making, disregard the work of others, and avoid legal as well as moral accountability for their actions (Clinard & Yeager, 1980). Managers often remain isolated from each other in their separate hierarchies of authority. Specialists fare no better with their separate functional duties. These conditions can foster irresponsible behavior and poor communication that lead to lawbreaking. In addition, difficulty arises in assigning blame to any one executive for illegalities carried out for the organization as a whole. In the case of *United States v. Pacific Hide and Fur Depot, Inc.* (1986), the jury found the company violated the Toxic Substances Control Act of 1976 when its general manager failed to manage properly the disposal of capacitors that contained PCBs. The defendant lacked actual knowledge of the violation because of the structural complexity of his company.

Not surprisingly, certain industries are more likely to commit environmental crimes than are others. Oil companies, among the leading violators in the survey by Clinard and Yeager (1980), pose environmental risks with their lawbreaking. Rebovich (1992) found that most illegally disposed wastes were generated by the chemical and petrochemical industries, although the actual spectrum of waste sources in the states he surveyed was much broader. He notes,

> Maine's cases evidenced textile-, wood-, and fishing-industry wastes whereas much of the New Jersey sample's wastes were derived from the chemical-producing and petrochemical industries. Pennsylvania and Maryland samples displayed a significant concentration of cases where primary waste sources were metal electroplating, galvanizing, and other metal treatment processes. . . . A waste-type source that was unique to the Maryland sample was that of pathological research waste. . . . The proper treatment of medical wastes has become a significant problem for Maryland. (pp. 34-35)

In sum, corporate environmental crime is more likely to be committed by corporate officers in a large, hazardous waste-producing firm in which a crime-facilitative culture is espoused.

Law Enforcement

Corporate environmental crime may occur when crime-prone individuals (with traits that predispose them to committing crime), occupying decision-making positions in a crime-prone firm (in which a culture that facilitates crime prevails), are motivated to violate environmental laws on behalf of corporate goals. The quality of law enforcement affects the likelihood of this outcome. Corporate crime, like street crime, can be viewed as a rational choice. Frank and Lynch (1992) argue that

> both corporations and individuals make an assessment of how big a risk they undertake if they choose to commit crimes. If there is little enforcement of the laws that pertain to the corporation, or if the enforcement agencies assigned to detect violations of law are small and underfunded, corporate actors might decide that the rewards from committing crime are greater than the chance of being apprehended. (p. 119)

Corporate environmental crime is probably encouraged by the weakness of environmental law enforcement. Environmental protection has been a concerted government effort only since the 1970s. Because the understanding of the nature and consequences of environmental pollution is still limited, the laws and regulations are incomplete. Moreover, the enforcement of existing environmental law lacks ample technical expertise, personnel, and funding. Thus, the detection of environmental crimes is flawed, and punishment of wrongdoers is uncertain. The environmental record of Allied Chemical Corporation illustrates how weak law enforcement breeds corporate environmental crime.

From the first, the company's Virginia plant, which produced Kepone, a highly toxic pesticide, was considered a model of bad environmental practices (Kelly, 1981). Kepone "dust flew through the air . . . saturating the workers' clothing, getting into their hair, even into [their] sandwiches" and creating a dense cloud of dust that rose at least 16 miles in the air and spread 64 miles through the river water around the factory (Stone, 1987, p. 122). Within the first 2 weeks of production, workers at the factory began to experience "Kepone shakes." By the time the plant was shut down, all the 133 workers tested revealed traces of Kepone in their blood. A hundred miles of the James River were closed to all fishing because of the contamination by Kepone. Thousands of pounds of Kepone still lie on the river bottom. The estimated cost of removal—$100 to $500 million—was prohibitive. The top managers of the plant were charged with 153 counts of violating the Federal Water Pollution Control Act (Kelly, 1981).

Government agencies were grossly remiss—some would say blind—in enforcing environmental laws against the facility. The Virginia Air Quality Resources Board, for example, maintained an air-monitoring filter only a few hundred feet from the plant. Unfortunately, Kepone was not on the list of chemicals the station had been told to monitor (Kelly, 1981). The Virginia Water Quality Control Board became aware of the Kepone problem in October 1974. It had the authority to shut down the plant but allowed the firm to correct the problem voluntarily. EPA investigators were also alerted to the crisis first in 1974 and then in 1975 but declined to investigate actively the situation. According to a study by Public Citizen, the number of workplace inspectors declined 17% and the follow-up inspections dropped by 86% during the Reagan administration. Moreover, inspectors cited fewer violations and imposed less severe penalties (Frank, 1993). The lack of vigorous law enforcement made the crime possible.

Conclusion

We have avoided a simple, single-factor explanation of corporate environmental crime. Following the theoretical framework of Frank and Lynch (1992), we have instead adopted an integrated approach that emphasizes a variety of influences. We have selected factors mostly from theories of corporate crime because corporate environmental crime is one type of this larger category of criminal activity. We have also added several distinctive factors to our explanation to reflect the special character and circumstances of environmental crime.

Corporate environmental crime, we argue, is the product of motivation and opportunity conditioned by the quality of law enforcement. Motivation has both structural (or macro) and individual (or micro) elements. When the drive for corporate success (usually expressed as greater profits or lower costs) greatly exceeds the legitimate means for achieving it, the structural groundwork for motivation is laid. Executives in this situation of strain may turn to illegal means to accomplish corporate aims. But the executives most willing to break the law on behalf of the corporation will often have some personal motivation as well, typically marked by fear of dismissal or some lesser loss, or personality traits, such as cunning, that are conducive to committing crime.

But motivation is not a sufficient condition for corporate environmental crime to occur. Two types of opportunity must also be present. First, the objective opportunity to commit crime must exist. Three circumstances provide this opportunity: a type of industry—such as oil or chemical production (as opposed, for example, to computer software)—that has a major potential impact on the environment; a large firm—in which muddled accountability and poor communication are more likely—within that industry; and a position of significant decision-making authority within that firm. Second, the subjective opportunity—the perception of opportunity by the lawbreaker—must exist. When an executive is socialized into a corporate culture that facilitates crime, he or she perceives more opportunity for crime. Such a culture fosters crime by stressing criminogenic norms of behavior such as amoral calculation and by providing rationalizations—techniques for neutralizing guilt—for criminal behavior. The executive who sees more criminal opportunities is more likely to act criminally.

Finally, the quality of law enforcement conditions both motivation and opportunity. If law enforcement is certain and severe, then opportunity and motivation are constricted by the high cost of crime—the great likelihood of apprehension and unacceptable punishment. If law enforcement is lax, misguided, or intermittent, then it is more likely that structural motivation will push firms in the direction of crime, that executives' crime-prone characteristics and sense of criminal opportunity will take hold, and that the objective opportunities to commit crime will expand.

Review Questions

1. What are the defining characteristics of corporate environmental crime?
2. Why is Hooker Chemical and Plastics Company often cited as the worst example of corporate disregard for the environment?
3. What are some of the chief ways companies jeopardize the health and safety of employees in the workplace?
4. How and why do U.S. corporations export environmental pollution to developing countries?
5. What motivates corporations to commit environmental crimes?
6. How does the quality of law enforcement affect the likelihood of corporations committing environmental crimes?
7. What are the chief features of the explanation for corporate environmental crime presented in the text?

CHAPTER 4

Organized Crime Against the Environment

The corporation founded to conduct legitimate business is not the only type of organization that commits environmental crime. The business enterprise undertaken expressly to profit from illegal activity has also been attracted to environmental wrongdoing. Indeed, criminal organizations, typically operating as corporations, have penetrated a variety of environmentally sensitive industries and now carry out a substantial portion of environmental offenses. In this chapter, we define the criminal organization and distinguish it from its legitimate counterpart. The chapter examines organized crime's domination of the hazardous waste disposal industry and presents a theoretical explanation for this form of environmental criminality.

Organized Crime Defined

Organized crime has been defined simply as "crime that is organized" (Bynum, 1987, p. 4), thus collapsing any distinction between it and corporate crime. Organized crime has also been narrowly defined as crime by the Mafia. The problems in defining organized crime well were recognized as early as 1976 by the Task Force on Organized Crime of the U.S. National Advisory Committee on Criminal Justice Standards and Goals (1976). They persist today (Hagan, 1994; Petrakis, 1992).

Nevertheless, most criminologists now agree that organized crime is characterized by hierarchy, financial profit through crime, the threat or use of force, corruption to obtain immunity, a code of secrecy, and restricted membership (Hagan, 1994). Moreover, they place organized crime along a continuum from semiorganized crime, which is locally based and only loosely organized, to fully organized crime, which criminally dominates—indeed often monopolizes—a service or product market and is run centrally as a national syndicate (Hagan, 1983; Ianni, 1973; Maltz, 1985; Smith, 1980). The concept of a continuum avoids the static model of a single type of organized crime, accommodating the different degrees to which this crime is indeed organized. We define organized crime as offenses by a continuing illicit enterprise that is hierarchically organized, principally engaged in criminal acts, and operated by resort to force, violent threat, or other illicit aggressive behavior. Although organized crime is committed by businesses founded to achieve criminal aims, corporate crime, in contrast, is carried out by firms that engage mainly in legal commerce.

Organized Crime and Hazardous Waste

Although environmental offenses range across a variety of industries from petrochemical refining, machinery manufacturing, and transportation equipment production to electric and gas utilities and sanitary services, organized crime against the environment is most strongly associated with the disposal of hazardous waste. The precise extent to which organized crime controls the waste disposal business is unknown, but its involvement is substantial as evidenced by state and local police investigative reports, trial transcripts, grand jury depositions, U.S. Senate and House committee hearings, news stories, and illegal dumpers' own testimony. Organized crime figures have played a prominent role in the industry for some time, especially in the Northeast and Midwest (New Jersey Superior Court, 1980; New York State Senate, 1980; U.S. House of Representatives, 1980, 1981b).

A number of factors have contributed to organized crime's infiltration of the industry. Since the 19th century, the federal and state governments have regulated solid waste enterprises that directly affect public health by granting licenses and permits to do business to private garbage haulers, incinerators, and owners/operators of landfills and dump sites (Savas, 1977). The government investigates violations of permits and punishes violators. Although this governmental control effectively protects public health by restricting the random disposal of human and industrial wastes, it has also created a new industry of garbage collection and disposal. The industry's profit potential eventually attracted organized crime figures. By the late 1950s, racketeers controlled garbage collection in many parts of the country (U.S. Senate, 1957).

More recent developments have drawn organized crime into toxic waste disposal in the 1970s. The amount of toxic waste to dispose of grew to astonishing levels by the end of the decade. Spurred by the breakneck pace of producing new chemicals, American industry, in the first four decades after World War II, annually created more than 380 billion pounds of solid wastes and 412 billion pounds of aqueous hazardous wastes from organic chemicals alone (Sarokin, Muir, Miller, & Sperber, 1985). As wastes proliferated, chemical companies sought alternative methods to get rid of them. Legitimate disposal by incineration, biological treatment, or chemical decomposition under company auspices was becoming cumbersome and expensive. For example, the cost of legally treating hazardous wastes in the 1970s ranged from $15 to $550 per 55-gallon drum. To cap matters, the Love Canal disaster in 1978 raised public concern about the environmental damage from chemical companies' dumping of toxic wastes.

Organized crime seized the opportunity created in the 1970s by the volume of hazardous water, the inadequacies of older techniques of disposal, and public alarm about chemical dumping. Organized crime began to move on the toxic waste disposal industry and shape it like the solid waste business (Block & Scarpitti, 1985).

Major criminal syndicates, especially Mafia families, became a dominant force in the industry in industrial states such as New York and New Jersey. Industry penetration by the Mafia was facilitated by the collusion and support of corrupt politicians and law enforcement officials (Block & Scarpitti, 1985). Organized crime mainly used three tactics to achieve prominence in the toxic waste disposal industry in these two states.

First, to eliminate competition and ensure high profits, organized crime bosses divided up the region into territorial monopolies based on the "property" claims of the different families (Szasz, 1986). According to this principle, a hauler was granted the exclusive rights to picking up solid waste in a given territory without competition from others. Organized crime bosses also purchased their own landfills in which they could dump hazardous waste from their territories (Block & Scarpitti, 1985). A New Jersey state police officer, in testimony before a Congressional hearing, described organized crime's control this way. "I am saying that someone operating in north Jersey and central Jersey areas, no way can operate unless somewhere, somehow, they are dealing with members of organized crime—given approval to deal in those territories" (U.S. House of Representatives, 1981b, p. 101). Territorial monopolies allowed for noncompetitive pricing of hazardous waste disposal and ensured huge profits for organized crime.

Second, the threat or use of violence was the most effective means of enforcing "property rights." If a legitimate firm engaged in toxic waste disposal in a territory assigned to organized crime interests, it was invited to join the criminal enterprise. Firms that resisted often became the targets of violence and intimidation. A case from Ramapo, New York, illustrates this process (Block & Scarpitti, 1985).

In the fall of 1975, the local planning board of Ramapo, New York, sought bids for a contract to manage the municipal landfill. The contract was awarded to Eugene Sorgine, a building contractor from nearby Mahwah, New Jersey. Sorgine had taken his company, recently up for sale, off the market after potential buyers could not meet his price. The Ramapo contract was a great windfall that reinvigorated his business's financial potential. Shortly after word of awarding the contract was publicized, Carmine Franco, head of the New Jersey Trade Waste Association, attempted to buy the Ramapo contract for a nominal fee, but Sorgine refused. In the following weeks, Franco became more persistent. He angrily pressured Sorgine at odd hours on the phone. Sorgine held his ground until the evening his house caught fire. His wife and children escaped unharmed, but the home itself suffered extensive damage. The next morning, Franco once again contacted Sorgine and asked him if he was now ready to sell his contract. Sorgine agreed. The transaction was completed by the end of the same business day. The selling price was even less than Franco's initial offer. Shortly after Franco took over the Ramapo landfill, Rockland County sheriff's officers observed his trucks illegally discharging hazardous liquid waste. The Ramapo landfill was finally closed in early 1984 by the New York state environmental commissioner after it was documented as the cause of contaminated drinking water in the area (Block & Scarpitti, 1985).

Third, organized crime figures advanced their control of the toxic waste business by corrupting local officials. They jockeyed for the inside track with state and municipal agencies that had jurisdiction over toxic waste disposal. The New Jersey secretary of labor, for example, was alleged to be closely associated with organized crime. A New York state senator jointly owned at least two landfills with a notorious organized crime figure. Public officials were bribed by organized crime members to ignore illegal dumping and keep it hidden from public scrutiny. For example, two organized crime figures applied in 1987 to open a new landfill in Chester County, Pennsylvania, after they had already poisoned at least three facilities in southern New Jersey, where they controlled much of the toxic waste disposal industry. When local residents protested to the Pennsylvania Department of Environmental Resources in 1987, they were told that the owners' history of poisoning New Jersey landfills was irrelevant. Permission to open the Chester County landfill was granted. In another case, two public works supervisors in Camden, New Jersey, were found guilty in the early 1980s of receiving kickbacks for allowing Mafia contractors to dump commercially generated debris, as well as toxic waste, at the city transfer station, which was restricted to receiving only local residential waste. After an 8-month investigation by the state's Environmental Crime Bureau, the two officials were sentenced to 6-year prison terms and required to forfeit their salaries earned during the life of the racketeering enterprise (Blumenthal, 1983; Epstein, Brown, & Pope, 1982).

Organized crime's influence extends to the local judicial system, which often imposes light sentences on mobsters who are found guilty of environmental crimes or treats their illegal activities with greater tolerance. Carmine Franco, the defendant in the Ramapo case, was indicted for a wide range of state environmental violations including falsification of state-mandated waste records, failure to disclose properly the presence of hazardous materials, restraint of trade, and racketeering. Nevertheless, he was only fined and prohibited from further involvement in the waste disposal industry in Rockland County, where the Ramapo landfill was located (Block & Scarpitti, 1985).

The Chemical Control Corporation of New Jersey, deeply immersed in organized crime, stored barrels of hazardous chemicals at a site where they leaked into the nearby Edison River. More alarming than this negligent behavior was the firm's deliberate dumping of chemicals into the river. The company incinerator ran nonstop night and day, producing foul-smelling odors, thick black smoke, and frequent nighttime ash and soot storms. State agencies received numerous complaints about the company's handling of waste. The Department of Environmental Protection noted that the firm's incinerator was in disrepair and appeared much too small to handle the volume of chemicals being processed. Nevertheless, neither a stack test to identify the pollutants entering the atmosphere nor nighttime inspections were conducted. In the next 2 years, landfills owned by the firm became organized crime's primary dumping ground for all the toxic waste carted from their territories in New York and New Jersey. Thus, in its brief 12-year history, the Chemical Control Corporation was transformed from a careless, sometimes illegal operation to a full-fledged criminal enterprise controlled by organized crime. In the end, it was not the justice system but a massive chemical fire that shut down the company (Block & Scarpitti, 1985).

The Tri-State Land Development Corporation and the Almordon Environmental Corporation, which operated in New York and Pennsylvania, were charged with illegally dumping toxic waste and diverting profits from the scheme to top Mafia bosses (Perez-Pena, 1993). According to a 60-count federal indictment, 14 defendants, including 5 from the Lucchese crime family, paid more than $500,000 in 1989 and 1990 to the Lucchese boss, Vittorio Amuso, and his underboss, Anthony S. Cass. The two companies operated illegal dumping ventures in Ulster County, New York, and Pike County, Pennsylvania. With the Lucchese family as a silent partner, the dumping netted more than $3 million in 2 years. The firms, without appropriate licenses, accepted construction and demolition waste, which routinely contained lead and other hazardous material. They also engaged in racketeering, made false claims to regulators in both states, coerced subcontractors into falsifying soil contamination tests, laundered money, evaded paying taxes, and committed mail and wire fraud. This case has been regarded as a "classic example of the infiltration of organized crime into the lucrative waste disposal business" (Perez-Pena, 1993, p. 6).

Hazardous Waste Offenses as Group Crime

Research before the 1990s has linked hazardous waste disposal to elements of traditional organized crime. Mafia families, organized into hierarchies, sought dominance in the industry by establishing exclusive property rights to regional territories, threatening nonunion firms with violence if they competed independently, and influencing local politicians and law enforcement officers through bribery or other techniques of corruption. Significant other research, however, by Donald Rebovich (1992) in *Dangerous Ground: The World of Hazardous Waste Crime* presents another perspective. Rebovich analyzed hazardous waste offenses and offenders in 71 cases from Maine, Maryland, New Jersey, and Pennsylvania. In 21 states, he interviewed law enforcement personnel who specialize in hazardous waste enforcement.

Group Crime

Rebovich (1992) concludes that in his four sample states, hazardous waste offenses did not result from industry takeovers by traditional crime families. The offenses were rarely committed as the "acts of a formal, criminal monolith," and the criminal units were not "as large or as centralized as traditional syndicate crime" (pp. 60-61). Little evidence supported the view that syndicate crime dominates the hazardous waste disposal industry. Instead, Rebovich found that generator offenses were criminally organized only "on the most fundamental level" or in "the workplace structure," and their organization usually took "the form of simple criminal conspiracies" or consisted of an "independent criminal unit" (pp. 60-61). The criminal arrangements were "primarily designed for illegal profit without the typical hallmarks of traditional syndicate racketeering (for example, threats of violence or corruption of officials)" (p. 60). Typically, criminal behavior was "loosely knit" and grew from "simple, individualized offenses, such as midnight dumping" (pp. 60-61).

Hazardous waste offenses, Rebovich (1992) argues, thus better fit the definition of group crime: crime committed by two or more people (as opposed to members of a more structured organization) for illegal profits and power, advanced by racketeering activities and, when appropriate, intricate financial manipulations (U.S. National Advisory Commission on Criminal Justice Standards and Goals, 1976). Rebovich (1992) discovered that most of the hazardous waste crimes were committed by multiple offenders operating in independent units. The hazardous waste conspiracies within treatment, storage, and disposal (TSD) facilities in New Jersey illustrate group crime being committed on two tracks in the workplace structure. The upper-level offenders—the owners and executives of the facility—consider criminality as a means to increase profits for themselves and the business as a whole. The lower-level offenders—for example, the yard worker and truck driver, who were hired because of their previous criminal records and scant technical knowledge—participate in illegal activity to keep their jobs. The group crime is supervised by a manager or higher-level executive but actually is carried out by a lower-level employee. Both levels join in the covert reward system of TSD legitimate and illegitimate profits. Thus, although criminality is typically confined to only a fraction of executives and owners in large generating companies, the criminality in the TSD workplace "pervaded all employment ranks" and is supported by a subculture into which all the firm's employees are socialized (Rebovich, 1992, pp. 100-101). As a result, removing or prosecuting one or two executives at the top is unlikely to halt criminal activity.

In the other three states that Rebovich (1992) studied, most detected group dumping offenses were committed by small generating firms with fewer than 50 employees. Because small firms lacked their own landfills, they had to contract with outside vendors to treat and dispose of their waste. As a consequence, their criminal behavior was quite visible. Large generators, in contrast, tended to protect themselves from discovery by disposing on site, a convenient but illegal alternative (Rebovich, 1992). Therefore, it would be misleading to conclude that large generators are not high-priority offenders.

Interfirm Connections

Group offenses by generating companies were carried out in conjunction with other waste-related firms. Thus, to understand group crime in the hazardous waste industry, interfirm relations must be examined. Two types of interfirm relations in group crime were identified (Rebovich, 1992). The first was shaped by criminal agreements between the generator, hauler, and TSD facility operator to dispose illegally of wastes at a savings to the generator and increased profit to the hauler or the TSD operator. Whether these generators knew that other members of the triad were acting illegally is uncertain. But it is clear that haulers either cemented ties with landfill operators to ensure acceptance of their waste or dispensed waste on their own land that was unapproved by the states.

In an alternative approach, a generator first formed a criminal alliance with the hauler who collected the waste and shortly thereafter disposed of it unlawfully. Other generators in the same industry then established an identical relationship with a criminal hauler. This shared practice by firms in the same industry helped legitimize in their own eyes their criminal waste disposal activities (Rebovich, 1992).

Group crime in the disposal of toxic waste in Maine, Maryland, and Pennsylvania exhibits "cooperative behaviors" but no monopolistic domination by a single criminal organization (Rebovich, 1992, p. 64). In addition, interfirm ties are not built or maintained by violence. No instances were uncovered where offenders protected their criminal relations by corrupting local officials. Instead, organized crime groups engaged in hazardous waste disposal tend to be loosely structured and flexible. They do not belong to a large, hierarchically structured organization. Their connections are shaped for the most part by the structure of patron-client ties, friendship, and other types of relationships.

Organized Crime in New Jersey

Although traditional organized crime had not infiltrated hazardous waste disposal in Maine, Maryland, and Pennsylvania, it was present to some degree in the New Jersey TSD industry. In 3 of the 23 New Jersey cases that Rebovich (1992) reviewed, officials of charged TSD facilities were identified as associates of a traditional criminal organization. More centralized control over a number of hauling, storage, and disposal firms was found. Violence was used to force a TSD's owner out of his facility. In the New Jersey TSD industry, criminal organization was more complex with some syndicate characteristics. Traditional organized crime, however, was not involved in the majority of hazardous waste disposal offenses in New Jersey.

In sum, Rebovich (1992) discovered a world of hazardous waste crime in which the intensity, duration, and methods of the criminal act are more likely to determine the criminal opportunities available in the marketplace than the association with and control by a criminal syndicate. The apparent contradiction between Rebovich's findings on group crime and Block and Scarpitti's (1985) discovery of monopoly control by organized crime in the hazardous waste disposal industry can be resolved. Each is viewing a different part of the beast. Together, they underscore the diversity of forms organized crime may take in disposing of toxic waste. They confirm the value of viewing organized environmental crime along a continuum: Territorial monopolies, controlled by organized crime families, lie at the top of the continuum, and group crime lies toward the lower end.

Explaining Organized Environmental Crime

Environmental crime by criminal organizations can be explained by insights from four theoretical perspectives: anomie, differential association, cultural transmission, and social control (Abadinsky, 1990).

Anomie

Anomie, as conceived by Merton (1938), is the structural strain in a society from culturally prescribed aspirations that exceed socially structured avenues for realizing them. When this discrepancy is great, people may compensate for the inadequacy of legitimate opportunity by engaging in criminal behavior. Crime becomes the illegitimate means to achieve legitimate goals. In American society, monetary well-being and material prosperity flourish as cultural goals. The doors of opportunity for economic success, however, are closed for some and only ajar for others. When people espouse the cultural end of economic success but the social structure denies them the legitimate resources to attain it, they may engage in crime. Since the 1940s, the chemical revolution has tremendously increased the volume of hazardous waste while adding enormously to the cost of its legitimate disposal. Illegal dumping has become an easy way to make not only quick but huge profits because anxious hazardous waste generators are eager to rid themselves of waste at the least cost. Organized crime, falling short of the American dream, may seize on this illegitimate opportunity to become "the embodiment of the great American success story" (Abadinsky, 1990, p. 46).

Differential Association

Merton's theory shows how a structural condition of society can generate the motivation in individuals to commit crimes. But it leaves unanswered the question of "why do some persons suffering from anomie turn to criminal innovation while others do not" (Abadinsky, 1990, p. 47). Sutherland's (1973) theory of differential association provides an answer. People learn how to commit crimes, he argued, mostly through primary group interactions—contact with others in intimate personal groups. What is learned within the socialization process includes not only the techniques of committing crime but also the motives, attitudes, and rationalizations that support it. A person becomes criminal after learning an excess of definitions favorable to violating the law over definitions unfavorable to violating the law. A case in New Jersey discussed by Rebovich (1992) illustrates this learning process:

> A yard worker, of a TSD facility adjacent to a waterway, commenced his employment with responsibilities of mixing wastes with solutions to produce usable byproducts. After several promotions, he found himself laboring near the water's edge, secluded from the rest of the facility, connecting waste-filled tanker trucks to a grounded hose.

Coworkers and supervisors alike maintained the hose was linked to underground holding tanks. The worker's confidence in this explanation was shaken after he witnessed wastes surfacing in the abutting waterway. The worker at first questioned the legitimacy of the activities, but became satisfied that the procedures were part of the normative structure. When reality eventually set in, as reported by the worker, he had become a fairly long-standing participant in the criminal activities and decided it was prudent to remain within the group and practice a self-imposed silence with other, newer employees at the facility. (pp. 54-55)

Cultural Transmission

The theory of cultural transmission stresses the importance for becoming criminal of a proper setting—ecological niches—in which education in the ways of organized crime is available. According to Cressey (1969), a leading proponent of this perspective, an organized crime group will survive only if it has "an institutionalized process for inducting new members and inculcating them with the values and ways of behaving of the social system" (p. 236). With regard to hazardous waste crime, these ecological niches are provided by the illegitimate TSD facility. Rebovich (1992) found that lower-level workers in the facility were selected because of their criminal records, lack of technical expertise about hazardous water, and ignorance about the consequences of environmental offenses. Their criminal conversion occurs in "normal day-shift activities," where they are given "marginally criminal assignments like the lateral stacking of incompatible wastes." They have exclusive contact with the facility's "core group" of veteran criminal disposers for committing overt offenses. Finally, they learn how to participate actively in "detection avoidance." This conversion process transforms the "novice employee from reluctant co-conspirator, to willing criminal partici-pant" in the criminal dumpers' world (p. 54). Within the illegitimate TSD facility, unlawful activities become the workplace norm, accepted by every employee. As a result, criminal activity could easily continue even if super-visory managers were removed from the setting and successfully prosecuted.

Social Control

Social control theory, propounded by Hirschi (1969), provides the most powerful explanation for the dominance of traditional organized and group crime in the toxic waste disposal industry. The theory of social control argues that internal and external restraints on behavior determine whether persons move in the direction of crime or law-abiding behavior. Internal restraints are produced during socialization under the influence of family, school, and other important groups. These can deter a person from committing crime in the absence of external authority by instilling a sense of guilt. External restraints, which induce a fear of being caught by authority and punished by law, are equally important in crime deterrence. The external restraints against environmental crime are especially weak for a number of reasons.

First, the implementation of environmental law is often lax. The Re-source Conservation and Recovery Act of 1976, for example, established a manifest system, which authorizes the states to register corporate generators of hazardous waste and to license hauling and disposal firms. Nevertheless, "in New Jersey, the state where organized crime intrusion into hazardous waste is most thoroughly documented, . . . [these] major provisions of the RCRA were poorly implemented and enforced" (Szasz, 1986, p. 10). Hauling permits were issued to any applicant who paid a nominal $50 fee. Interim disposal permits were also freely granted to landfills, even those with no real disposal facilities (U.S. House of Representatives, 1980, cited in Szasz, 1986).

The Resource Conservation and Recovery Act required documentation of the movement of hazardous waste "from cradle to grave"—from the generator, through the transporter, to the shipment's final arrival at a licensed disposal site. Until 1980, however, New Jersey never assigned a single person to monitor the manifests being filed in the state capitol (U.S. House of

Representatives, 1981a). "Once a license was obtained, lax supervision of the manifest system made illegal and unsafe disposal of hazardous waste a relatively straightforward low-risk activity" (Szasz, 1986, p. 11).

Second, inspections of hazardous waste disposal are often improperly conducted. Inspectors are often unfamiliar with treatment apparatus or inattentive during inspections. Inspectors were described by hazardous waste workers in Rebovich's (1992) study as so "slow" that the owners of the illegal TSD facility were able to stay "several steps ahead of them" (p. 36).

> Some of the inspectors that were coming to the site, they didn't know what was going on. All they would look at is the pipes. They just asked which way the material went. They weren't really interested in retention time, you know. They asked you but never stayed and observed and took samples. (p. 36)

The failure by inspectors to thoroughly examine treatment apparatus permitted facilities to continue operating criminally for a protracted period. The inspectors' investigative naïveté also allowed offenders to anticipate inspection cycles and consequently avoid being detected (Rebovich, 1992).

Third, corruption of state workers also weakens the external restraints against environmental crime. State regulators of hazardous waste were sometimes co-opted by illegitimate operators. They were tempted with generous promises of corporate jobs on resigning from their regulatory posts. State inspectors and law enforcement officers sometimes went on to serve with TSD facilities as full-time employees or part-time security guards. The criminal facilities took full advantage of these former state workers' expertise to avoid legal pitfalls and uncover loopholes (Rebovich, 1992).

Fourth, state personnel sometimes engaged in knowing regulatory neglect. They permitted illegal, even harmful, practices because they believed no other reasonable choices existed (Marino, 1982). State regulatory agencies often faced intractable questions. Where is all the garbage going to go if we close down landfills? Who is going to pay for cleaning up landfills known to be poisoned (Scarpitti & Block, 1987). When legitimate solutions were hard to find, the tolerance of illegitimate operations rose. Regulatory neglect was also rationalized as an incentive to businesses to relocate or remain in the region. A Maryland assistant attorney general remarked,

> They say, "Well this is a nice city to be in. I'd like to set up my company in this city." It improves the employment market. The company moves here,

hires people—it's good for the city. It's not that the city is interested in just violating the environment per se. It's that it presents a more positive business climate if you have lax regulations. . . . These are matters where our enforcement philosophy is quite different than the city's. (Rebovich, 1992, p. 89)

Review Questions

1. What is the text's definition of organized crime?
2. What factors influenced organized crime's infiltration of the hazardous waste disposal industry?
3. Why does Rebovich prefer to characterize hazardous waste offenses as group crime?
4. How does Rebovich's perspective differ from that of Block and Scarpitti?
5. What are the chief features of the explanation for organized environmental crime?

CHAPTER 5

Environmental Crime by the Government

Corporations and criminal combines are not the only organizations that commit environmental crime. Government is a third type of organizational offender. What sets the government as a criminal apart is its responsibility for enacting and carrying out law. The lawmaker and enforcer may be the lawbreaker. Crimes by the government have a special poignancy because the government is charged with protecting the people from crime. That criminal organizations engage in environmental crime does not surprise us. Environmental crime by corporations may seem an inevitable consequence of doing business. But when the government, which is empowered to protect the environment, commits crimes against it, we are especially indignant—although in these cynical times, no longer startled.

Governmental Crime Against the Environment Defined

Disagreement about the definition of governmental crime abounds (Barak, 1991; Chambliss, 1989; Douglas & Johnson, 1977; Friedrichs, 1995a; Geis & Meier, 1977; Kauzlarich & Kramer, 1993; Kramer & Michalowski, 1990; Sharkansky, 1995). The controversy between the strict legalist and the social legalist approaches to the study of crime underlies this dispute.

The strict legalists restrict crime to offenses that are prohibited by law and therefore punishable by incarceration. The social legalists cast a wider net: Crimes include significant moral wrongs whether or not they are expressly banned by law.

Social legalists dispute the strict legalists' claim that the criminal law accurately accounts for the full catalog of wrongdoing deserving of punishment as criminal behavior. They point to the government's self-interest in exempting itself from its own definitions of crime and punishment. For reasons of self-preservation alone, government, as the author of law and the final arbiter in society, is unlikely to define its misbehavior broadly as crime or to submit to the criminal law's sanctions. Some actions by government will be agreed on by all nations as crimes—assassination, terrorism, piracy, and fraud, for example. But others, such as the environmental damage of war, copyright theft, and the privations of collectivized agriculture, may cause enormous injustice and even violate universal human rights without being acknowledged as crimes (Barak, 1991). If the strict legalist approach is adopted, then a wide range of government wrongs must be excluded from analysis.

International law offers the type of broader standards that social legalists prefer for defining governmental crimes. By embodying principles of freedom, social justice, equal opportunity, and due process, international law presents a more satisfactory basis for designating a variety of grievous wrongs as crimes by the government. Although international law shines a morally brighter light on governmental wrongdoing, it is enforceable in practice only by consent among nations—which is to say, infrequently. Governmental crimes consequently may be recognized by international law, but they are rarely prosecuted. No state has ever voluntarily relinquished its sovereignty to an international prosecutor or court with broad powers to try crimes by the government, and the prospects for creating such an agency are dim (Molina, 1995).

With these difficulties of conception and enforcement in mind, we adopt the following definition. Governmental crime is illegal, environmentally harmful activity "carried out from within or in association with governmental status" (Friedrichs, 1995a, p. 74). Governmental offenses are defined as crimes by domestic law, principles of international law, or the provisions of international agreements. Although international tribunals are unlikely to succeed in prosecuting governmental crimes against the environment, we include international law as an authority for defining these offenses. This concession to the social legalist perspective seems warranted here.

Offenses by lower levels of government may be readily redefined as crime by higher levels of government. For example, in the federal system in the United States, national laws may define certain offenses by states, counties, and municipalities as crimes. But there is no higher source than the national government—except the Constitution itself—to declare of what its crimes may consist. Because the national government acknowledges few of its misdeeds as crimes, some guidance from international law is appropriate if the environmental offenses of nation-states are to be fully discussed.

Governmental crimes against the environment may entail abuse of power, corruption in office, and a variety of political scandals, but it stands in contrast to state crime, whereby criminal action is carried out as an expression of official policy. Governmental crime against the environment can be committed by agencies, officeholders, workers, or government-supported organizations from the municipal through national levels. Personal gain may result, but this is not the wrongdoer's chief objective. Finally, governmental crime against the environment may consist of the commission of acts that violate environmental law or principles or the failure to enforce the law or carry out administrative duties.

Crimes of commission are illustrated by the military's generation of millions of pounds of hazardous waste in connection with manufacturing, testing, and operating weapons (Goewey, 1987); the release in wilderness areas of large amounts of pesticides from U.S. Forest Service agricultural activities (Breen, 1985); the immense disposal of medical wastes by Veterans Administration hospitals (Breen, 1985); radioactive discharges at federal facilities for producing power or weapons-grade nuclear material (U.S. General Accounting Office, 1986); and deforestation prompted by the U.S. Forest Service's selling off millions of acres of logging rights in national forests to private timber firms (DeBonis, 1991). Crimes of omission are exemplified by the negligence of the South Carolina State Water Control Board in apprehending Kepone polluters, delays by local and state government in protecting victims of the environmental crisis at Love Canal, and the EPA's failures to strictly enforce a variety of environmental regulations, especially against the military. We turn now to examining in more detail important examples of governmental crimes against the environment.

Crimes of Commission

Nuclear Testing by the
Atomic Energy Commission

Before the first light of dawn on January 27, 1951, an Air Force B-50 bomber banked left over juniper and Joshua trees and dropped an atomic bomb on the desert west of Las Vegas. The flash of light awakened ranchers in northern Utah. The concussion shattered windows in Arizona. The radiation swept across America, contaminating soil in Iowa and Indiana and the coastal bays of New England. Thus began nuclear testing, the most prodigiously reckless program of scientific experimentation in U.S. history. Between 1951 and 1963, the government detonated 126 nuclear bombs in the sky above the 1,350-square-mile Nevada Test Site (Gallagher, 1993). Each explosion sent aloft a cloud of radiation roughly equal to the release from the Chernobyl nuclear disaster in the former Soviet Union.

At that time, the serious effects of nuclear testing were not considered an environmental issue, let alone an environmental crime. Nuclear testing continued after the passage of the first environmental laws in the 1970s. From 1945 to 1989, more than 1,800 nuclear bombs were detonated at more than 35 sites. One quarter of these tests took place in the atmosphere, and one third of the remaining underground tests are believed to have leaked radiation (Finger, 1991).

The U.S. Public Health Service has documented that nuclear testing by the U.S. government poisoned soil in Virginia, milk in New England, wheat in South Dakota, and fish in the Great Lakes (Gallagher, 1993). The main victim of the nuclear testing program, however, according to a team of Congressional investigators, is "our own people" (Gallagher, 1993, p. xvi). Army infantry men were ordered to observe the test from unprotected trenches. In 1982, 1,200 downwind residents in the Southwest, victimized by nuclear testing, brought a lawsuit against the Atomic Energy Commission (AEC). Ninety-eight witnesses described how exposure to dangerously high radiation from the Nevada testing had killed family members and friends. Secret files of the AEC discounted "downwinders" as "a low-use segment of the population" (Gallegher, 1993, p. xxiv).

Although the AEC privately acknowledged the environmental danger of radiation, it refused to sound any public alarm. Committed to maintaining nuclear superiority over the Soviet Union during the Cold War, supporters in Congress and the White House joined the conspiracy of silence. Finally, in 1978, President Jimmy Carter reversed a 30-year policy and ordered relevant AEC files opened to public scrutiny. An AEC conspiracy to hide its environmental record was exposed: The agency had lied in Congressional hearings, destroyed documents, given false testimony in court, and denied in the media any harm to the public. The courts eventually ruled in victim lawsuits that a terrible miscarriage of justice had occurred and that the AEC had perpetrated a fraud (Gallagher, 1993). Not until 1990 did Congress pass the Radiation Exposure Compensation Act, which recognized the human toll from nuclear testing and provided modest stipends to some families of victims.

Disposal of Hazardous Waste by the Military

Bristling with sophisticated technology, the U.S. military leads the world in destructive capacity. Not surprisingly, it is also the largest polluter in the country (Minister, 1994). The EPA has placed more than 100 military sites at the top of the National Priorities List for environmental cleanup. Thousands more require eventual cleanup as the result of haphazard disposal, spills, and leaks of hazardous materials (Calhoun, 1995). The U.S. Department of Defense (DOD) has identified approximately 15,000 contaminated sites in about 1,600 military bases around the country. As much as 99% of high-level radioactive waste is attributed to military sources (Finger, 1991). The military generates more than a ton of toxic waste every minute, creating a more ominous environmental threat in a year than the top five U.S. chemical companies combined (Minister, 1994).

The military has routinely violated bans on ocean dumping by discarding waste fuel, paint, paint thinners, and cleaning solvents at sea. For example, a sailor testified at Congressional hearings that while on sewage and scullery detail aboard the USS *Abraham Lincoln* in the late 1980s, he was ordered to dump 200 garbage bags overboard every day. The garbage contained raw sewage as well as hazardous wastes. A fellow seaman was ordered to throw paint, solvents, and plastics into the ocean. Another seaman, serving aboard the USS *Juneau* from 1984 to 1988, routinely threw empty cans and solvents overboard (Alibrani, 1993).

A retired Navy pilot came forward in 1980 to tell New Jersey environmental officials that he participated in three dumping missions. Flying from a field near Philadelphia, he and his crew on each of three trips dumped more than 6 tons of nuclear wastes into the ocean. Another retired Navy pilot divulged that he had undergone six similar missions in San Diego (Sharkansky, 1995). The Line Air Processing Company apparently flushed 37 million gallons of radioactive water from a uranium processing plant into five wells that once supplied drinking water. The firm had recommended this method of disposal "because our law department advises that it is considered impossible to determine the course of subterranean streams, and, therefore, the responsibility could not be fixed" (p. 41).

The U.S. General Accounting Office reports that from 1946 to 1970, most ocean dumping occurred at four major sites off the U.S. coast. One site was 140 miles southeast of Sandy Hook, New Jersey; the second was 220 miles southeast of Sandy Hook. Together, these two sites accounted for 50,000 containers. The third site, where 4,000 containers lay, was located in Massachusetts Bay, only 12 miles east of Boston. Finally, the fourth site, holding roughly 45 containers, lay off the Farallon Islands, 50 miles west of San Francisco. Secret dumping at unknown sites is thought to vastly exceed these totals. The General Accounting Office notes the dismal record keeping of dumping projects: "The federal government has no complete and accurate catalogue of information on how much, what kind, and where low-level nuclear waste was dumped because detailed records were not required" (National Advisory Committee on Oceans and Atmosphere, 1984, p. 85).

The intentional disposal and discharge of toxic wastes inside military bases are also rampant. For example, an investigation at the Naval Air Engineering Center in Lakehurst, New Jersey, revealed that more than 3 million gallons of contaminated fuel, hydraulic fluid, solvents, and other highly toxic chemicals had been dumped into the ground during the previous 2 years. In 1980, highly toxic acrylonitrile was detected in the ground at 35,000 times the maximum level allowed by EPA (Shulman, 1992). The Lakehurst base sits at the northern tip of the Pine Barrens, a federal wilderness area and home to the largest aquifer in the Northeast. The aquifer is the chief source of water for southern New Jersey. Denver's Rocky Mountain Arsenal, a U.S. Army installation, holds the disgraceful honor of having created earth's most toxic square mile, a nearly hundred-acre basin of deadly chemicals (Shulman, 1992).

Environmental Damage During Wartime Military Operations

Although the military may not recklessly or intentionally dispose of hazardous wastes, no domestic environmental law bans the use of inhumane, indiscriminate, disproportionate, or treacherous weapons in a war for reasons of environmental protection. International law, however, does contain such a prohibition. The 1977 Special Arms Control Treaty prohibits military use of environmental modification techniques as a means of destruction in war or any other hostile action (United Nations General Assembly, 1976). The term *environmental modification techniques* refers to methods that alter the dynamics, composition, or structure of the earth (U.S. Congress, 1978). Environmental modification techniques pose a widespread, long-lasting, or severe threat to the environment (U.S. Arms Control and Disarmament Agency, 1990). Their use, by this standard, constitutes a governmental crime against the environment.

U.S. military operations during the Vietnam War wreaked environmental havoc on the country. Three tactics in particular would probably have been banned as environmental modification techniques under the 1977 Special Arms Control Treaty had it then been in effect. Defoliants, sprayed from low-flying planes, stripped plants of foliage and, indeed, killed plant life in general if doses were repeated or high. Defoliation was intended to destroy food crops, thereby starving the enemy, and to clear roadways of plant life (Zilinskas, 1995). Second, heavy earth-moving equipment physically leveled ground cover such as trees and bushes to reduce the risk of ambush. But in the process, the land was severely damaged, and local ecosystems were destroyed (Johnstone, 1971). Finally, rainmaking was widely practiced to make roads impassable for vehicular traffic, destabilize hillsides along roads, and flood rivers so that bridges and other river crossings would wash out (Zilinskas, 1995). Intelligence sources estimate that rainfall increased 30% in rainmaking areas and hampered enemy transport of supplies (U.S. Congress, 1988).

Although these operations had specific military objectives, they clearly caused widespread, long-lasting, and severe harm to the environment. About 12% of Vietnam's landmass was damaged by defoliation and land clearing. Of commercial-quality timberland, 1 1/4 million square meters were destroyed by defoliants, as well as 5 to 11 million square meters of unmarketable timber. Replacing lost nutrients, restoring a balance among species, and regrowing mangrove forests on defoliated or physically cleared land are long-term projects. Reversing erosion will take decades (Zilinskas, 1995). The National Academy of Sciences concluded that ecological damage from herbicides in South Vietnam—a U.S. ally—may take a hundred years to heal. The study noted substantial damage to inland tropical forests and destruction of the coastal mangrove swamp forests, a major breeding ground for fish and shellfish (Finney, 1974).

While U.S. military operations in Vietnam ruined vegetation, land, and waterways, human beings—including Vietnamese and American soldiers—were also victimized. Agent Orange, a widely used defoliant in Vietnam, contains the toxic chemical dioxin. Minuscule doses of dioxin—in some cases a few parts per trillion—have caused death, cancer, birth defects, and other disorders in laboratory animals. Pregnant test animals who have been fed food with just one part dioxin per trillion have produced an unusually large number of stillborn and dying offspring (Regenstein, 1982). Exposure exceeds these laboratory levels in many parts of Vietnam. During the peak spraying years of 1967 through 1969, approximately 3 gallons of Agent Orange per acre were blanketed on an area of South Vietnam about the size of Rhode Island and Connecticut combined (Gough, 1986). Insisting at the time that Agent Orange was nontoxic to humans, the U.S. Army continued using it until 1970.

By 1974, the National Academy of Sciences found that an alarming number of South Vietnamese women exposed to Agent Orange gave birth to babies with cleft palates, twisted limbs, and incomplete spines and faces (Council on Environmental Quality, 1981). The incidence of a rare form of cancer of the liver increased fivefold during the time of U.S. defoliation, presumably as the result of being exposed to dioxin (U.S. Senate, 1974).

The Veterans Administration has estimated that several hundred thousand U.S. veterans of the Vietnam War may have been exposed to Agent Orange (Council on Environmental Quality, 1981). Congressman David Bonior, himself a Vietnam veteran, believed that "all 2.5 million Vietnam veterans may have been exposed to the herbicide because of its entry into the food chain and water system" (U.S. House of Representatives, 1979, p. 7). More than 12,000 Vietnam veterans filed medical disability claims between late 1979 and early 1982 asking for compensation based on exposure to Agent Orange. They reported a wide range of problems, including defects in offspring, cancer, nervous disorders, dizziness, personality changes, chronic coughing, impotence, liver and kidney disease, muscular weakness, loss of sex drive and appetite, insomnia, blurred vision, ringing in the ears, and skin rashes. Veterans filed a class action lawsuit against Dow Chemical Company and other firms. Eventually, the defendants agreed to one of the largest out-of-court settlements in U.S. legal history. Although the federal government was protected against lawsuits by the doctrine of sovereign immunity, it deserved to be the real defendant. The government had experimented with Agent Orange for many years and knew about its toxicity as early as 1962 (Wilcox, 1983). It nevertheless contracted with chemical firms to produce Agent Orange for wartime use (Schuck, 1987). More recently, veterans of the Persian Gulf War have charged the DOD with covering up the extent of their exposure to poison gas and other toxic materials of war.

The U.S. Department of Energy and Federal Weapons Production Facilities

The federal government is the nation's largest business. It owns almost one third of the land in the United States, operates 27,000 installations and 387,000 facilities, and employs more than 3 million workers (Calve, 1991; U.S. Bureau of the Census, 1992). Its enormous variety of activities includes construction, manufacturing, telecommunications, transportation, agriculture, publishing, medical care, generation of electricity, and, most important, production of weapons (Breen, 1985).

These activities often pose serious risks to the environment, just as the commerce and industry of private business do. For instance, more than 20,000 federal installations across the country have reported environmental contamination on their grounds. For fiscal year 1993 alone, nearly $10 billion was allocated for the cleanup of federal facilities (Doyle, 1993). In this section, we focus on the systematic disregard of environmental laws at federal weapons production facilities, under the supervision of the U.S. Department of Energy (DOE).

The DOE, established by President Carter, oversees producing nuclear materials, assembling nuclear components into warheads, and designing and testing nuclear weapons (Lamperti, 1984). It operates 17 facilities, employs more than 100,000 workers, and spends more than $8 billion annually (Kauzlarich & Kramer, 1993). The DOE carries out most of these programs under contract with large corporations such as General Electric, Lockheed Martin, and DuPont. In general, contractors design, develop, and manufacture the nuclear weapons, whereas the DOE owns the equipment and materials in the production facilities and supervises the contractors' activities. The contractors perform the day-to-day operations within the weapons production facilities, where they must meet all DOE environmental, health, and safety requirements. The DOE oversees the contractors' performance by conducting appraisals and audits of their work and ensuring compliance of the entire complex with environmental law. The National Academy of Sciences, however, has argued that "DOE directives to their contractors are often vague," providing "the corporation with a great deal of latitude in the interpretation of DOE orders" (cited in Kauzlarich & Kramer, 1993, p. 13). Severe violations of environmental law result at these federal facilities. The longest-standing offense has been the mishandling of the immense radioactive and other toxic wastes left by producing nuclear materials. The cost of correcting the damage would be enormous.

> In 1986, the Savannah facility generated over 200,000 gallons of waste each day, and the Hanford plant has dumped over 200 billion gallons of radioactive and hazardous wastes since its inception in 1942. Indeed, the contamination wrought by nuclear weapons production is so severe that the General Accounting Office estimates the cost of getting the complex into compliance with applicable environmental laws would be a startling 250 billion dollars. (Kauzlarich & Kramer, 1993, p. 14)

The Hanford Nuclear Reservation, in Washington near the Columbia River, was America's major source of plutonium from 1945 to 1986. From late 1944 through 1955, plant operators secretly released an estimated 53,000 curies of radioactive iodine—the equivalent of a major nuclear accident—into the surrounding atmosphere. In addition, millions of curies of radioactive material were released at least until 1970 directly into the Columbia River (Frank, 1993). The Hanford facility sits on more radioactive waste than does any other producer of nuclear material. More than 1,300 waste sites within its perimeter—trenches, tanks, ponds, sand-covered pits, and underground storage cribs—store 1.4 billion cubic meters of hazardous materials. Leaks from these sites are believed to have contaminated the groundwater beneath almost a quarter of the reservation (Gerber, 1992). In addition, each of 177 huge tanks at Hanford holds more than 4 million liters of chemical and radioactive waste. A potentially explosive mixture of gasses was discovered in the late 1980s to be leaking from some of these tanks (Dan, 1990).

More than 13,000 people living near the Hanford Nuclear Reservation have probably received significant dosages of radiation from secret emissions at the facility in the 1940s (Shulman, 1992).

Although the current level of airborne radiation considered safe by the U.S. government for civilians living near nuclear weapons plants is 0.025 rads per year, a study found that the level of radiation in a large number of residents living in the vicinity of the plant during and after World War II may have accumulated in excess of 33 rads during a 3-year period. In addition, a small number of infants and children could have accumulated doses of radiation in their thyroid glands as high as 2,900 rads during the same period (Shulman, 1992). Residents have also been affected by drinking milk from cows that grazed on contaminated grasses near the facility and drinking water and eating fish from the Columbia River (Steele, 1989). The Hanford Nuclear Reservation is the most seriously contaminated nuclear production site in the United States. It has been labeled "the dirtiest place on Earth" (Fishlock, 1994, p. 37).

At the Rocky Flats Nuclear Weapons Plant in Colorado, safety and contamination are also major concerns. The plant, operated by Rockwell International Corporation, was partially closed in October 1988 after two employees and a DOE inspector inhaled radioactive particles (Gerber, 1992). Evidence revealed that plutonium and toxic chemicals had been released into the surrounding air and soil at Rocky Flats for nearly 35 years (Johnson, 1988). An estimated 200 million gallons of wastewater were sprayed on a 17-acre parcel that drained into the Great Western Reservoir and nearby streams. In addition, 275,000 tons of plutonium were dumped and buried at the plant. Rocky Flats violated the Resource Conservation and Recovery Act by disposing of hazardous waste and discharging radioactive materials without permits (U.S. Congress, 1988).

The Fernald Feed Materials Production Center near Cincinnati has also been a source of worrisome disclosures. The complex, which began in 1952, was shut down in December 1984 after the DOE disclosed that during a 3-month period, excessive amounts of uranium dust and oxides had been released through ventilating systems (Gerber, 1992). Hearings by the Senate Governmental Affairs Committee in 1985 and 1987 revealed that more than 230 tons of radioactive material from the plant had leaked in the Greater Miami River Valley during the preceding three decades. Thousands of kilograms of uranium dust had been discharged into the atmosphere and surface water. Five million kilograms of radioactive and other hazardous substances had been disgorged into pits and swamps, permitting percolation into groundwater (U.S. Congress, 1985). This contamination prompted nearby citizens in 1986 to file a lawsuit against the plant. A settlement of $78 million compensated Fernald's neighbors for lost property values and medical tests (Associated Press, 1989).

Deforestation by the U.S. Forest Service

Clear-cutting of forests ranks high as a "green crime" (Frank & Lynch, 1992). Although tropical deforestation has become a celebrity issue around the world, the destruction of old-growth forests in the United States has aroused much less attention. Untouched, old-growth forests once covered much of the lower 48 states. Today, about 96% of these virgin forests, including California's original coastal redwoods, have been cleared away (Miller, 1992).

Deforestation is a direct result of the clear-cut, contributing to the greenhouse effect and the extinction of plants, animals, and insects world-wide. It will "eventually affect humans, as global temperatures rise, coastal flooding occurs, pollution and respiratory illnesses increase, and the planet's natural balance is thrown off kilter" (Frank & Lynch, 1992, p. 89).

Private timber cutters are not solely responsible for this problem. The U.S. Forest Service also plays a key role in the destruction of old-growth forests on public lands. Before World War II, the major timber companies logged primarily on private land. By clear-cutting privately owned old-growth forest as quickly as possible, they maximized profits: Timber brings financial returns, whereas uncut timber incurs property taxes (Newton & Dillingham, 1994). World War II witnessed an abrupt increase in timber demand at a time when much of the more accessible privately owned land had already been cut. In response, the Forest Service began its transformation from "guardian to arm of the timber industry" (Miller, 1992, p. 18). By the postwar era, it was the "federal timber company" (p. 30).

The philosophy of the modern Forest Service encourages exploitation. The Forest Service Manual emphasizes that a key object of the agency is to make available "the timber, water, pasture, mineral, and other resources of the forest reserves . . . for the use of the people. They may be obtained under reasonable conditions without delay. Legitimate improvement and business enterprise will be encouraged" (Robinson, 1990, p. 46). In keeping with this aim, the Forest Service has gone into the business of selling trees and making money from the sale. Indeed, half its annual budget is covered by the proceeds of timber sales (Miller, 1992).

The agency acts as an auxiliary of the lumber industry, instead of a protector of public assets or at least a skilled entrepreneur of natural resources. To facilitate access by commercial timber companies to public forests, the Forest Service constructed a huge network of roads. The agency is now considered the country's biggest constructor of roads, overseeing a road grid that is eight times longer than the entire federal interstate highway system (Heritage Foundation, 1991). The more roads the Forest Service builds, the more trees are cut, and the bigger the budget the agency can obtain and perpetually underwrite. Not only is the mission misguided; it fails to turn a real profit for the taxpayer. Economists estimate that the Forest Service loses up to $200 million a year (Newton & Dillingham, 1994). The agency has been accused of selling trees so cheaply "that loggers would be foolish to say no. It [the Forest Service] builds roads, pays rangers, absorbs the risks of fires and insects, then sells at a loss" (p. 121).

The Forest Service overestimates the number of trees ready for harvest. A mapper for the Forest Service claimed that the government often plots "phantom trees" on computer maps of areas stripped by clear-cutting. This deceptive practice allowed the agency to report falsely that nearly three quarters of an area of clear-cut land in Idaho contained mature trees. The Forest Service overestimates the potential harvest of old-growth forests in the Pacific Northwest by about 20% (U.S. Department of Agriculture, 1992). Overestimation helps perpetuate the Forest Service in the timber business. It persuades the large timber companies that there are more trees on the land than there actually are. Stirred by the prospects of a large timber harvest, the timber companies invest millions of dollars in lobbying Congress and the federal government to open the forests to cutters. And the Forest Service remains in the business of selling public forests for money.

Finally, the Forest Service understates the environmental effect of its timber sales. By law, the Forest Service is required to prepare an impact statement before any timber is sold or lands are mined. With half the agency's budget revenue derived from timber sales, it is strongly tempted to skew impacts in favor of cutting. Forest Service agents who put together big timber sales are more likely to get promoted, and those who speak out against timber sales or their detrimental effects are more likely to get transferred (Miller, 1992). A researcher hired by the Forest Service to assess the impact of tree harvesting on rare plants found herself out of a job when she refused to alter her assessment conclusions from "will be affected" by deforestation to a more ambiguous "might possibly be affected" ("Forest Service Stops Whistle Blowers," 1992). A Forest Service manager, a veteran of 32 years, was fired after he told a Congressional committee in sworn testimony that there is "a pattern of lawlessness" in the agency. According to him, the Forest Service "had become comfortable with lying to the public, ignoring long-festering problems, and serving the timber industry as government agent of environmental destruction" rather than environmental protection (Earth First, 1992b, p. 2). The manager was given a direct reassignment after he failed to meet timber quotas demanded by Idaho and Montana politicians. He told the House Civil Service Subcommittee that the quotas applied to his region were impossible to meet without breaking federal environmental protection laws (Earth First, 1992b). In sum, "Agency managers ignore ecological impacts and environmental laws alike in their push to meet timber targets and please agency administrators, local industry, and members of Congress." (Earth First, 1992a, p. 1).

The Forest Service manages national forests as a business operation to make money, not as ecosystems to preserve. This approach has been ruled illegal by Robert M. Parker, Chief Judge of the U.S. District Court of the Eastern District of Texas. He held that the agency "violated the National Forest Management Act's requirements to maintain biodiversity and to limit clear-cutting, seed tree and shelterwood logging" ("Judge Halts," 1993, p. 1).

Crimes of Omission

A crime of omission is the offense of failing to act when there is an obligation to act. If the failure is willful, wanton, and reckless—and a person is killed as a consequence—the offense could elicit a charge as serious as manslaughter. The government is bound by a host of specific laws; more generally, it has moral and legal obligations to its citizens to fulfill its constitutionally prescribed aims. When the government deliberately fails to meet these statutory or constitutional obligations, it is guilty of crimes of omission (Henry, 1991). Such offenses might include woefully insubstantial flood relief, dangerously constructed public housing, and shoddy police protection. When public school systems are unaccountable and negligent in enforcing minimal academic performance by students, they may be committing crimes of omission (Cabrera, 1995). Schools are thereby failing to fulfill part of their social contract, professional mission, and statutory obligation to offer individuals education to their potential. The government's failure to protect the environment entails crimes of omission. The government often fails to discharge its responsibilities and carry out its obligations with respect to environmental protection. The consequences are just as severe as—sometimes more devastating than—the damage from environmental crimes of commission (Henry, 1991; Ross, 1995)

The Departments of Energy and Defense at Weapons Production Facilities and Military Bases

The DOE, as supervisor of operating contractors' activities, is responsible for compliance with environmental law at federal weapons facilities. The EPA allows the DOE, in effect, to regulate its facilities' controlled radioactive releases into ground and surface water, radioactive waste production, and radioactive leaks into water. The DOE is consequently obligated to issue directives to facility contractors about obeying environmental law and standards. In addition, its field offices must conduct appraisals and audits on the contractors' work to detect and correct immediately potential environmental problems. The DOE has dragged its feet in carrying out these duties. In some cases, it has even refused altogether to comply with environmental laws. The burden of DOE's responsibilities lies with these environmental laws: the Clean Water Act of 1972, the Clean Air Act of 1970, and the Resource Conservation and Recovery Act of 1976. For many years, the DOE argued that its activities were exempt from the Resource Conservation and Recovery Act under the national security provisions of the Atomic Energy Act of 1954 (Kauzlarich & Kramer, 1993; Reicher & Scher, 1988).

The DOE described its operations at its Rocky Flats facility as "patently illegal" and "in poor condition generally in terms of environmental compliance." It then ignored the problems and even rewarded the operating firm with bonuses for their "protecting" the environment as evidenced in its regulatory practices and cleanup techniques (Abas, 1989, p. 22).

DOE directives to weapons facilities on environmental standards have often been vague (National Academy of Sciences, 1987), resulting in confusion or lack of compliance. For example,

> In the 1987 DOE-UNC contract, the DOE ordered UNC to "operate and monitor the N Reactor and support facilities in a safe, secure, and environmentally sound manner, to achieve a fiscal year production goal of 705 KMWD with less than 24 unscheduled outage days." While this directive may be legally inclusive, and thus rather direct in nature, the DOE does not provide the contractor with the specific methods to achieve compliance with applicable environmental issues. It is in this sense that the DOE order could be considered relatively vague. Additionally,the above clause seems to indicate that the DOE is sending a message to the contractor that, while safe and environmentally sound procedures of waste disposal (which are unspecified) are important, it is equally important that precise production quotas are met. (Kauzlarich & Kramer, 1993, p. 13)

The DOD, like the DOE, avoided its environmental obligations on lands under its control. For example, the Comprehensive Environmental Response, Compensation, and Liability Act (CERCLA) requires the cleanup of hazardous waste sites, especially those on the National Priorities List. More than 17,000 military properties are threatened with potential contamination; a hundred of these are at the top of that list. The DOD took 6 years to develop a plan for cleaning up thousands of contaminated sites under its control (Shulman, 1992). By 1993, cleanups were under way or completed at 34% of the National Priorities List's nonfederal sites, almost four times the rate of remediation at federal—mostly military—sites (Doyle, 1993). The Emergency Planning and Community Right-to-Know Act of 1986 provides another illustration of DOD dereliction. The law grants communities a right to know about hazardous waste use and storage in their area. Private industry has cooperated with the EPA in proffering the required information. The EPA then publicizes the findings through its database, the Toxic Release Inventory. The DOD, in contrast, has refused to release such information. The Lakehurst Naval Air Engineering Center, for example, dumped more than 3 million gallons of carcinogenic aviation fuel and other toxic chemicals into the ground, threatening to contaminate southern New Jersey's water supply. Lakehurst officials hid the full extent of their knowledge of the contamination at the base from outside agencies and the public (Shulman, 1992). At the Cornhusker Ammunition Plant in Nebraska, the Army withheld information for 2 years about dangerously high levels of explosive compounds contaminating nearby drinking water wells. The public was treated like "mushrooms," with the Army keeping them "totally in the dark" (p. 75). Because the military severely restricts public access to information about its environmental noncompliance, most citizens are unaware of the environmental dangers at military installations across the country. The facilities delay or sometimes avoid altogether their statutory obligations to clean up the environment they have despoiled (Minister, 1994).

The Environmental Protection Agency

The chief purpose of the federal EPA, created in 1970 by executive order of President Nixon, was "the protection, development, and enhancement of the environment" (Lewis, 1985, p. 4). It assumed responsibility for air pollution control, water quality maintenance, solid waste management, pesticide registration and control, and radiation standards (Lewis, 1985). The EPA focuses mainly on two major fronts: enforcing environmental laws against industry and developing scientific standards to ensure a safe and healthy environment. Critics argue that the EPA failed in its mission and has deteriorated into a bureaucratic agency without a soul (Cahn & Cahn, 1985). It has committed a variety of crimes of omission, as the following review of its failures underscores.

EPA's Enforcement Efforts Are Often Weak

The EPA, to cite one example, has been criticized for not effectively enforcing the Clean Water Act's permit program in Region IV and the Chesapeake Bay Region. Weak enforcement resulted mainly from poor management, inaction against chronic violators, and ineffective use of civil and administrative penalties (Adler & Lord, 1991). EPA oversight of state enforcement programs is also extremely weak. Each of the major environmental laws, such as the Clean Water Act, the Resource Conservation and Recovery Act, and the Clean Air Act, allows state governments to assume primary control over environmental regulation in their regions. As a condition for assuming regulatory control, however, a state must meet minimum federal standards for pollution abatement and control. The EPA retains the legal authority to enforce federal law in states that fail to take timely and appropriate action. In reality, EPA often ignores or downplays inadequate state enforcement. For instance, the Clean Air Act, enacted in 1970, required each state to produce a state implementation plan for fulfilling air pollution standards for airshed within its boundaries by 1979. By 1977, however, Congress was forced to extend compliance deadlines to 1982 when it became apparent that few states could meet the requirement. In May 1982, 2 months before the new deadline, EPA concluded that 31 states still failed to meet the air quality standards mandated by Congress.

During the period of noncompliance, the EPA was to have imposed sanctions on states in violation; penalties included a prohibition on any new stationary source of air pollution and the withholding of federal grants to highways and to pollution control and sewage treatment facilities. Deadlines came and went with no sanctions imposed (Rosenbaum, 1994).

The agency's administration of the Superfund program has fallen far short of expectations (Hynes, 1989). Armed with a $1.6 billion bankroll, the EPA was mandated to rank, investigate, and clean up in 5 years the nation's 400 most serious hazardous waste sites. In its first decade of running the Superfund program, EPA took more than 5 years just to assess and classify the average hazardous waste site. Comprehensive cleanups have been so rare that EPA cannot realistically calculate the cost or time for cleaning up a site (Hynes, 1989). EPA has focused its entire efforts on industrial waste sites and abandoned dump sites. Problems of environmental contamination that do not fit this model are neglected. For example, urban soil contains high levels of lead, and farmers' wells are compromised by pesticides, but EPA has largely ignored these sources of environmental contamination (Hynes, 1989).

EPA Fails to Enforce Some
Environmental Laws Altogether

Under the Federal Insecticide, Fungicide, and Rodenticide Act (FIFRA) of 1972, the EPA is authorized to evaluate every pesticide planned or in use, weighing its benefits to agriculture against the harm of residues to food consumers and the environment. Where the risks are high, the EPA may ban, restrict, or relabel the pesticide. In 1986, the U.S. General Accounting Office found that the EPA, during FIFRA's 14-year history, had failed to evaluate the safety of the majority of chemical pesticides in use. The General Accounting Office concluded that at its current pace,

> EPA will not finish its review and reassessment of the safety of pesticides in use until well into the twenty-first century. Until this is completed, we will not know the full environmental and health risks of the fifty thousand older pesticides which are still in use, primarily in agriculture. (Hynes, 1989, pp. 149-150)

The EPA has also refused to implement and enforce the provisions of the Resource Conservation and Recovery Act. Under this act, the EPA was charged with regulating the disposal of toxic wastes but for 2 years failed to translate the act into concrete regulations. As a consequence, approximately 260 million pounds a day of toxic chemicals were deposited in the environment without federal regulation (Regenstein, 1982). When regulations were finally devised, loopholes and other deficiencies made them ineffective. For example, operators were required to care for their dump sites for only 20 years after they closed, far too short an obligation, according to critics. Future "Love Canals" were likely to occur; indeed, they were "probably already happening across the country" (p. 156). Congress found the regulations so wanting it estimated that leakage from 80% of identified waste sites could have continued unchallenged (U.S. House of Representatives, 1979).

Although the Resource Conservation and Recovery Act established a monitoring system "from cradle to grave" for tracking toxic wastes, the EPA did not put it into effect until November 1980. To beat the deadline, chemical companies rushed to dump thousands of tons of hazardous and toxic wastes that they had stored on their property for months or even years (Regenstein, 1982).

The EPA has excluded many extremely toxic pesticides from regulation by choosing to ignore "such obviously relevant properties as infectiousness, radioactivity, or teratogenicity and mutagenicity that have the ability to harm unborn children or cause genetic alterations" (Regenstein, 1982, p. 157). The EPA has mishandled licensing procedures for firms or individuals handling hazardous wastes. It granted temporary permits to thousands of hazardous waste sites without confirming that they were safe. The agency was aware of more than 8,300 unregistered sites yet took no action against them. The

General Accounting Office's analysis of sample EPA inspection reports uncovered that 122 of 127 facilities violated current regulations (Regenstein, 1982).

EPA's Reluctance to Pursue
Criminal Enforcement Undermined
the Effectiveness of Some Laws

By 1972, the major federal environmental statutes contained criminal provisions. Nevertheless, during the entire decade of the 1970s, only 25 criminal environmental cases were prosecuted at the federal level (Cohen, 1992b). There were no full-time criminal investigators at the EPA. Criminal environmental investigations were assigned randomly to EPA offices around the country (Adler & Lord, 1991). A stronger public voice against pollution prompted a somewhat more aggressive effort at enforcement by the EPA in the early 1980s. In 1981, the EPA established the Office of Criminal Enforcement to specialize in criminal pollution cases. These initiatives did signal a greater commitment to criminal enforcement. In fiscal 1986, for example, 129 indictments were returned, compared with only 43 indictments years earlier (McMurray & Ramsey, 1986). But compliance and cleanup through civil enforcement remain the main priorities of EPA.

EPA Is Partly Responsible for
the Military's Noncompliance
With Environmental Law

The EPA has interpreted environmental statutes loosely with respect to military facilities. As a result, military compliance with environmental regulations has often been lax. For example,

> EPA ruled that unused ordnance—including chemical weapons—is not a waste product for purposes of RCRA, even when stored or buried. This creates a sizable loophole in the RCRA scheme. At the Jefferson Proving Ground in Madison, Indiana, for instance, the Army expended 23 million rounds of ordnance over the last fifty years. The land now contains more than one million unexploded bombs, mines, and artillery shells, some thirty feet below the surface. Since EPA defines hazardous waste to exclude unexploded bombs, the Jefferson Proving Ground would not be subject to a cleanup order

if it were not also contaminated with radioactive and toxic wastes. (Minister, 1994, pp. 151-152)

The Government's Role in the Love Canal Disaster

Love Canal has become a synonym for toxic waste disaster. When a thousand families were forced to escape the toxic dangers beneath their homes and flee a Niagara Falls neighborhood in upstate New York in the late 1970s, public condemnation centered on Hooker Chemical and Plastics Corporation. The chemical company had buried hundreds of 55-gallon metal drums containing nearly 22,000 tons of toxic refuse, including dioxin, in part of an uncompleted canal—a mile-long ditch 115 yards wide and 25 feet deep—purchased from the city of Niagara Falls in 1920. Less concern has been voiced about the role the government at various levels played in the case. We refocus attention here on how government's negligence and carelessness contributed to the environmental disaster at Love Canal.

The Niagara Falls Board of Education

By 1953, Hooker Chemical had filled its ditch with toxic waste and topped it with soil. The site was deeded over for $1 to the local school board, which built a new elementary school there. A neat subdivision of bungalows quickly blanketed the area. The Niagara Falls Board of Education, eager to find land for a new school, abandoned caution in accepting Hooker's largesse. The board knew the history of the Hooker site as a chemical waste dump. Although the deed did not specify exactly what and how much toxic waste was buried on the property, it did claim to exempt Hooker from further liabilities stemming from the dump. This waiver of responsibility acknowledged the presence of chemical wastes at the site that would cause injury or death, requiring subsequent transfers of ownership of the property to include a warning about the potential danger (Albanese, 1984).

Hooker even insisted that the school board inspect the site before buying it (Zuesse, 1981). Finally, the school board's own attorney advised that the deed planted liability with the board. He urged hiring a chemical engineer to assess chemical hazards at the site before taking title (Mokhiber & Shen, 1981). But the Niagara Falls school board, pressed by financial hardship and the urgent need for classrooms, ignored the warnings, disregarded the counsel of others, unanimously accepted the property, and built a school atop a toxic waste dump.

The Niagara County Health Department and the City of Niagara Falls

In the two decades before the environmental movement, the residents of Love Canal noticed the chemical oddities of their neighborhood but did not link them to risks of illness or death. Black sludge seeped through basement walls, oozed into backyards, and belched up from swimming pool drains. Terrible odors hung in the air. Most residents accepted these discomforts as the necessary price of living at the edge of a gritty industrial city. By the late 1970s, however, articles in the local press publicized the environmental dangers of toxic dumping by Hooker Chemical, and residents began seeking relief. But the response of local officials was unsympathetic, even hostile. The Niagara County Health Department opposed a major cleanup, arguing that containing the material within the neighborhood was preferable to releasing it directly into the Niagara River. Indeed, department officials threatened legal action against Love Canal residents for disposing of the invading chemicals from their basements into the city's sewer system. The department claimed that pumping chemical sludge into the city's sewer system would poison fish and algae in the Niagara River. Residents of Love Canal would be fined $25 for each violation ("Dump Site Toxic Chemicals," 1976). Abandoning consistency, department officials subsequently assured residents that no evidence existed that toxic residues seeping from the waste landfill posed any imminent health threat to the families along its perimeter. They promised, in any case, that the condition would be corrected before any health hazard did occur ("No Evidence on Toxic Residues," 1977).

The department eventually proposed a $400,000 project to contain the leaching chemicals. The city government of Niagara Falls, however, rejected the plan, citing limited funds. As the health risk drew international news coverage, the city government was embarrassed into action. Its initial efforts to isolate the seeping chemicals, however, were stymied by its refusal to pay the cleanup costs. The option of evacuating residents was rejected, leaving homeowners to manage on their own with the effects of toxic leakage during the winter of 1977-1978.

New York State Government and
the New York Department of Public Health

Not until August 1978—2 years after the dangers at the dump had been made public—did the New York State Department of Public Health intervene. The commissioner declared that Love Canal was an official emergency that imperiled the health of the general public (Mokhiber & Shen, 1981). Yet he favored evacuating just pregnant women and children younger than 2 years. Residents were enraged: If their community was a peril, they reasoned, everyone should leave.

When the state in 1979 offered to pay for the temporary relocation of any pregnant woman, the assistance usually arrived too late to prevent injury to her fetus. To qualify for relocation generally, proof of sickness was required. The standard was so stringently applied that many residents failed to qualify for assistance in 1979. Evacuation was initially limited to families living directly over the dump site, although many experts believed the toxic waste had migrated further afield, placing more peripheral families at risk. In sum, the state's response was uncharitable and slow. Not surprisingly, residents of Love Canal believed that the government actually worked against, rather than for, them (Mokhiber & Shen, 1981).

Explaining Environmental Crime by the Government

Government, especially at the federal level, is not just an environmental lawmaker but also an owner and supervisor of facilities that pollute. Indeed, the military is the nation's largest polluter. The EPA exercises only the loosest supervision over military pollution; it fails to enforce vigorously many environmental laws. State and local governments have compiled a blemished record, with negligence and indifference scattered among their efforts at environmental protection. Some of these actions are serious enough to constitute environmental crimes by the state.

We are unaware of any comprehensive theory that explains these criminal acts by government. We discuss, instead, three important factors that influence this type of crime.

Goal Attainment

Rational goal theory proposes that organizations are driven to maximize attainment of their most central goals (Gross, 1978, 1980; Needleman & Needleman, 1979; Vaughn, 1982, 1983). Business seeks to maximize profits and market share (Clinard & Yeager, 1980). Government seeks to maximize national security and power. The zealous dedication to such strongly held legitimate goals may, however, set off illegitimate activity. Powerful missions may prompt illegal behavior. The pressure to make it can make things come undone. Goals that must be achieved at all costs may indeed incur great costs. If international relations are determined largely by the power among nations, then goal attainment that ensures national security or enhances national power will be vigorously engaged. If these goals have a high moral cast, then their pursuit may take on the quality of a moral mission and seem to justify the sacrifice of more conventional law-abiding behavior.

The postwar era after 1945 pitted the United States against the Soviet Union in a global ideological, economic, and geopolitical competition. The international goal of the nation became winning the Cold War and containing Soviet communism. Superiority in nuclear weapons became a key feature of this goal. By matching or beating every Soviet advance in nuclear technology, the United States deterred most Soviet aggression. By stockpiling these destructive weapons, the United States successfully exercised its global economic and political authority and gained great advantage over those countries that did not possess their own nuclear arsenal (Kauzlarich & Kramer, 1993). One cost of this goal attainment was damage to the environment. To achieve nuclear superiority, the government encouraged weapons facilities to employ the most effective and efficient means of production, regardless of their adverse environmental consequences (Kauzlarich & Kramer, 1993). In the name of the Cold War, the U.S. military's record of environmental contamination was simply ignored.

The U.S. defoliation program in the Vietnam War fits a similar pattern. Environmental concerns were trumped by the higher aim of winning the war and containing communism before it spread throughout Southeast Asia. Defoliation was intended to expose "enemy forces, facilities, roads, ambush sites, infiltration routes, and enemy locations from the air, ground, or water" and to destroy the enemy's food resources, thus diverting scarce manpower to transport food from far-off supply depots (U.S. Department of the Army,

1971, p. 29). Environmental integrity, as well as the health of Vietnamese civilians and U.S. and allied soldiers, was sacrificed on the altar of higher ambitions.

Legal Doctrine

Legal doctrines buffer the agencies of federal government from prosecution for environmental crimes. The doctrine of *sovereign immunity* protects federal officials (indeed governmental workers at all levels) from personal liability for acts taken within the scope of their duties. It bars any meritorious lawsuit against the federal government unless it has consented to being sued. Consent must be clear and unequivocal. Without such consent, governmental immunity from suit is complete. Although all major federal environmental statutes explicitly waive sovereign immunity, three factors shield the federal government from litigation (Minister, 1994). First, waivers of immunity are unclear and even contradictory among environmental laws. For example, although most of the statutes waive immunity from federal penalties for failing to control pollution or transport toxic wastes properly, they do not say whether the federal government is still protected from state and local penalties. Second, courts have frequently held that federal facilities are immune from penalties and civil fines (Minister, 1994). In *U.S. Department of Energy v. Ohio* (1992), the U.S. Supreme Court held that federal facilities do not waive sovereign immunity from punitive fines and penalties under the Clean Water Act and CERCLA. Third, the amended Federal Torts Claim Act provides low-level federal employees with immunity from lawsuits against liability in most common-law tort actions. A federal employee would not be personally liable, for example, if the negligent storing of toxic soda ash resulted in injury to others (Herm, 1991).

Another legal doctrine that discourages prosecution of environmental crimes by federal agencies is the theory of the *unitary executive,* which holds that the executive branch is an indivisible institution under the exclusive authority of the president. One part of the executive branch may not sue another. That would be tantamount to the president suing him- or herself (Steinberg, 1990). Instead, legal action between sister agencies must be resolved internally. By executive order in 1986, President Reagan invoked this doctrine to eliminate almost all of EPA's authority to enforce CERCLA at federal facilities by requiring the U.S. Department of Justice (DOJ) to approve any enforcement actions. The DOJ, however, narrowly interpreted President Reagan's order to prohibit suits by one executive agency against another (Stever, 1987). In 1990, a special task force established by the nation's governors and attorneys assessed the result of the Reagan order.

Under federal environmental statutes, federal agencies are directed to comply with federal and state environmental laws to the same extent as private facilities, but many have failed to do so. Although the EPA is aware of numerous violations, its enforcement powers have been crippled by a DOJ policy prohibiting the EPA from filing lawsuits or issuing unilateral enforceable orders against its sister agencies. Hamstrung by the DOJ's unitary theory of the executive, the nation's chief environmental watchdog is forced to sit by as basic environmental statutes and regulations are routinely ignored at federally owned facilities (Shulman, 1992).

Because the DOJ and EPA were banned in the Reagan years from prosecuting federal and military facilities for environmental crimes, the states became solely responsible for undertaking criminal actions against these installations. Their hands were tied, however, by another legal doctrine—*federal supremacy,* which holds that the federal government is supreme within its sphere of action and state law therefore cannot interfere. The doctrine protects federal power from infringement by the states. It extends to federal employees immunity from state prosecution for actions taken in pursuit of their lawful duties (Herm, 1991). This immunity is not absolute; to qualify for it, employees' acts must have met certain criteria. In practice, however, this condition has made little difference. States have been mostly unable to regulate federal facilities because the executive branch resists their imposition of fines, penalties, or other sanctions. The federal government's posture toward local government has been the same.

The supremacy doctrine applies only to the federal government. It does not shield state and local agencies from liability. In practice, however, these lower levels of government are protected from suits by the reluctance of elected officials and citizens to have judgments and fines paid for by the only available source of funds—tax revenues. Citizens—or their elected representatives—are placed in the position of suing themselves. This dilemma confronted the residents of Love Canal.

> Governments obtain their money through taxes, so a successful claim will
> likely be recovered through tax increases. Therefore, when governmental

bodies become defendants, citizens can only sue "themselves" inasmuch as they are the source of the government's assets. This situation makes the inability of citizens to sue the Superfund for damages an especially serious problem. (Albanese, 1984, p. 58)

In sum, unsupportive legal doctrine cripples environmental law enforcement against the government. As was true in the case of corporate environmental crime, wherein external controls on behavior are badly compromised, crime may flourish. Weak law enforcement against the government encourages environmental crime by the government.

Institutional Capability to Enforce the Law

Government agencies may possess the will but lack the institutional capability to protect the environment effectively. Indeed, their deficiencies may be so grave that they commit serious crimes as one aspect of a larger failure to implement public policy. Rosenbaum (1994) has systematically evaluated the institutional and policy deficiencies that enfeeble EPA and leave it defenseless against the environmental crimes of other government agencies it is supposed to regulate.

The EPA suffers from *overload*—too much to do. The agency "cannot possibly do all the things its various mandates tell it to do" (Rosenbaum, 1994, p. 131). It must regulate approximately 1,500 reportedly hazardous air pollutants under the Clean Air Act. It must evaluate more than 50,000 pesticides under FIFRA. It must test approximately 60,000 chemicals under the Toxic Substance Control Act and the Resource Conservation and Recovery Act. The major environmental statutes "cover an enormous range of ecological problems, technical or scientific expertise, regulatory activity, and geographic space" (p. 126). The 1990 amendments to the Clean Air Act fill 800 pages of small print.

The EPA is hampered by *limited resources.* "No domain of federal policy making requires a greater diversity of technical information and professional skills than environmental regulation" (Rosenbaum, 1994, p. 124). Its budget, most of which goes to the Superfund Trust and to the states as grants, has not kept pace with its staff and resource needs. For example,

Employees in Research and Development, whose work is essential to creating
an adequate science base for rule-making, decreased from 2,300 to 1,800
between 1981 and 1992. In mid-1991 only three of EPA's twenty-three major
programs were appropriately monitored with adequate indicators. (p. 132)

EPA is subjected to *excessive oversight.* The EPA's programs fall under
the jurisdiction of at least 20 Senate and House standing committees, and
nearly 100 subcommittees in both chambers (Rosenbaum, 1994). These
committees monitor EPA's regulatory policies and conduct impact analyses
of EPA's regulations. From 1981 to 1989, the average review time for EPA
rules was 64 days, longer than any other federal agency. These reviews
hamper timely rule making. "No other federal agency is exposed to such
sustained and critical oversight" (p. 130). The EPA is Congress's "designated
whipping boy" (p. 131). Besieged by Congressional critics, the EPA is almost
"predestined to large programmatic failure and policy subversion" (p. 125).

The EPA suffers from *bureaucratic pluralism.* The EPA bureaucracy
encompasses exceptionally diverse managerial, professional, geographical,
and political interests. This intensifies the agency's preoccupation with
power struggles, value conflicts, and statutory bickering. For example, each
EPA program office—the agency's most important operational unit—"lives
with its own statutory programs, deadlines, and criteria for decisions, and
usually possesses a steel grip on large portions of its office budget, to which
it is entitled by the laws it enforces" (Rosenbaum, 1994, p. 127). The Office
of Toxic Substances alone claimed $1.6 billion of EPA's budget in fiscal year
1992 for waste site cleanup. EPA's regional offices—intermediaries between
the states and headquarters—frequently defend state positions and interests
in conflicts over policy and practice. Finally, the states—the actual enforcers
of environmental statutes—are themselves a power within EPA because of
the Congressional delegations standing behind them.

The EPA *lacks a clear and coherent mission.* Public agencies need a
statutory charter that explicitly declares their mission or primary policy
objectives if they successfully are to defend their programs and justify their
allocation of resources. Nevertheless,

No organic act of legislative charter clearly defines EPA's mission or helps
to set its policy priorities. Created in 1970 through an executive reorganization, the agency's mission is the sum of all individual laws it administers—a
conglomeration of legislative acts written at different times and for different
purposes and bereft of overall coherence. (Rosenbaum, 1994, p. 125)

EPA must implement 10 major—and a host of minor—statutes with inconsistent, often competing, goals.

The EPA constantly faces *arbitrary and demanding deadlines.* The EPA most often violates environmental laws by not meeting legislatively mandated deadlines, which are usually unreasonable and unrealistic. For example, the EPA was required to "write 55 major air pollution control rules within two years, list 189 toxic air pollutants for which the agency must write standards for all major sources, and specify a schedule for writing each standard" (Rosenbaum, 1994, p. 132). By 1988, EPA had already inherited 800 statutory deadlines. They reflect profound legislative distrust. The EPA is left with little room to maneuver as it struggles to carry out confounding, sometimes unfeasible, regulatory tasks (Rosenbaum, 1994).

Finally, the EPA is split by *fragmented authority.* At least 27 other federal agencies and bureaus share regulatory authority with EPA over the environment and occupational health. For example, more than 25 federal laws deal with some aspect of toxic and hazardous waste management. Their administration involves not only the EPA but the Food and Drug Administration, the Department of Transportation, the Consumer Product Safety Commission, the Department of the Interior, and five agencies in the Department of Agriculture. This fragmentation of authority creates a large cast of aggressive competitors for EPA money, personnel, and authority. As a consequence, coordinated pollution management is impossible.

Institutional deficiencies were also at work in the Love Canal disaster. Limited resources for a new school heavily influenced the Niagara Falls Board of Education in its fatal decision to accept a free site with a dangerous history. The county public health department failed to correct hazardous conditions at the site when its investigation was cut short by the withdrawal of city funds. New York State health officials rejected survey findings spelling out the crisis because they would have made a compelling case for the costly evacuation of several hundred additional families. In addition, New York State government was slow in finally relocating residents of Love Canal because of the overwhelming financial burden (Mokhiber & Shen, 1981).

Environmental crimes of omission are more often the result of weak institutional capability than of the calculated subversion of policy. Inadequate capacity has its origins more in administrative and political problems than in criminal design. Consequently, it can best be corrected by additional funds, better legislation, or more astute management (Sharkansky, 1995).

Review Questions

1. What is the text's definition of governmental environmental crime?
2. What is the difference between crimes of commission and crimes of omission?
3. What are important examples and evidence of governmental crimes of commission against the environment by the U.S. military, the U.S. Department of Energy, and the U.S. Forest Service?
4. What are examples and evidence of governmental crimes of omission by the U.S. Department of Energy, the U.S. Department of Defense, and the U.S. Environmental Protection Agency?
5. What were the chief failures by local, county, and state governments in the Love Canal disaster?
6. In what ways are the following legal doctrines in opposition to environmental law enforcement against the government: the doctrine of sovereign immunity, the theory of the unitary executive, and the doctrine of federal supremacy?
7. What deficiencies in institutional capability weaken the EPA's enforcement efforts?

CHAPTER 6

Personal Environmental Crime

The environmental offenses we have examined so far have their roots in collectivities. The agents of the offenses have been individuals, but they are almost always acting on behalf of, for the benefit of, under the direction of, or in the name of corporations, organizations, or government. The offenses they commit are large scale—from the catastrophes of Love Canal, Bhopal, and Rocky Flats to lesser disasters and bad conduct that still wreak serious environmental or human damage. The offenses are *crimes,* after all, rather than civil wrongs, under the law precisely because their effects are significant. These two characteristics—an organizational context and a serious impact—are absent in a fourth type of offense that we examine in this chapter: personal environmental crime.

Personal Environmental Crime Defined

Key Characteristics

Personal environmental crime is distinguished by five key characteristics. First, it refers to infractions by individuals, outside their occupations or jobs. They usually act alone—without organizational affiliation—in their capacity as citizen or consumer in everyday life. Second, personal environmental crime is widely practiced by ordinary people who lack criminal profiles: Virtually everyone has done it at least once, and some do it fairly often. Third, the offenders do not think of their acts as crimes, although the law does. Fourth, the offenders suffer little stigma by committing these crimes; their public reputations as law-abiding citizens are not damaged. Finally, although the environmental impact of a single crime is usually not serious, the cumulative effect of many incidents may be.

Types of Personal Environmental Crime

Two principal types of personal environmental crime can be identified. Household crimes, probably the most common type, are committed for convenience. They offer the prospect of doing things more easily or simply, if illegally. They often present opportunities for modest profit or savings as well. As environmental regulation of the home expands, the variety and volume of household crimes will grow. Depending on the jurisdiction, household crimes include dumping household appliances, refuse, construction waste, and other material at forbidden sites; improperly venting sulfur dioxide and other toxic particulates into the atmosphere from home heating systems; disposing of paints, varnishes, lacquers, oil, gasoline, and other toxic chemicals down household drains; piping home sewage into waterways or too near freshwater supplies; improperly separating garbage for recycling; violating restrictions on leaf, newspaper, and garbage burning; and ignoring limits on water use during droughts.

The second type of personal environmental crime is recreational. Recreational crimes occur in the course of avocations, hobbies, vacation pursuits, and other venues for personal enjoyment. They are most common to hunting, boating, fishing, camping, and other outdoor pursuits that treat scenic land and waterways as playgrounds. These sites are frequently public grounds managed by the government on behalf of the citizenry. They include beaches, bays, oceans, rivers, lakes, national and state parks, primitive wilderness areas, forests, high desert plains, marshlands, estuaries, and a variety of other natural wonders. Recreational users may view their common ownership of these facilities as a license for abuse. With no private owners in sight—and police scarce—disrespectful use by some visitors is encouraged. Recreational crimes, like household crimes, may be motivated by the prospect of convenience or modest financial improvement. They may also result from sheer negligence.

Recreational crimes, especially in their cumulative effect, pollute pristine areas, diminish limited resources, or damage the wilderness and its flora and fauna. As urban areas encroach on recreational preserves and patronage grows, recreational crimes will accelerate. They include dumping garbage and fuel from recreational boats; failing to pack refuse out of wilderness areas; driving recreational vehicles such as dune buggies, motorbikes, snowmobiles, and jet skis in prohibited areas; hunting or fishing for endangered species, out of season, or beyond legal limits; ignoring fire bans in parched countryside; collecting protected flowers and plants; and harvesting wilderness crops or mining resources for personal use.

The Criminological Heritage

Environmental crime is a neglected topic in criminology, so it is not surprising that personal environmental crime has garnered even less attention. Its existence, however, is anticipated by the modest literature on what has come to be called *folk crime,* the everyday deviance committed by ordinary citizens (Ross, 1961, 1983). In this vein, Gabor (1994) argues that criminality is a matter of degree, rather than an absolute condition. Most people will conform to rules. A minority will deviate slightly from them, and an even smaller number will deviate from them substantially. The degree of deviation is inversely linked to the number of deviants. Thus, although a few people are chronic offenders, whose lives revolve around criminal acts, most of the public is at the other extreme, engaging in illegal activities only occasionally.

This framework receives confirmation in a number of studies. For instance, 97% of a random sample of nearly 1,700 men in New York City admitted to having committed at least one criminal infraction during their adolescent years (LeBlanc & Frechett, 1989). Wolfgang's famous cohort study of young Philadelphia males revealed a tripartite structure for criminal behavior: A large majority committed at least one offense, a smaller number engaged in crime occasionally, and a tiny group carried out many offenses (Tracy, Wolfgang, & Figlio, 1990). The U.S. Department of Transportation discovered that a majority of motorists routinely violated traffic rules (Ross, 1983).

Folk crime's domain is the lesser infractions of everyday life that tend not to damage the law-abiding reputation of the average citizen. Sometimes known as avocational crimes (Friedrichs, 1995b; Geis, 1979) or mundane crimes (Gibbons, 1983), these offenses involve routine, even dull instances of opportunistic lawbreaking, which receive little publicity in the media and scant attention from the criminal justice system. They include traffic violations; tax evasion; failure to pay parking fees, tolls, telephone charges, and other fees for services; customs evasion; unauthorized copying of copyrighted material (books, audiotapes, and videos); coupon fraud; buying fenced goods; and littering.

So the widespread existence of personal environmental crime should not surprise us, although criminological research has not shed any empirical light on its nature and extent. To begin filling in the picture, the first author (Situ, 1997) undertook a study of illegal solid waste dumping, wastewater disposal, and other environmental infractions by ordinary citizens in New Jersey. The rest of this chapter reports on that study.

Personal Environmental Crime in New Jersey

Methodology

New Jersey presents an interesting setting for the study of personal environmental crime. New Jersey state and local governments have taken pains to protect the environment and to punish environmental offenders (DeCicco & Bonanno, 1988). The state enacted a rich profusion of environmental laws, many of which are more stringent than federal regulations. In addition, it has established environmental task forces in many counties.

For this study, 154 environmental case reports and reports on 150 environmental violation suspects from 1992 through 1994 in a southern New Jersey county were examined. The case reports provide information on accidents reported to the county environmental task force, including their nature and location. The suspect reports provide demographic data for constructing profiles of environmental offenders. In addition, a questionnaire was given to 100 New Jersey citizens to assess public reaction to environmental crime and to identify personal environmental crimes that escape detection by authorities. Finally, interviews were conducted with 20 public officials who deal with environmental offenses. They ranged from police officers in a county environmental crime task force and a chief investigator in a county prosecutor's office to state park wardens and investigators in a county utilities authority. Five environmental offenders were also interviewed.

Types of Environmental Offenses

Analysis of the 154 case reports revealed that most offenses involved the intentional dumping of solid wastes, a criminal misdemeanor. The wastes were hazardous materials, construction and demolition debris, household electrical appliances, and vegetative waste. The most popular dumping sites for these materials were wooded areas, the ends of secluded dirt roads, and vacant lots or abandoned buildings. The illegal dumping was conducted mostly in secret and at night. Approximately 90% of the dumping was detected only several days after the fact. In one extreme case, 5 years expired before the dump sites were located.

Investigators from a county utilities authority reported that in northern New Jersey, the collecting of recyclables and trash without a permit was a serious problem. Violators arrived at night, removed curbside trash in residential areas, and sold it for cash. Largely because of theft, the tonnage of collected recyclables in one township decreased by almost 50% during a 3-year period.

Illegally discharging sewage wastes into public waters was a common violation of environmental laws identified by investigators of the New Jersey State Police Marine Bureau. People illegally release their wastewater in one of three ways: through open-ended pipes leading from their homes directly into bulkheads or open-ended septic tanks buried under beaches, through septic pipes that are disconnected from city sewage systems, and through buried pipe without sewage systems.

Prosecution of Personal Environmental Offenses

Under New Jersey law, the crime of illegally dumping solid wastes or discharging wastewater requires proof that the offender acted with purpose, intention, or knowledge. Investigators interviewed in this study were convinced that most illegal dumping or discharging was done intentionally. Because crime scenes were usually located in remote areas, far from traffic or the offenders' places of work, accidental dumping was implausible. Illegally discharging wastewater required the deliberate alteration of existing systems. Septic pipe, for example, does not disconnect from city sewage systems on its own; someone has to disconnect it knowingly.

Nevertheless, only four of the incidents in the 154 case reports were disposed of criminally. Reports from the marine police indicated only one case in which a violator was criminally charged. Illicit drugs and handguns at the crime scene, rather than the environmental violation itself, prompted the criminal indictment.

Prosecutors are reluctant to bring criminal charges against citizens who commit personal environmental crimes. First, evidence of a serious impact from the violation is hard to establish. Ordinary citizens, for the most part, dump or discharge nontoxic materials, which do not pose the imminent danger of death or serious bodily injury or environmental destruction. Second, proving the criminal intent of the ordinary citizen is difficult even when investigators are convinced that most violations are intentional. The prosecutor must prove beyond a reasonable doubt that the violator clearly understood the relevant laws and the environmental impact of his or her infraction. In practice, criminal charges are brought only when the violation seriously damaged or endangered the environment and also involved nonenvironmental criminal acts such as arson, theft, or the illegal possession of guns.

The Offenders

The study uncovered no pattern of distinguishing characteristics among citizens who commit personal environmental crimes except that men are overwhelmingly more likely than women to dispose of waste and other material illegally. This probably reflects the typical household division of labor. But the absence of any broader profile of offender qualities confirms the view that personal environmental crime is widely committed.

Explanations of Personal Environmental Crime

Selling recyclables stolen from curbsides is clearly crime with an economic motive. Dumping tires, rugs, used engine oil, old cars, furniture, electrical appliances, and construction materials in unauthorized disposal sites is a money-saving convenience for the violator. Shore homeowners who discharge their wastewater into the ocean save the cost of sewage fees and installation charges for septic tanks and sewer pipe.

Admitted offenders interpreted their behavior as noncriminal. This rationalization is evident in the following excerpt from an interview with a violator of Title 13 of the New Jersey Conservation and Development Act.

Q: What have you dumped?

A: Concrete, blocks, scrap steel, and wood.

Q: Why?

A: Nowhere else to put it. So I dumped them on wooded farmland, which was a public property.

Q: Did you make or save money on the disposal?

A: Yes, no dumping fee. It is free.

Q: Did you know that it is illegal to dispose of solid waste at an unauthorized site?

A: Yes, I knew. But I didn't know why they made it illegal. What I dumped was just a little bit and will be grown over in no time. I really don't see who is hurt.

All offenders, from the street to the suite, justify and reinterpret their criminal behavior (Gabor, 1994; Ryan, 1971; Sykes & Matza, 1957; Yockelson & Samenow, 1976). A common justification by ordinary citizens who commit personal environmental crimes is the denial of injury or the absence of victims. The offenders of illegal dumping are often strongly committed to this view. In addition, they believe that dumping nontoxic waste illegally is a trivial wrong that the law overcriminalizes. Of the 100 respondents to the questionnaire in this study, 90% agreed that the disposal of hazardous waste should be strictly prohibited but that dumping trash in the woods causes no harm. The government should concentrate its attention on "real" crimes, they insisted.

Law enforcement officers are also caught in a conflict between their personal views and the laws requiring their full enforcement. For them, the priority is to combat street crimes. To stop illegal dumping is an "additional duty," which can be ignored when time and energy are not available. The following view by one officer is typical:

I don't want to see our environment vandalized. But I just don't have the time to check out the trash around, to find out who the dumper is, when I am told a 911 caller is waiting for my help!

Although forest wardens concurred that illegal dumping was a serious problem in forests, their heavy workload has forced them to allocate limited manpower to combating more harmful activities, such as wildland arson, illegal poaching, and cutting trees, and ensuring safety in state parks. "We just don't have time to post our rangers on a forest road to wait for someone to dump their garbage into the woods," complained an assistant director of a state park and forest service.

According to opportunity theory (Nettler, 1982), people may be predisposed to act in a certain way, but the circumstances they encounter will also affect the way they act. For example, people are more likely to commit theft when unmonitored property beckons, defenseless targets present themselves, and the prospects of punishment seem low. These factors underlie many of the decisions to commit personal environmental crime, which this study examined. The New Jersey Pine Barrens, the largest wilderness area on the east coast with more than 3 million acres of unimproved land and hundreds of miles of unpaved roads, offer an alluring setting for offenders to dump their waste illegally without fear of detection. In addition, weak law enforcement has convinced solid waste dumpers that they have little risk of being apprehended and punished. Rangers from the State Division of Parks and Forestry oversee activities in most of the Pine Barrens. Personnel in the region, however, are spread thinly. For example, Wharton State Forest, which covers 200 square miles of the Pine Barrens, is severely understaffed. The Environmental Crime Task Force, the chief protector of the environment at the county level, has suffered budget cutbacks in recent years. Although regular police officers exercise responsibility for detecting and investigating environmental offenses, their main concern is still street crime. Thus, environmental infractions committed on county property are handled mainly by the public health department, an administrative agency with no police powers. Weak law enforcement reduces the likelihood of punishment and encourages personal crimes against the environment by ordinary citizens.

Review Questions

1. What are the key characteristics of personal environmental crime?
2. What are the defining features of the two types of personal environmental crime—household crime and recreational crime?
3. Why could personal environmental crime be considered a variety of folk crime?

4. What are the chief findings of Situ's study of personal environmental crime in New Jersey?

CHAPTER 7

Combating Environmental Crime

Enforcement

Law enforcement is the government's effort to keep people honest. It consists of controlling crime—investigating criminal incidents and apprehending offenders—and preventing crime—keeping the rest of us law-abiding. Crime control occurs after it is too late, so to speak; crime prevention takes place before it is too late. Crime prevention results partly from enforcement action—monitoring people who might break the law and checking the places where crimes are likely to occur. But it also derives from the deterrent effect of criminal justice: Certain, swift, and appropriately severe punishment of wrongdoing persuades people to obey the law. Enforcement is not solely—indeed, not mostly—a function of government, however. There are two other "cops." We obey the law mostly from habit or conviction: An internal cop, introjected from family and social life, keeps most of us on the right side of the law most of the time. A social cop—our neighbors, coworkers, and other associates, to the extent that these communities still exist in our lives—monitors our activity and applies mostly informal sanctions against misbehavior. As a consequence, criminal justice workers from the government are enforcers of last resort—backups to the inevitable imperfections of the other two. But when the other cops fail massively, the government's policing may become overwhelmed—called on to do more than it possibly can.

All three cops—conscience, community, and government—help enforce environmental laws. People in firms, organizations, and on their own who are not constrained from violating environmental laws by their moral code or the influence of their associates may be constrained by the administrative or civil enforcement efforts of government. This work of compliance relies on standards and deadlines, testing and monitoring, giving funds and withholding them, authorization and certification and their denial, administrative orders and injunctions, and civil damages and fines. In the belief that administrative and civil techniques often fail, criminal enforcement has been added to the mix. Environmental laws with criminal sanctions—heavy fines and imprisonment—draw on the power to shame and stigmatize offenders with criminal records. In this chapter, we examine the environmental law enforcers at the federal, state, and local levels of government; their responsibilities in criminal justice (especially their approaches to investigation); and their rivalries.

Environmental Law Enforcement at the Federal Level

The EPA and the DOJ are the leading federal enforcers of criminal environmental law. This was not always the case. Prior to 1980, the EPA almost exclusively sought civil sanctions, penalties, and injunctive relief against violators, despite the opportunities provided by the most recent environmental legislation for criminal enforcement as well. In June 1978, the EPA departed from past civil practice by issuing extensive guidelines to process cases in the criminal mode. The EPA hereby acknowledged for the first time the need for criminal sanctions in its regulatory arsenal as thousands of air and water pollution sources violated deadlines in the Clean Air Act and the Clean Water Act (McMurray & Ramsey, 1986). But the agency committed no personnel to the task of criminal enforcement. There were neither any criminal investigators within the agency nor any criminal attorneys to prosecute environmental offenders. Civil and administrative enforcement continued to be the major approach to violators.

The DOJ, for its part, did not actively pursue criminal enforcement until the late 1970s, although it had the power to do so earlier under a variety of environmental laws, the oldest of which dates from 1899. As the decade drew to a close, the DOJ responded to the same mounting frustration that prompted modest steps by the EPA. Civil procedures and sanctions were not containing a rising tide of regulatory violations. The DOJ created a new Environmental Enforcement Section in which criminal enforcement was one priority. More important, it established the Environmental Crime Unit in the Land and Natural Resources Division. Staffed by attorneys with expertise in criminal and environmental law, the unit was dedicated to the investigation and prosecution of environmental crime (Starr, 1986).

The DOJ's increased emphasis on criminal sanctions stimulated important changes in the EPA's orientation to enforcement. In early 1981, the EPA opened the Office of Criminal Enforcement. A year later, the agency hired its first group of criminal investigators—federal law enforcement officers with the authority to serve and execute criminal search warrants, make arrests, carry weapons, protect witnesses, and generally enforce the criminal provisions of statutes under the EPA's jurisdiction (Starr, 1991). By 1991, the EPA's criminal enforcement staffing had grown to more than 110 investigators assigned among 10 regional offices around the nation. To consolidate criminal enforcement efforts, the Criminal Investigations Division and the Criminal Enforcement Counsel Division were merged into the Office of Criminal Enforcement in early 1991. This reorganization accelerated the agency's response to high-priority criminal matters (Strock, 1991).

Under this new federal scheme, the EPA identifies and investigates environmental violations. When the EPA wishes to criminally prosecute a violator in the U.S. court system, it recommends the case to the DOJ for prosecution. The recommendation is reviewed by DOJ attorneys in the Environmental Crimes Unit, and the department makes the final decision whether to file the case. If the case goes to trial, the DOJ legally represents the EPA in court, although EPA's legal and technical staff remain actively involved in the case (EPA, 1990). Interagency cooperation obviously is critical to prosecuting environmental criminals successfully, yet discord has marked relations between the two groups. The EPA often referred cases to the DOJ prematurely, failing to carry out thorough investigations. As a result, the DOJ declined almost 60% of the EPA's criminal referrals from 1979 through 1981, to take one early period of marred cooperation. The DOJ was simply unable to pursue these referrals in the absence of the necessary investigative groundwork (Starr, 1991). To surmount the problem, training programs were instituted for the EPA technical and legal staff at the Federal Law Enforcement Training Center. This training has ensured that EPA cases are better prepared and targeted against polluters before their submission to the DOJ.

The EPA's activities in criminal enforcement have also been bolstered since 1981 by the FBI. In 1986, 35 special agents from the FBI's White-Collar Crimes Section were given additional responsibility for investigating federal environmental crimes (Matulewich, 1991). Although the FBI focuses mainly on hazardous waste cases and conducts investigations on only 30 cases per year on request from the EPA, its participation in environmental law enforcement reflects broader cooperation among the federal government agencies than in the past.

Environmental Law
Enforcement at the State Level

Two factors have contributed to the increasingly important role that the states have played in environmental law enforcement since the mid 1970s. First, virtually every federal environmental statute enacted in the 1970s gave state governments enormous responsibility for implementing environmental regulations in their jurisdictions. Second, as the states' role in federally directed environmental policy continued to grow under the "new federalism," many states passed their own environmental statutes, and nearly all states created their own environmental agencies to enforce these state laws and administer state programs (Haskell & Price, 1973; Jessup, 1990).

State enforcement activities typically include monitoring emissions, effluent, and environmental quality; inspecting facilities; levying and collecting fines; issuing notices of violation and administrative orders; invoking civil and criminal penalties; and revoking permits. Although state environmental agencies generally set environmental goals and standards, design and implement regulatory programs, issue permits, and conduct inspections, the state police and attorney general's office are usually in charge of criminal enforcement (Edwards, 1996). The state police specialize in criminal investigation, whereas the office of the attorney general focuses on prosecution. Attorneys general in many states have established environmental crime task forces. In the early 1980s, only Louisiana, Maryland, Michigan, New Jersey, New York, and Pennsylvania employed specialized units to deal with environmental crimes on a full-time basis. By 1991, 29 states had environmental crime task forces or their equivalents (Rebovich, 1996). The task force brings together personnel from different agencies to coordinate operations and overcome interagency inertia or resistance.

We focus here on the role of the state police in criminal investigation of environmental crime, drawing on a review by Edwards (1996). State prosecution of environmental offenders by the attorney general's office is discussed in Chapter 8.

Jurisdiction

Most state police organizations are active in investigating "highway-oriented" crimes, especially the illegal transport of hazardous materials and the illegal disposal of hazardous and nonhazardous waste (Edwards, 1996, p. 207). In addition, some state police agencies investigate other offenses, such as air pollution, industrial explosions, pesticide infractions, and wetlands violations.

Perceived Roles

The state police role in attacking environmental crime varies from one jurisdiction to another. In many states, they are the exclusive investigators of environmental crime. In California, Kentucky, New Jersey, South Dakota, and Texas, they carry most of the burden but share some responsibility with others. In some states, their only task is assisting other agencies on request (Edwards, 1996).

Personnel

Most officers assigned to environmental crime are street-level police, not administrative personnel. The numbers of officers in the state police working on environmental crime range from 3 to 98. Most state police agencies rely on external sources of legal advice, principally the state attorney general, county prosecutors, and state departments of environmental protection, rather than on an in-house environmental attorney (Edwards, 1996).

Facilities and Equipment

State police agencies have acquired special equipment for their fight against environmental crime, including "air-sampling equipment, protective gear (boots and gloves), spill kits, fire turnouts, radiation equipment, video cameras and other photographic equipment, and reference publications" (Edwards, 1996, p. 222). Several states have set up toll-free 800 numbers on which to report environmental incidents. Arizona, California, Idaho, Illinois, Kentucky, and Texas deploy specialized vehicles, in addition to the standard police car, for environmental work. Only Arizona, Arkansas, and Nebraska perform most of their environmental testing at an in-house laboratory. Most states refer their lab work to outside facilities operated by state departments of health or environmental protection or to private laboratories (Edwards, 1996).

Training

By 1991, more than 1,000 police officers had attended training programs on environmental investigation (EPA, 1994). Training hours range from 4 in Wisconsin to 60 in California. Training is conducted in-house or by state environmental protection agencies, the FBI, regional hazardous waste organizations, the Federal Law Enforcement Training Center, or the U.S. Department of Transportation. The variety of trainers and training hours reflects the absence of national standards (Edwards, 1996).

Levels of Activity

The rise in reported environmental incidents, arrests, and convictions for various environmental crimes suggests that states are gradually turning to the criminal options in environmental regulation. There is a wide discrepancy among the states in the rate of response, however. Some states such as California, New Jersey, and Oregon are more committed to environmental crime enforcement than are others such as Arkansas, Kentucky, and Mississippi. There is, as well, a substantial difference between states in the number of reported incidents, arrests, and convictions (Edwards, 1996). This difference may be due to the amount of training the police investigators received, the difficulty in obtaining criminal evidence, lack of public awareness about environmental crime, or the strategy of using criminal sanctions only as a threat (DiMento, 1993).

The findings of Edwards and others (O'Brien, 1991; Rebovich, 1986, 1992; Ringquist, 1993) underscore the expanding entrance of the state police into criminal environmental enforcement. The most important lesson from this new venture for policing is the need for interagency cooperation. The environmental task force and the investigative or prosecutorial strike force were devised expressly to meet this challenge. These special units are meant to avoid duplication of effort by coordinating civil, criminal, and administrative responses and effectively allocating available resources.

Environmental Law Enforcement at the Local Level

In recent years, growing numbers of counties, cities, and municipalities have attacked a wide range of potentially devastating environmental problems. Local law enforcement agencies, including city police, county sheriffs, and fire departments, have become the "eyes and ears" of the community in detecting illegal environmental activities because of the routine mobile presence in local areas (Hammett & Epstein, 1993a). Some local prosecutor's offices have augmented their efforts by creating environmental task forces to which their own investigators are assigned. Others have relied on outside law enforcement agencies to develop criminal cases. By identifying a community's most pressing environmental concern, local law enforcers have gained public support and enlisted additional resources from local governments (Pollock, 1992).

Local enforcement programs are dominated by one of three agencies: the police, the prosecutor, or a local environmental protection agency (Epstein & Hammett, 1995). In police programs, the county sheriff or the major police department in the area has primary responsibility. In Broward County, Florida, for example, the sheriff's office was assigned in 1990 to handle environmental problems. In Portland, Maine, the city police department is the leading environmental law enforcement agency (Epstein & Hammett, 1995). In programs operated by the prosecutor, an environmental task force or county strike force tackles environmental crime. Essential to the force's operation are law enforcement, technical, and laboratory components (Hammett & Epstein, 1993b). The force usually consists of a sergeant, detective, several investigators, and assistant prosecutor (Epstein & Hammett, 1995). In some jurisdictions, a public health agent is also included. This arrangement aids close coordination among prosecutors, environmental crime investigators, and regulatory agents.

The final approach is an environmental agency-based program, in which the police department and regulatory agency formalize their relationship by contract. For example, the Palm Beach County Sheriff's Office assigns, by written agreement, two deputies to the Palm Beach County Solid Waste Authority to supervise criminal investigation. The authority pays the two officers' salaries and benefits, vehicles, uniforms, and supervisory costs (Epstein & Hammett, 1995).

Approaches to Investigation

Environmental crimes pose unique challenges to traditional law enforcement methods. Hazardous waste sites and materials spills may pose life-threatening danger to investigating officers themselves. The technical nature of environmental incidents and the absence of proximate victims may complicate detection and reduce leads. Environmental crime cases "are characterized by their inordinate demands on investigative time and resources; [they require] extraordinary discipline and expertise in evidence gathering" (Mustokoff, 1981, p. 28). Traditional law enforcement methods are not incompatible with solving environmental crimes. "Hazardous waste crimes and their perpetrators are being pursued in the same aggressive manner that a burglar, armed robber, or rapist would be" (Maioli & Staub, 1988, p. 4). Clearly, a combination of both innovative and traditional tactics is required for the relatively uncharted realm of environmental law enforcement.

Reactive Investigation

Investigations are either reactive or proactive. The first gathers information from complaining citizens, whereas the second builds on self-initiated inquiry. Although citizen complaints are the main source of leads on traditional crime, the records of health departments and regulatory agencies are the most important source of information for environmental crimes. By inspecting facilities for routine compliance, regulatory agents most often identify specific environmental problems. The Atlantic County Environmental Crime Task Force (New Jersey), for example, assesses roughly 650 cases prepared each year by the local health department (Epstein & Hammett, 1995). Criminal investigations often emerge from such compliance inspections. According to the law enforcement officer's guide for environmental criminal enforcement (EPA, 1990), regulatory inspectors should call on the EPA criminal investigation staff when they encounter circumstances such as these:

Conflicting data—when the company has two sets of records on the same incident or its comonitoring data [are] not consistent

Conflicting stories—when an inspector is told one thing and sees something quite different, either in records or through observation

Unsubstantiated data—when the inspector is given monitoring data for which there is no supporting record or documentation

Deliberate actions—when an employee says he or she was told to do something the inspector knows to be illegal

Claims of ignorance—when an employee claims to be unaware of established requirements but the inspector discovers records in the company's files showing knowledge of those requirements or where coworkers make statements during interviews showing that the employee had knowledge (pp. 14-15)

Real estate filings and the records of fire departments and licensing boards are also important sources for detecting violations. For instance, improperly storing waste frequently causes fires. When plant sites are routinely inspected for their fire hazard, the illegal disposal or storage of hazardous waste is often discovered (Mustokoff, 1981). Licensing agencies have information about business operations, company officers and owners, and annual reports.

Another source of leads is citizen complaints, many of which are received as anonymous calls to toll-free numbers. More than one third of cases in four sampled states were from citizen complaints. In most of these cases, the reporting citizens were neighbors of firms that transported, stored, and disposed of hazardous wastes. They usually observed illegal activities, viewed stored drums, or smelled unusual odors (Rebovich, 1992). Other complying witnesses include business competitors of violating firms, their employees, and the offenders themselves. Violators become leads to many other suspects who are involved in similar activities (Epstein & Hammett, 1995). The key question for investigators in opening an investigation is how reliable the complaint is. "The reliability of the original complaint often sets the tone for the entire investigation [influencing] the competence of decision-making, absence of bias, and verification of documents and observation" (Mustokoff, 1981, p. 39).

Proactive Investigation

Until the early 1980s, proactive investigations of environmental violators were uncommon (Mustokoff, 1981). As environmental criminal enforcement became a part of regular policing, however, local police—as the eyes and ears of the community—took a more proactive posture (Hammett & Epstein, 1993a). Their most typical technique—randomly patrolling in local areas—lent itself quite naturally to detecting environmental abnormalities. More recently, new tactics and guidelines have been incorporated into proactive investigations.

For proactive investigations, police officers are trained to observe promising indicators of illegal environmental activity. Four leading indicators are reviewed here (Brewer, 1995).

Abnormal Activity

Abnormal activity is "a change in normal patterns of activity, [such as] an unusual amount of night-time truck activity in an area where several abandoned warehouses or other storage buildings are located [or tank trucks] parking at the end of a lot, pumping material from one truck to another" (Brewer, 1995, pp. 9-10). The discriminating issue is whether a given activity seems unusual. Does it differ notably in appearance or operation from what is normal?

Offensive Odor

Foul smells often point to the presence of hazardous materials. A leading trainer suggests, "If officers encounter a smell that burns their eyes, mouth, nose, and skin, they should leave the area immediately, contact local public health officials or state environmental regulatory personnel and seek medical attention, particularly if the burning sensation continues" (Brewer, 1995, p. 10).

Unusual Appearance

The environment tends to have a normal appearance. When pollution intrudes, looks may change. In looking for departures from the normal, officers should ask the following:

> Is there a discharge of colored water coming from a pipe draining into a clear stream?
> Is smoke too dark to see through being emitted from a stack?
> Is a pipe leading from a plant to a body of water discharging visible solids or leaving a sheen on the water? (Brewer, 1995, p. 10)

For example, an area of dead grass or damaged vegetation near drainage pipes may indicate a water pollution violation.

Mysterious Moment

Is there something secretive or suspicious about activities? Examples are a bulldozer

> operating at night in a marsh or wetland, [a truck] pouring waste water into a sewer on the side of a road, [or someone] dumping garbage in barrels, cans or bags where it probably should not go, for example in the back of a parking lot, in an alley, in the woods, or in someone else's trash dumpster. (Brewer, 1995, p. 10)

These actions usually indicate that illegal environmental activities are under way.

A successful proactive approach to investigation has been developed by the Los Angeles County Environmental Strike Force and the California

Highway Patrol Hazardous Waste Unit. Individual companies that were suspected of illegal activity in hazardous waste transportation and disposal were targeted. During the surveillance, investigators witnessed several violations committed by transporters. As a result, a number of federal and state charges were filed against violators. The illegal transportation of hazardous waste into Mexico was also detected. Cases filed with the Los Angeles district attorney's office all led to convictions (Police Practice, 1991).

Training for Law Enforcement

Training for environmental investigations poses a special challenge because hazardous substances may present an immediate threat to the life and longer-term dangers to the health of investigators (Matulewich, 1991; O'Brien, 1991). As a consequence, enforcement personnel should be schooled in basic criminal investigative techniques such as "witness interviewing, warrant preparation and execution, gathering and analyzing documents, collecting evidence samples, and maintaining the chain of custody of evidence" (Hammett & Epstein, 1993a, p. 35) and in specific methods for responding to and detecting environmental crime while maintaining safety. Environmental incidents usually involve spills, leaks, releases, or illegal discharges of hazardous substances. The correct response by police officers to calls for assistance is often to make no response (Brewer, 1995). A thorough knowledge of state and federal environmental laws is critical in identifying environmental offenses. Sometimes, a harmful environmental act may be permitted by a regulatory agency as an exception to a particular statute. Under this circumstance, further criminal investigation probably would not be pursued (O'Brien, 1991).

The Los Angeles Police Department has developed an effective training program for law enforcement personnel that is based on long experience with the emergency management of hazardous materials, environmental investigations, and hazardous materials transportation enforcement. The general objectives of their training are to

Create an awareness of the potential threat presented by hazardous substances and the circumstances under which they may be encountered

Provide an understanding of the tactics and sources of information available to minimize the risk of injury to department personnel, the public and the environment

Create an awareness of the resources and agencies responsible for managing hazardous materials incidents, investigating environmental crimes and regulating the transportation of hazardous substances

Ensure that appropriate hazardous materials exposure records are maintained and, where necessary, arrange for medical monitoring (Gates & Pearson, 1991, p. 15)

The Los Angeles Police Department offers different levels of training to law enforcement personnel, depending on their job function and exposure to hazardous substances. For example, "first respondents"—patrol and traffic officers and supervisors—are usually trained in awareness and operations. Awareness training focuses on becoming familiar with "basic hazard communication systems and appropriate personnel safety precautions, [the knowledge of] appropriate evacuation/isolation distances and notification requirements, [and an understanding of] the Incident Command/On-Screen Manager systems" (Gates & Pearson, 1991, p. 15). Operations training centers on "appropriate courses of action, . . . personal protective equipment and safety precautions, . . . evacuation and isolation consideration, . . . command post operations, . . . interagency liaison, coordination and communication, . . . decontamination procedures, . . . legal considerations, . . . and appropriate documentation" (p. 16).

More sophisticated technical training addresses the needs of personnel in specialized assignments who must directly handle hazardous materials or offer technical information to inform decisions by others (Gates & Pearson, 1991). Hazard identification, assessment, incident cleanup requirements, and notifications required by state and federal regulatory agencies are the core subjects of training at this level.

Four regional environmental enforcement associations—in the Midwest, Northeast, South, and West—bring together environmental regulatory agencies, attorney general offices, law enforcement agencies, and local prosecutor associations from each area. They provide members with enforcement skills training, professional networking opportunities, and valuable information sharing.

Although most comprehensive training in criminal environmental enforcement is sponsored by state or regional agencies, short courses are now offered by some county and local facilities. They focus on specific topics, such as recognition of environmental crime, collection and control of evidence, report writing, interviewing techniques, and personal safety (Epstein & Hammett, 1995).

Methods of Obtaining Evidence

The purpose of investigation is to obtain both incriminating and exculpatory evidence. After a complaint is issued or suspected activity is detected, the next important task is uncovering evidence that supports or repudiates a crime.

Investigative Techniques

Although most police departments are novices at investigating environmental crime, pioneering practitioners have identified some effective techniques for hazardous waste investigations. These include some combination of "(1) surveillance; (2) surreptitious monitoring; (3) . . . search and seizure warrants; (4) statements made by targets, co-conspirators, and other witnesses to the crime; and (5) . . . the grand jury" (Mustokoff, 1981, p. 36). More recently, Wright and Imfeld (1991) have advocated the following techniques for successful investigations:

Stationary, moving and aerial surveillance to document ongoing criminal activity

Long-range photography and closed-circuit television to document probable cause

Tracing the origins of drum and barrel markings to manufacturers and purchasers

Remote monitoring devices to gather evidence

Consensual monitoring of informants and cooperating witnesses to obtain first-hand incriminating statements

Grand juries, which may result in unexpected evidence through compelled cooperation (p. 3)

Traditionally, the court has allowed observation from a stationary or moving vehicle to establish probable cause for a search warrant on targeted facilities. But it has restricted electronic surveillance, such as long-range photography and video filming, from aircraft. In *Katz v. United States* (1967) and *Berger v. New York* (1967), the U.S. Supreme Court made electronic surveillance subject to the Fourth Amendment requirement for a warrant (Mustokoff, 1981). As a result, only consensual electronic surveillance was possible without a warrant at that time. More recent decisions of the court have expanded warrantless electronic surveillance (Maioli & Staub, 1988). Consent is no longer required if the intercepted communications occur in a public place. In New Jersey, for example, suspected illegal discharges into waterways were confirmed by investigators who set up long-range cameras on nearby bridges (Rebovich, 1992). If the interception takes place in an area where there is a reasonable expectation of privacy, however, either consent or a court order is needed (Maioli & Staub, 1988). Such areas include "curtilage," such as "a courtyard, garden, or enclosed space of grounds immediately surrounding a dwelling house [and] any land or building immediately adjacent to a dwelling" (Epstein & Hammett, 1995, p. 32). In the cases of *United States v. Dunn* (1987) and *Florida v. Riley* (1989), the U.S. Supreme Court ruling held that "a barn located 60 yards from the defendant's home, but not within a fence surrounding the house, was not within the curtilage of the home" (Epstein & Hammett, 1995, p. 30). Therefore, from a location in open fields, police officers could peer inside a barn despite the defendant's reasonable expectation of privacy. Furthermore, the aid of a flashlight did not render the inspection an unconstitutional search.

Surveillance's greatest value is in detecting a pattern of continuous violation of environmental law. Single instances of off-loading or discharge are likely to be dismissed in court as an accident or mistake. The cost of both visual and electronic observation can be substantial, however, depending on the background information investigators already know. If they do not know, for example, when dumping will take place, time is wasted in waiting. In addition, the cost of surveillance by helicopter, high-altitude flight, or satellite usually exceeds the budgets of law enforcement agencies (Mustokoff, 1981).

Surreptitious monitoring, like electronic surveillance, of toxic dumping has raised legal concerns. Courts have ruled that prior authorization is required for surreptitious entry to install recording and transmitting devices. Court precedent, however, has been to grant requests for surreptitious entry if it is the only means by which the government could obtain evidence. The courts have also been more tolerant of surreptitious monitoring that is confined to an industrial or warehouse site, rather than a private residence (Mustokoff, 1981).

The grand jury is a powerful tool for investigating environmental crime. There are two advantages to using the grand jury. First, the grand jury can issue subpoenas compelling people to appear as witnesses. Failure to comply is grounds for immediate arrest (Riesel, 1985). Second, the grand jury proceeding is secret, and neither the alleged offender nor his or her attorney can routinely attend or cross-examine. This secrecy and strict confidentiality encourage witnesses to testify more willingly without fear of reprisal. Thus, the grand jury greatly facilitates evidence gathering and allows the government to construct a case without exposing its strategy before the trial starts (Segerson & Tietenberg, 1992).

If the budget permits, the undercover operation also can be a noteworthy strategy:

> In the cases where agents assumed undercover identities, the information obtained proved to be highly productive in that it affirmatively established not only the criminality of offender actions but allowed greater insights into the criminal relationships between employees within the offending firm. (Rebovich, 1992, p. 82)

Undercover officers from Portland, Maine, tracked linked waste hauling operations throughout much of the Northeast. An undercover operation in New Jersey led to the discovery of violations involving 30 companies (Epstein & Hammett, 1995).

The tracing of drum identification markings, waste sample analysis, and dye testing are also basic techniques. Abandoned drums containing illegal hazardous wastes can often be traced to drum manufacturers and then to generators and hauling firms. Dye testing is useful in locating the sources of discharge in sewers and waterways and for identifying hazardous discharges themselves.

Search and Seizure

Search and seizure fulfills a number of vital aims in environmental crime investigation: securing samples for laboratory analysis, viewing the crime scene, gaining access to relevant documents, conducting interviews, and possibly even observing the crime taking place. The search and seizure provisions of the Fourth Amendment pose special difficulties for the investigation of environmental crime. The basic constitutional protection against unreasonable search and seizure is the warrant, issued by an appropriate court when probable cause that a crime has occurred is shown. Environmental investigators often have trouble demonstrating probable cause. If residents complain about foul odors from an unauthorized dumping site, investigators need a reliable lab analysis to confirm the presence of hazardous waste. Without the lab analysis, they cannot establish probable cause for a search warrant. But to enter the property and take samples for a lab test, they need a warrant. The same evidence that verifies a crime is also necessary to justify a warrant (Mustokoff, 1981). Moreover, a pattern of community complaints about health problems or environmental damage from a nearby toxic waste dump will weigh significantly in a judge's decision to issue a warrant. But serious violations may not arouse community alarm because their damaging effects to health or the surroundings are invisible or long delayed (Mueller, 1996).

Under some circumstances, search and seizure can occur without a warrant. Three types of warrantless searches are most commonly available to investigators of environmental crimes. First, they can be part of statutorily authorized inspections, such as routine fire code, sanitation department, and building code inspections. If these inspections disclose the illegal storage of hazardous substances or other environmental violations, the evidence is admissible in court. For example, the California Health and Safety Code authorizes state patrol officers to "stop and inspect any vehicles reasonably suspected of transporting hazardous wastes" (Hammett & Epstein, 1993b, p. 52). In many jurisdictions, the evidence obtained by regulatory personnel can be used against offenders in criminal courts (Nixon, 1992). Almost everywhere, a regulatory investigator's records that confirm a violation are accepted by the court in support of probable cause.

Environmental investigators may also conduct warrantless searches with voluntary written consent from property owners or users. When warrantless inspections are not authorized by the law or when probable cause for a search warrant is absent, consent inspections offer the only legal alternative. Suspects of environmental crime are generally more willing to consent to searches than are suspects of traditional crime. Pollution violators tend to believe they are innocent and in compliance. They worry, as well, that failing to cooperate will only prompt an investigator's hostility or suspicion (Hammett & Epstein, 1993b).

Finally, open storage facilities are often subject to warrantless searches. In *Dow Chemical Company v. United States* (1986), the U.S. Supreme Court held that warrantless aerial surveillance and photography of a Dow chemical plant did not constitute an illegal search under the Fourth Amendment because the defendant lacked a reasonable expectation of privacy in the open areas of the industrial complex.

Thus, although the exclusionary rule is still theoretically applicable to environmental crime cases, it is rarely used in practice because a warrantless search and seizure can almost always be conducted. The central question becomes whether the normal protection against unwarranted search and seizure can be too easily avoided in environmental cases.

Regulatory Agencies and Enforcement Issues

Enforcement is the government's response to people and organizations that fail to obey the law. Environmental law is not simply a collection of statutes on environmental subjects. Instead, it is a complex system of civil and criminal statutes, regulations, and guidelines, which a wide variety of government agencies promulgate and enforce. As a consequence, the single most important requirement for effective environmental law enforcement is cooperation between regulatory agencies and traditional law enforcement officials.

The Importance of Interagency Cooperation

Although regulatory structures differ from state to state, health departments, environmental protection agencies, sewer authorities, fire departments, and the Occupational Safety and Health Administration are the key regulatory actors in the local enforcement of criminal environmental law. State environmental protection agencies are charged with the overall responsibility for regulatory implementation, including permits, inspections, and the development and monitoring of environmental protection programs. Other agencies help implement regulations and collect information on compliance and violations.

Regulatory agencies generally perform four duties in enforcing criminal environmental law. First, they notify the police or prosecutors of potential environmental crime. By conducting routine inspections or compliance monitoring, and by responding to materials incidents such as accidents, spills, and fires, regulatory agencies are able to detect violations at regulated facilities. Second, they collect evidence as part of their duties on routine inspections and emergency responses to substantiate violations. Such evidence may be used in any resulting enforcement action to bring the facility into compliance (EPA, 1990). Third, they preserve samples of suspect hazardous substances for lab analysis. Sample taking is a critical part of criminal investigation, which must be conducted with care if testing is to be valid. As a consequence, in many states, technicians from regulatory agencies are the only personnel who are allowed to collect site samples (Hammett & Epstein, 1993a). Fourth, they provide a variety of other technical support for investigations. For example, investigations of hazardous waste crimes may call on the following technicians from regulatory agencies (Wright & Imfeld, 1991):

Technical specialists, such as engineers, chemists, and geologists, who can give guidance on what to sample and how to sample properly

Equipment operators for digging equipment, barrel handling devices, remote sensing and sampling devices, and a variety of hand-operated equipment necessary for unearthing buried evidence

Health and safety specialists who can give advice regarding the dangers of possible exposure to hazardous substances and advice on what equipment and methods to use in order to maximize the protection of search personnel

Regulatory agency personnel to evaluate documentary and physical evidence to determine whether the continued operation of the company would jeopardize the public's health (pp. 4-5)

Thus, although regulatory agencies are not law enforcement organizations as such, they are vital to investigating environmental crime (Matulewich, 1991). The law enforcement community is not qualified to conduct environmental enforcement on its own. As a report on environmental crime investigations in Palm Beach County, Florida, concludes (Pearsall, 1994),

Most law enforcement officers have little or no idea of the existence of the complex array of environmental control laws with all the exceptions, changes and omissions. We are naive when it comes to the scientific background needed to put together an environmental pollution case. Neither do we understand or have the knowledge to safely deal with the illegal disposal of hazardous waste. Civil regulatory agencies have this knowledge and the resources to document evidence of a violation. Both criminal and civil agencies must work together in order to succeed. (p. 1)

Obstacles to Interagency Cooperation

The ideal of interagency cooperation is difficult to achieve in reality. The single biggest obstacle is "regulatory mind-set" (Hammett & Epstein, 1993b, p. 38). The philosophy of cooperative regulation shapes regulators' reaction to environmental violations (Scholz, 1984). The highest value is placed on persuasion and voluntary compliance. Most firms are given the benefit of the doubt for having good intentions. Regulators assume that companies will be cooperative and correct violations if given a reasonable opportunity. Persuasion, rather than legal action, is thought to be most effective in getting violators to comply with the laws. This regulatory mind-set contributes to the tension between regulators and personnel in criminal law enforcement, who believe that the deterrent effect of criminal prosecution should be exercised. In Alameda County, California, for example, "Regulators tend to view the glass as half full and they want to fill it up obtaining compliance from the violator. The D.A. meanwhile sees the glass as half empty and seeks to prosecute the thief who stole the missing half" (Hammett & Epstein, 1993b, p. 39). Regulatory mind-set has also contributed to insufficient training in collecting evidence, delaying the decisions to refer cases to the prosecutor, overlooking violations, and considering criminal prosecution only as a last resort (Hammett & Epstein, 1993b).

Regulatory mind-set blinds regulators to the harsher reality of venality, deception, and narrow self-interest by violators. Relying on persuasion or voluntary compliance can encourage abuse of the law and disregard of people's health (Frank & Lynch, 1992). Regulatory agencies tend to be captives of the industries they regulate (Chambliss & Seidman, 1982; Simon & Eitzen, 1993). Agency capture is a process "whereby the agency adopts the values and orientation of the regulated industry" (Frank & Lynch, 1992, p. 135). Regulators' zeal to punish violators may be compromised by fears that the local community will lose jobs if the polluter moves away or economizes. They may agree that for the sake of economic prosperity, excessive regulation by zealous enforcement agents should be avoided. As a result, they tend to compromise with violators. "Let's be reasonable" becomes the motto of many regulatory agencies. Enforcement officers who seek criminal sanctions are branded as unreasonable (Frank & Lynch, 1992).

Regulators may also avoid criminal prosecution as unfamiliar ground. They may worry about being embarrassed if they lose a battle in court (Frank & Lynch, 1992). They often maintain relationships with firms, which make them sensitive to business pressures for seeking noncriminal enforcement.

For all these reasons, they tend to be more patient with violators than criminal enforcers would be, giving firms many opportunities to comply with environmental law (Hammitt & Reuter, 1988). Violators may work for just this outcome. For example, hazardous waste offenders often co-opt regulators to avoid punishment (Rebovich, 1992). By promising regulators a generous corporate position after their resignation or retirement or offering a part-time job with a seductive salary, offenders are able to pressure, influence, and even control regulators. Not surprisingly, some regulators become advocates for regulated firms and sacrifice the regulatory agency's primary mission of protecting the public (Clinard & Yeager, 1980).

Approaches to Interagency Cooperation

Current efforts toward interagency cooperation are designed "to ensure that criminal, civil, and regulatory actions are applied in a coordinated and appropriate fashion, based on resource availability and the characteristics of violators and violations" (Epstein & Hammett, 1995, p. 33). Several models of interagency cooperation attempt to meet these goals.

The Alameda Model

Interagency cooperation in Alameda County (California) is formalized by a guidance document. Under this agreement,

> Police responsibilities include identifying criminal civil violations, locating and interviewing witnesses, and assisting in the collection of physical evidence. The fire department is to call health department personnel to the scene when chemicals are involved and to assist in scene documentation and evidence sample collection. The county hazardous materials response team is assigned to procure and preserve evidence and to assist police, fire, and health officials in formulating technical questions that will aid the prosecution in the preparation of its cases. (Hammett & Epstein, 1993b, p. 33)

Each agency to the agreement operates independently, but its work is coordinated by the guidance document to serve the common goal.

The Los Angeles Model

Interagency cooperation in Los Angeles County is achieved through the Los Angeles County Environmental Crime Strike Force. Representatives from 20 state and local law enforcement and regulatory agencies are permanently assigned to develop criminal environmental cases under the county prosecutor's leadership. No written agreement covers strike force procedures, however. In contrast to the Alameda model, the Los Angeles approach relies on informal interagency cooperation, rather than a formalized structure, to enforce group decisions. The commitment of participants to environmental law enforcement is the key to success of the Los Angeles model. If an agency fails in its obligations, other members would disapprove (Hammett & Epstein, 1993b). An informal structure, however, has become essential to the strike force. It consists of the following:

A law enforcement component to conduct criminal investigations

A technical component with a capacity to conduct health risk assessments and collect samples at the scene of alleged violations

A laboratory component to conduct analyses of samples, maintain the chain of custody of evidence, and provide expert testimony at trial (p. 3)

Law enforcement and regulatory personnel resolve disputes by informal criteria that clarify whether an incident should be handled administratively or criminally. The seriousness of a violation, the intent and environmental record of the violator, and the amount and toxicity of the substance are taken into consideration by regulatory agencies in deciding actions (Hammett & Epstein, 1993b).

The Los Angeles County Environmental Crime Strike Force has been widely emulated around the country. Critics argue, however, that its informality reduces effectiveness through time. This approach is most often modified by adopting memoranda of understanding to discourage jurisdictional fights among competitors for the position of lead agency (Hammett & Epstein, 1993b). In western New York, the interagency strike force worked successfully for some time as an informal group and then solidified its already proved relations by an agreement. To this end, a temporary task force is formed to bring agencies together for formal meetings and training sessions for a specified period. After adequate training occurs and inter-agency relationships prosper, relevant staff work together informally as needed on specific cases without formal meetings with the larger group (Hammett & Epstein, 1993a).

Whatever the form of interagency cooperation, decisive leadership is crucial to its well-being. Generally, the prominent involvement of the prosecutor is required (Hammett & Epstein, 1993b). The successes of interagency cooperation in Los Angeles County, Cook County (Chicago), Jefferson and Gilpin Counties (Colorado), and Monmouth County (New Jersey) are all due mainly to the leadership of their district or local prosecutors. Police begin to divert resources to investigate environmental crime only when they have confidence in prosecutors' commitment to pursuing cases vigorously (Epstein & Hammett, 1995). Once the commitment of prosecutors is secured, regulatory agencies that are traditionally reluctant to refer cases for criminal prosecution can become strong advocates of criminal enforcement (Hammett & Epstein, 1993b).

Review Questions

1. What are the respective roles of the U.S. Department of Justice and the U.S. Environmental Protection Agency in the enforcement of environmental crime laws?
2. What is the role of the state police in investigating environmental crime? (Discuss jurisdiction, perceived roles, personnel, and levels of activity.)
3. What are the three main types of environmental enforcement programs at the local level?
4. What are the major features of reactive investigations of environmental crime?
5. In proactive investigations, what are the primary indicators of illegal environmental activity?
6. What are the main investigative techniques for obtaining evidence in environmental crime cases?
7. What types of search and seizure are typical in investigating environmental crimes, and what constitutional issues do they raise?
8. Why is interagency cooperation so important for successful enforcement of environmental criminal law, and what are the main obstacles to achieving it?
9. What are the two main models of interagency cooperation in environmental enforcement?

CHAPTER 8

Combating Environmental Crime

Prosecution

Although federal environmental statutes have incorporated criminal sanctions since the Refuse Act of 1899, environmental offenses were not criminally prosecuted until the 1970s. As public awareness of environmental problems has grown, criminal sanctions against "midnight dumpers" and other water and air polluters have gained public approval, although their use is hardly commonplace. Indeed, the criminal prosecution of environmental violators is still rare in occurrence, limited in scope, and beset with difficulties. In this chapter, we first review criminal prosecution of environmental crime at the federal, state, and local levels. We then examine key problems that may hamper—or result from—this approach.

Criminal Prosecution at the Federal Level

Environmental prosecution at the federal level has made bold strides since the 1980s. Although the earliest federal prosecution dates from the 1970s, the entire decade tallied only 25 criminal environmental prosecutions (Habicht, 1987). Cases accelerated in the 1980s and 1990s but still take only the smallest bite out of the thousands of violations. In 1986, for example, 94 criminal indictments were entered, and 67 convictions were won (Hutchins, 1991). 1993 was a record year for criminal prosecutions under the nation's environmental laws: The DOJ obtained 186 indictments with a 90% conviction rate. From mid-1983 to mid-1994, the DOJ filed environmental indictments against 1,255 corporate and individual defendants: 931 of them were convicted or plead guilty; more than 299 years of imprisonment were served by the guilty (Cartusciello & Hutchins, 1994).

From 1983 to 1991, half of environmental crime prosecutions were for violations of the Resource Conservation and Recovery Act or CERCLA. A quarter were for water pollution offenses. The remaining quarter covered false statements and violations of the Toxic Substance Control Act, the Clean Air Act, and the Federal Insecticide, Fungicide, and Rodenticide Act. Of prosecutors' targets, 70% were individuals. Of these, 35% were company owners or presidents; 17% were corporate officers, board directors, or vice presidents. Managers and supervisors made up 29% of defendants, whereas the remaining 19% were nonsupervisory personnel (Hutchins, 1991). About 30% of indictments were against corporations. These firms were mostly small, with less than $1 million in sales or fewer than 50 employees (Cohen, 1992a).

These achievements have convinced some experts that criminal enforcement of environmental laws is now a national priority, leaving environmental offenders nowhere to run or hide (Marzulla & Kappel, 1991; Thornburgh, 1991). Although the number of criminal prosecutions has grown, it has not kept pace, however, with the explosion in enforcement actions. From mid-1981 to mid-1991, administrative actions consistently constituted about 90% of federal enforcement. Civil actions took up about 8% to 9%, and criminal prosecutions held steady at about 1% to 2% of the total (EPA, 1992). Clearly, criminal prosecution remains the exception rather than the rule (Bennett, 1990).

The dishearteningly minor role for criminal prosecution is confirmed by other data. If the 82 successful prosecutions by the DOJ in fiscal year 1992 are measured against the 258,860 generators of hazardous waste during the same year, then "only .0317% of the regulated population were criminally convicted for violating environmental law" that year (Ross, 1996, p. 68). For the previous year, the comparable figure is 0.02%. Not surprisingly, a survey of 500 leading industrial corporations found that nearly two thirds were involved in significant environmental illegalities (U.S. House of Representatives, 1990). A minuscule number of convictions obviously packs little deterrent power. If criminal prosecutions are relatively rare, criminal sanctions do little to deter. Finally, convicted federal environmental offenders on the average receive the low end of the range of available federal penalties:

> The average fine is only one-fifth of the maximum allowed. Even the middle-level defendants generally do not spend more than a few months in jail. The average fines for environmental violations that threaten the health and safety of entire towns, regions, and watersheds remain well below the statutory minimum for an armed mugger. (Adler & Lord, 1991, pp. 808-809)

Consequently, corporations calculate that it is financially much cheaper to risk paying a fine, which averages approximately $100,000, than to cover the cost of complying with hazardous waste regulations (Ross, 1996).

Meager federal prosecution is due largely to three factors. First, modest criminal prosecution reflects modest resources. In criminal cases, a criminal environmental investigation is performed by the National Enforcement Investigation Center, a technical resource and investigative unit of the EPA (EPA, 1985a). After being thoroughly developed and reviewed, the case is referred to the DOJ for prosecution. Roughly 150 EPA criminal investigators, however, had to oversee 258,860 generators of hazardous waste in 1991, for example. Each investigator was thus responsible for regulating approximately 1,700 generators in that year (Ross, 1996). The EPA has consequently concentrated its limited investigative resources on the most egregious instances of environmental misbehavior. Many polluters are not targeted by the EPA; they therefore never face criminal prosecution by the DOJ. The failure to prosecute is compounded by inadequate resources at the DOJ. When the number of criminally prosecuted cases for which there was a guilty verdict has increased, the number of entered guilty pleas has risen as well. The heightened prospect of being found guilty in a trial encourages violators to plead guilty in negotiations with the prosecutor. This added payoff, which augments the number of convictions, is diminished when the DOJ prosecutes fewer cases to a successful verdict (Adler & Lord, 1991).

Additional resources alone will not maximize enforcement effectiveness. A second brake is EPA's refusal to make criminal prosecution a high priority. By contrast, in states such as Pennsylvania and New Jersey, all cases are first screened for potential criminal prosecution by the attorney general's office. Only those cases not pursued are left for administrative or civil

handling (Starr, 1991). The EPA does not follow this approach. More funda-
mentally,

> EPA is an agency accustomed to including a broad array of scientists,
> administrators, and lawyers to resolve scientific disputes. The agency is
> uncomfortable with the need in criminal cases to limit sensitive enforcement
> information to a few critical decision-makers who must then make hard
> yes-or-no decisions in which "reasonable doubts," not scientific consensus,
> is the operative standard. (Starr, 1991, p. 914)

Third, the EPA's lack of independent enforcement authority contributes
to weak federal prosecution. The necessity of referring all cases, regardless
of their size and complexity, to the DOJ duplicates efforts by the two
agencies. This not only wastes the already limited resources of both agencies
but also pushes the EPA into the reactive posture of referring only major
criminal actions to the DOJ while ignoring lesser violations that might be
stopped before they escalate (Adler & Lord, 1991).

Criminal Prosecution at the State Level

Prior to the 1970s, the states were the middlemen in environmental
protection, the administrative stratum between an increasingly powerful
federal government and municipalities (Haskell & Price, 1973). They acted
for the most part in accordance with a Washington-based agenda while under
intense political pressure from local officials (Davis & Lester, 1989). Federal
and state environmental laws of the 1970s and 1980s altered this status by
empowering the states with the primary responsibility for enforcement
(Bowman, 1984, 1985; Crotty, 1987). Unfortunately, little research has been
conducted to assess the consequences of this change (Cohen, 1992a).

In general, the attorney general in a state holds the main responsibility
for criminally prosecuting environmental violators, at the request of state
environmental agencies (EPA, 1990). Of 38 attorneys general who responded
in a recent survey, 26 reported their office had jurisdiction to prosecute one
or more categories of environmental crime. In Wisconsin, for example, the
attorney general's office is responsible for prosecuting more than 11 types
of environmental offenses. In a few states such as Indiana and North Carolina, however, the office provides legal advice only (Edwards, 1996).

Under the auspices of the attorney general, environmental prosecution typically features interagency cooperation to coordinate responses, allocate resources, and avoid overlapping effort. In Arizona, for example, the attorney general has adopted a team approach with three regional task forces working up environmental prosecutions. Experienced prosecutors and criminal investigators in the attorney general's office are granted full police powers to prepare and handle environmental criminal cases (Hammett & Epstein, 1993a).

In New Jersey, criminal prosecution became a priority of the state attorney general's office as early as 1978 in response to sharply rising incidents of illegal hazardous waste dumping in the middle 1970s. The office's Toxic Waste Investigation/Prosecution Unit was the first unit of its type in the United States (Rebovich, 1992). Since then, New Jersey has continued to act aggressively in environmental criminal prosecution. In 1982, the unit grew into the Environmental Prosecutions Section, consisting of personnel from the state police, the Department of Environmental Protection, and the U.S. attorney general's office for the district of New Jersey. In 1990, the position of state environmental prosecutor was created to coordinate the state's effort on environmental crime. The state environmental prosecutor supervises the prosecution of important environmental cases, cooperates in multistate cases, and fosters the development and training of county environmental task forces (Hammett & Epstein, 1993a).

The responsibilities of attorneys general for prosecuting environmental crimes vary from state to state. In Maryland, for example, prosecuting attorneys are in charge of both civil and criminal enforcement of environmental statutes. In New Jersey and Pennsylvania, in contrast, prosecuting attorneys face a clear division of these responsibilities (Rebovich, 1992). Under California law,

> The attorney general has primary responsibility for civil and appellate matters but has no original jurisdiction in criminal cases. However, if the district attorney declines to prosecute a case, the A.G. may pursue the prosecution. Also, if a district attorney's office declines prosecution, the case can be referred to the A.G. for possible civil proceedings. (Hammett & Epstein, 1993a, p. 45)

Moreover, the volume of state prosecutions of environmental crime varies widely. Two factors contribute to the variation. First, although many state environmental crime units have the authority to deal with violations across municipal and county lines, they may lack the resources to prosecute infractions at small sites and respond to emergencies as quickly as the local or county unit. Second, the criminal jurisdiction of the attorney general is sharply limited. For example, the attorney general does not have access to the grand jury process. This jurisdictional obstacle impedes the attorney general's participation (Hammett & Epstein, 1993a).

Other obstacles frustrate successful prosecution of environmental crime at the state level as well. For states such as Maryland, South Dakota, Colorado, Maine, Missouri, New Jersey, and Vermont, agency success is blocked mainly by a shortage of funds and properly trained investigators. Arizona, Louisiana, Minnesota, New York, North Carolina, Texas, Utah, and Wisconsin also report a need for more resources for environmental law enforcement (Edwards, 1996). Inadequate laws, the lack of statutory authority over distant violators, and judges' misperceptions also weaken the struggle against environmental crime.

Criminal Prosecution at the Local Level

Local prosecutors have grown to become a critical force in the battle against environmental crime. The nature and scope of environmental crime, after all, are determined by patterns of local industry and business. Consequently, local prosecutorial agencies are more familiar with the particular environmental problems and needs of local communities than are state and federal prosecutors. Moreover, the more than 2,800 district attorneys nationwide represent an important resource for environmental prosecution. A national survey confirms the significance of local prosecutors in fighting environmental crime (National Institute of Justice, 1994). Among 100 local prosecutor's offices in jurisdictions with more than 250,000 residents, approximately half operate special environmental prosecution units. More than half of the 100 offices assign full-time prosecutors to environmental offenses, and more than three quarters assign part-time prosecutors to them. More than 71% of offices reported that prosecutors routinely participate in the investigation of environmental offenses. These efforts yielded a dramatic increase in criminal prosecutions. Between 1990 and 1991, prosecuted cases in the sample nearly doubled from 381 to 756—a 98% increase. In the first half of

1992, criminal prosecutions eclipsed those for all of 1991, rising from 756 to 882, a 17% increase and a 132% increase over total criminal prosecutions for 1990 (National Institute of Justice, 1994).

The importance of local prosecutors is also revealed by examining prosecutorial procedure in environmental cases. A study of five local prosecutor's offices shows prosecutors getting involved as soon as an environmental offense is identified by a local law enforcement agency and the case is referred (Hammett & Epstein, 1993a). In some counties, prosecutors give direction to a series of investigative activities, such as collection of background information on the suspected firm or individual, surveillance of suspects, and gathering of additional evidence to support a criminal prosecution. Prosecutors almost always render legal advice in preparing and executing a search warrant. They determine whether lab findings meet legal requirements for prosecution. They prepare expert witnesses for testimony on lab results. Their most important task is deciding whether the evidence warrants criminal charging. If it does not, civil or administrative prosecution will be pursued. Some prosecutors have the authority to initiate these alternatives; others must refer the cases to the state attorney general or another designated official. After formal charging, the prosecutor may negotiate a plea agreement or proceed to trial. Finally, the prosecutor advises the court on sentencing and assists in imposing and collecting fines (Hammett & Epstein, 1993a).

Although the local prosecutors' role in environmental criminal prosecution is clearly indispensable, their success depends on joining needed expertise with resources. The environmental task force, led by the prosecutor, best achieves this union of personnel from diverse law enforcement and regulatory agencies with financial resources and technical capacity (Edwards, 1996; Hammett & Epstein, 1993a; Matulewich, 1991; National Institute of Justice, 1994; Rebovich, 1996).

Other factors contribute to successful prosecution as well. First, support and leadership from the top of the prosecutorial agencies are critical to local prosecution efforts. The county district attorney usually plays this key role by formalizing a task force to institute a training program. An especially calamitous pollution case may prompt a shift of resources to environmental prosecution. The crisis raises the public's consciousness about the dangers of environmental crime and spawns a new constituency demanding criminal prosecution. Such a case also frequently offers important lessons in the value of interagency cooperation. Finally, successful prosecution results from sufficient resources. Because many environmental cases are costly to prosecute, limited resources often hamper effective prosecution (Hammett & Epstein, 1993a).

Environmental Criminal Liability

The Scope of Corporate Criminal Liability

Industrial corporations are a primary target of environmental criminal prosecution because they generate, transport, and store so much of the nation's hazardous waste. Corporate criminal liability for environmental violations is an important weapon in the battle to deter environmental misbehavior. The court has increasingly accepted plaintiff arguments for corporate criminal liability in cases in which a firm's misdeeds led to injury, illness, or death. For example, Film Recovery Systems, Inc., was convicted in 1985 for the death of a worker who was not protected from poisonous substances at the work site (Nittoly, 1991). Borjohn Optical Technology, Inc., was found guilty of violating the Clean Water Act. The firm ordered employees to dump toxic waste into the public sewer system. Thereby exposed to poisonous chemicals, the workers risked serious illness (Weidel et al., 1991).

Attempts to impose criminal liability on firms do not go unchallenged. Corporate defendants are likely to cite the well-established doctrine of *limited corporate liability,* which holds stockholders liable only for the amount of their initial investment and not personally liable for the debts of the corporation (Easterbrook & Fischel, 1985). Limited liability provides operating flexibility and financial benefits to a corporation, but it can also be used, critics argue, to screen illegal behavior from public scrutiny (Kane, 1991). Corporate criminal liability challenges this doctrine by holding a company's stockholders, who probably have few managerial skills and no involvement in production, responsible for the shortcomings of managers and workers.

The traditional doctrine of mens rea assumes that liability should not be imposed unless the accused committed a wrongful act with intent. Corporate criminal liability complicates this long-standing view because a corporation, as a social construction rather than a human person, possesses no mental state. Therefore, it is difficult, if not impossible, to prove that a corporation intended to act in an illegal manner (Doerr, 1985).

In the past decade, however, important theories have been advanced to support the concept of corporate culpability. The theory of agency, for example, argues that a principal corporation (parent) is held responsible for the acts of its wholly owned subsidiary (agent). This theory was invoked in the *Exxon Valdez* case. The *Exxon Valdez,* an oil supertanker, ran aground on Bligh Reef in March 1989, spilling 240,000 barrels of oil into Alaska's Prince William Sound. The United States charged Exxon Shipping Company, the owner of the *Exxon Valdez,* and its parent, Exxon Corporation, with five criminal counts each for causing this environmental catastrophe (Raucher, 1992). Limited corporate liability would have protected Exxon against these charges, but the government was clearly basing its decision to prosecute on agency theory. The government claimed it need prove only an agency relationship between Exxon Corporation and Exxon Shipping. It offered evidence not only that Exxon Shipping acted on behalf of Exxon Corporation but also that its policy decisions, operations, and personnel training were under the direct control of Exxon Corporation. The court embraced agency theory, accepted the evidence, and imposed corporate criminal liability on the parent company for the environmental violation of its subsidiary agent.

A second theory bolsters corporate criminal liability by holding a corporation responsible for the acts and intent of its top management (Doerr, 1985). In *United States v. Frezzo Brothers, Inc.* (1970), the government not only brought suit against two executives of Frezzo Brothers, Inc., who allowed the firm to discharge sewage into a stream during an 8-year period, but also named the corporation as a defendant. Both the executives and the corporation were found guilty. The corporation was fined $50,000, and the executives each received jail sentences of 30 days and fines totaling $50,000 (Doerr, 1985).

A third theory bases corporate criminal liability on the firm's failure to establish procedures for preventing accidents or disasters. In the *Exxon Valdez* case, the government noted that Exxon Shipping had assigned a captain to the ship who had a serious drinking problem and a helmsman who lacked the necessary skills to perform his duties. The company failed to ensure competent control of the ship, thereby breached maritime regulations, and incurred felony criminal liability (Raucher, 1992).

Another theory expands the definition of knowledge that is required for establishing corporate culpability. In the traditional version of mens rea, the intent to commit a crime is proved by actual knowledge of the violated statute. In many environmental statutes, knowledge of the violating actions—not the law that prohibits the actions—is a sufficient basis for intent. In the case of *United States v. International Minerals and Chemical Corporation* (1971), for example, the defendant was charged with knowingly violating a regulation that prohibited the shipment of hazardous materials without a permit. The court held that *knowingly* in the statute pertained only to knowledge that the material shipped was hazardous—not to knowledge of the existence of the regulations (Weidel et al., 1991).

The doctrine of collective knowledge "allows the collective knowledge of a corporation's employees, acquired within the scope of their employment, to be imputed to the corporation" (Weidel et al., 1991, p. 1122). Therefore, a corporation can be guilty of a knowing violation even when no single employee has full knowledge of all aspects of the violation. In other words, when the aggregated information of a number of employees presents a full picture of the crime, the corporation itself can be viewed as having knowledge of the violation.

Finally, the doctrine of strict liability does not require mens rea at all to sustain a conviction. In ignoring the defendant's intent, the strict liability doctrine allows for "punishment of individuals who, because of deception, unwittingly commit prohibited acts" (Levenson, 1993, p. 403). Strict liability has been traditionally applied to public welfare offenses that usually cause widespread harm to public health, safety, or welfare. These offenses often occur when widely distributed goods do not comply with reasonable standards of quality, integrity, disclosure, and care. An example of this crime might be the wholesale marketing of salmonella-tainted meat to supermarket chains around the country. Public welfare offenses can have severe effects. Consequently, the statutes governing them do not include intent as an element of the crime (Harris, Cavanaugh, & Zisk, 1988). Because environmental crime is viewed as one type of public welfare offense, the doctrine of strict liability has been adopted in some environmental statutes (EPA, 1984). As a result, the prosecution's burden of proof under such statutes is lower than that under statutes requiring mens rea. The case of *Ohio v. Budd Co.* (1980) illustrates the abandonment of traditional mens rea in favor of strict liability. The Budd company was successfully sued after an employee noticed an oil slick near a tank but failed to report the spill. Appealing the conviction, the corporation argued that Ohio had to demonstrate that the company intentionally violated water pollution statutes. The Ohio Court of Appeals held that "Ohio's pollution law was a strict liability statute and therefore culpability was not required to find a person guilty of the offense" (Doerr, 1985, p. 663).

The doctrine of strict liability relieves the state of the difficult task of proving intent. The doctrine is applauded by some as an effective way of guaranteeing more corporate convictions for environmental violations (Milne, 1988-1989). Many scholars, however, are critical of the doctrine. Some argue, for example, that the strict liability doctrine operates under an irrebuttable presumption. Some level of culpable intent is present once an impermissible act is committed; therefore, punishment is justifiable (Abrams, 1982; Hippard, 1973). Sometimes, however, this basic presumption is uncertain. Some defendants have spent several years in prison despite having taken extraordinary efforts to comply with the law (Levenson, 1993). In these cases, the strict liability doctrine is considered unjust.

The Scope of Individual Criminal Liability

The criminal provisions of environmental statutes apply to any *person* broadly defined who commits a violation. *Persons* may be knowing participants in illegal acts, but they may also be responsible corporate officers. Knowing participants include individuals who knowingly dispose of hazardous waste without a permit, purposely discharge sewage into public water, or fail to report an oil spill to the authority. Most environmental statutes also hold individual corporate officers criminally liable in their official capacity for directing or authorizing violations of the law. For example, an executive is liable when he or she did not illegally dump hazardous waste him- or herself but still ordered or approved its being done (Seymour, 1989). In *United States v. Ward* (1982), the owner of an electrical transformer storage company was criminally charged for disposing of toxic substances in violation of the Toxic Substances Control Act of 1976. The owner had hired a vendor to dispose of PCB-contaminated oil, and the vendor dumped the oil illegally. To impose criminal penalties on individual corporate officers, they must willfully violate the law or at least know that the probable consequence of their action is illegal.

The criminal liability of corporate officers extends even further, however. Under the responsible corporate officer doctrine, a corporate official is subject to criminal liability even though he or she did not personally commit the illegal act or possess personal knowledge of criminal behavior by a subordinate. The doctrine overrides mens rea's traditional requirement of intent. Here, prosecution need show only that the officer's corporate position granted the officer the authority and responsibility to prevent or promptly halt a violation. The responsible corporate officer doctrine holds an especially high risk of criminal liability for senior corporate officers, who are not usually involved in the daily affairs of the firm. In the case of *United States v. Northeastern Pharmaceutical and Chemical Corporation* (1986), the corporation's president was named the defendant. Although he knew that the firm produced toxic by-products, he did not know the exact method of disposal, which involved dumping the waste on a nearby farm.

The responsible corporate officer doctrine is not identical to the concept of strict liability. The differences are illustrated by the case of *United States v. Dee* (1990). William Dee, Robert Lentz, and Carl Gepp were chemical engineers in high-level supervisory positions at the Chemical Research, Development, and Engineering Center, the largest of 40 organizations engaged in military research. At the time the case was tried, Dee was the head of the munitions directorate within the center, Gepp was the chief of the pilot plant, and Lentz was Gepp's boss with responsibility for supervising pilot-scale process studies on waste disposal and pollution abatement. Each official had 15 to 20 years of experience in chemical engineering. They were familiar with the dangers of the various chemicals used in projects. In January 1984, they were informed that their lab wastes were improperly draining through the sanitary treatment system. The problem was disregarded, however, and illegal disposal continued. In January 1986, Dee and Lentz were warned of significant leakage of chemicals stored at the old pilot plant. But until the summer of 1986, inspections revealed that hazardous wastes still remained at the plant site, and chemicals were leaking from the drums stored there. In spring 1986, employees at the newer pilot plant disposed of thousands of hazardous chemicals in an open field during a cleanup of the complex. Dee and Lentz disagreed with the safety office's assessment that the wastes were creating an environmental and health hazard. They therefore did not make cleanup of the site a priority. At their trial, they were found guilty of violating the Resource Conservation and Recovery Act for improperly treating, storing, and disposing of hazardous wastes and doing so without a permit.

The defendants appealed the conviction on the following grounds: (a) The government failed to establish that they had "intent" to violate the

Resource Conservation and Recovery Act because they did not know that their actions constituted a violation of the act; (b) the conditions that existed at both pilot plants were the result of circumstances beyond their control; and (c) the evidence was insufficient to establish their involvement in the criminal activity that was alleged in each count of the indictment (Barrett & Clarke, 1991). The Fourth Circuit rejected these arguments and affirmed the conviction.

The main issues raised by this case are what the term *knowingly* meant under the Resource Conservation and Recovery Act and whether the defendants, as upper-level managers, could be held criminally liable for the actions of their subordinates. There are two interpretations of the *knowing* provision to be taken into consideration here.

> Under a broad interpretation of the "knowing" provision, the government only needs prove that the defendant "knows" that he is treating, storing, or disposing of a material and that the defendant is aware of the general nature of that material. Under a restrictive interpretation of the provision, the government need only prove that the defendant "knew" that he was specifically violating RCRA and that the defendant "knew" each element of the offense. Such a restrictive interpretation is inconsistent with RCRA's overall regulatory goal. (Barrett & Clarke, 1991, p. 873)

In the *United States v. Northeastern Pharmaceutical and Chemical* case, the court adopted the first of these interpretations. The court also embraced the responsible corporate officer doctrine in holding Dee and his associates criminally liable for actions they did not either know of or participate in. The doctrine served as a guidepost for the jury, setting forth key factors from which to infer the requisite intent under the Resource Conservation and Recovery Act (Barrett & Clarke, 1991). These factors include "(1) that a RCRA violation occurred within an officer's area of supervision and control; (2) that the officer had the authority or power to prevent or correct the violation; and (3) that the officer knowingly failed to do so" (p. 874). Thus, the responsible corporate officer doctrine is not a simple copy of strict liability. Instead, "inferred knowledge" must be demonstrated to hold a corporate officer liable for offenses that endanger the public welfare. As a result, the knowledge requirement under the Resource Conservation and Recovery Act is stretched but not broken.

The responsible corporate officer doctrine has been extensively applied to more recent cases. In *United States v. MacDonald and Watson Waste Oil*

Co. (1991), the court held that the position and responsibility of executives or their previously obtained information were sufficient evidence of knowledge. In *United States v. Britain* (1990), the director of public utilities for the city of Enid, Oklahoma, was convicted of violating the Clean Water Act by improperly discharging pollutants into navigable waters. The defendant appealed on the theory that he was not a criminally liable "person" as defined under the statute because he was neither a permittee nor a responsible corporate officer of the discharging permittee. The court rejected this argument based on the interpretation that a "responsible corporate officer," to be held criminally liable, would not have to "willfully or negligently cause a permit violation." Instead, the willfulness or negligence of the actor would be imputed to him or her by virtue of his or her position of responsibility. These recent cases represent the "broadest application yet of the responsible corporate officer doctrine in the environmental law setting" (Harig, 1992, p. 156).

This discussion reveals two types of criminal liability against corporate officers (Seymour, 1989). The first is direct criminal liability. Under this version, the government must show that a corporate officer personally authorized illegal acts by subordinates, tolerated their commission, or knew of their consequences. The second is indirect criminal liability, as specified under the responsible corporate officer doctrine. Under this version of liability, the court does not require any evidence of the officer's direct participation or acquiescence in criminal behavior by a subordinate. The government needs only to introduce evidence regarding the nature of the corporation and the defendant's position and responsibilities in it. "Courts typically have been willing to impose indirect criminal liability only when the corporation is small and highly centralized" (p. 345). The influence a senior officer exercises over a small firm is considerably greater than the influence of an executive in a large, publicly held corporation.

> In a large corporation with many departments, a high-ranking corporate officer may have no authority or involvement in many spheres of corporate activity. Rather, plant managers, area supervisors and other relatively low-ranking employees often have broad power with respect to a matter within the scope of their authority. In such cases, senior corporate officers may be able to avoid indirect liability for the wrongful acts of subordinates because they are simply too distant from the transaction to be charged with a responsible share of liability. (Seymour, 1989, p. 345)

The potential for criminal liability for senior officers in large corporations still remains, however. In *United States v. Park* (1975), for example, a corporate president was criminally convicted despite his delegation of operational authority to others in a large firm.

Prosecutorial Discretion: Civil Versus Criminal Charging

Introduction

Environmental enforcement can pursue administrative, civil, or criminal remedies. If an administrative approach to an environmental case is followed, the case is handled by a quasi-independent judicial system within the executive branch, rather than by independent courts. This alternative is less expensive for involved parties than a court proceeding, but it provides less protection of the violators' rights (Segerson & Tietenberg, 1992). Moreover, the available remedies for administrative violators are somewhat limited. They are confined mainly to directed relief, such as issuing an order to stop the sale or distribution of an unregistered or misbranded pesticide, revoking permits, debarring violators from governmental contracts, and imposing fines. During the 1980s, for example, more than 90% of environmental disputes with the federal government were dealt with administratively (EPA, 1990).

Although administrative penalties are directly imposed by a government agency's order without the need for court involvement, civil penalties can be imposed only by judicial actions filed in civil court. Although civil penalties are not necessarily more severe than administrative penalties, civil proceedings are usually used to deal with more serious violations or complex cases because the "courts have more latitude in assigning punitive damages, can resolve difficult points of law and can establish precedents which lay the groundwork for future cases" (Segerson & Tietenberg, 1992, p. 55). Civil penalties are generally meant to deter further violations of environmental statutes rather than to punish (Selmi, 1986). Their primary purposes are to bring the violator back into compliance and to dissuade the violator from further noncompliance (EPA, 1985b). Civil actions resulting principally in fines, however, are ineffective as a tool of deterrence. Fines are typically calculated by companies as an ordinary cost of doing business and are ultimately passed on to the public in the form of higher prices (McKibben, 1992).

Criminal prosecution has been called the nuclear weapon of the environmental enforcement arsenal (Marzulla & Roistacher, 1990) because of its powers to incarcerate and stigmatize. Criminal, like civil, proceedings are conducted in the courts. Because the EPA lacks authority to prosecute, civil and criminal cases must be referred to the DOJ for bringing charges against environmental violators. The rules for gathering evidence are more restrictive in criminal proceedings than in civil proceedings. The standards of proof necessary for a criminal conviction are much higher than they are for a civil finding of guilt. In a civil trial by jury, a mere majority can convict, but in a criminal felony trial, the jury's guilty verdict must be unanimous. In the past, civil proceedings had been commonly interpreted as a measure of the EPA's enforcement performance. Although criminal enforcement has increased dramatically in recent years, civil and administrative actions continue to be the mainstay of environmental enforcement by the federal government (Arbuckle, 1993a).

Although the 1990s have been declared "the dawn of a new era" in criminal environmental prosecution (Nittoly, 1991, p. 1125), prosecutorial discretion has emerged as a vexing concern. Prosecutors have wide latitude to reject and steer cases as they see fit. From 1979 through 1981, for example, the DOJ declined nearly 60% of EPA's criminal referrals (Starr, 1991). Although specific data are unavailable, the total number of convictions from 1983 to 1994 contained a substantial number of bargained guilty pleas (Cartusciello & Hutchins, 1994). Prosecutors may also raise or lower charges, dismiss or abandon a case at many points, refuse to plea bargain, and influence sentencing, just as they do with traditional criminal cases. A former federal prosecutor of environmental crimes (Riesel, 1985) noted, "The prosecution of adultery and the violation of environmental statutes have at least three things in common. Enforcement is selective and erratic, and the consequences are often harsh" (p. 10065). The high level of prosecutorial discretion in environmental cases results from four factors: the lack of a central review system, the absence of clear guidelines from environmental agencies, a low level of culpability among offenders, and attitudinal resistance to placing environmental offenders on the criminal docket.

The Lack of a Central Review System

Although a central review system governs civil environmental enforcement, it is absent in criminal enforcement (Gaynor, Remer, & Martman, 1992). In general, in civil enforcement an EPA attorney prepares a referral package, which is subject to a formal internal EPA review. If the referral package is approved, it is forwarded to the Enforcement Section of the DOJ's Environmental and Natural Resources Division. There, the referred case is reviewed by a trial attorney and his or her supervisors, including the chief or deputy chief of the section. Finally, the case is presented for formal approval by the assistant attorney general for the environment, who must sign the complaint before the case can be filed. These centralized review procedures ensure that the government's minimum standards for civil prosecution will be met and that the applicable environmental law is uniformly interpreted (Gaynor et al., 1992).

In the case of criminal enforcement, however, U.S. attorneys—federal prosecutors—may commence prosecution and start criminal environmental investigations without consulting the Environmental Crimes Section of the DOJ (Gaynor et al., 1992). Thus, although the section plays a critical supervisory role in handling civil environmental cases, it becomes a bystander because criminal prosecution is carried out by a U.S. attorney. This "relatively laissez-faire framework" severely restricts the oversight of environmental criminal prosecution, increasing the possibility for U.S. attorneys to abuse their discretionary power (p. 7).

The Absence of Clear Guidelines

As late as 1988, neither the DOJ nor the EPA had articulated clear guidelines for exercising prosecutorial discretion on criminal violations of environmental statutes (Seymour, 1989). As early as 1982, the EPA did list significant factors in deciding to pursue a criminal action. These factors included the extent of environmental contamination, material impact on EPA's regulatory functions, and the defendant's history of noncompliance (EPA, 1982). Given their lack of specificity and the absence of any further interpretation, however, these standards provided few practical guideposts for prosecutors. Moreover, they contained enormous discretionary leeway in contrast to EPA's more precise guidelines for civil prosecution. In addition, two of the guidelines for civil prosecution focused on a history of noncompliance and willful misconduct, respectively, which are also normally requirements for criminal prosecution.

Finally, in 1991, the DOJ issued more explicit criteria. *Factors in Decisions on Criminal Prosecutions for Environmental Violations in the Context of Significant Voluntary Compliance or Disclosure Efforts by the Violator* outlines six key factors for deciding whether to mount a criminal prosecution of an environmental offense. The first factor is a voluntary, timely, and complete disclosure of the noncompliance. "Particular consideration should be given to whether the disclosure substantially aided the government's investigatory process and whether it occurred before a law enforcement or regulatory authority had already obtained knowledge regarding noncompliance" (p. 3). The second factor is cooperation. Full and prompt cooperation is essential, whether in the context of a voluntary disclosure or after the government has independently learned of a violation. "Consideration should be given to the violator's willingness to make all relevant information available to government investigators and prosecutors" (pp. 3-4).

The third factor is the extent to which a violator has undertaken preventive measures and compliance programs. Prosecutors should consider the existence and scope of any regularized, intensive, and comprehensive environmental compliance program. "Particular consideration should be given to whether the compliance or audit program includes sufficient measures to identify and prevent future noncompliance and whether the program was adopted in good faith and in a timely manner" (DOJ, 1991, p. 4). Fourth, the pervasiveness of noncompliance must be considered. The more pervasive the noncompliance, the more likely there may be systemic or repeated participation in illegal acts. Fifth is any evidence that the violator took internal disciplinary action against employees who violated company environmental compliance policies. Finally, consideration should be given to the extent of any subsequent compliance efforts to remedy continuing noncompliance. By these standards, a leading candidate for criminal prosecution would be a company that did nothing to prevent a major violation, still ignores—and will repeat—it, hid the violation and has not been forthcoming about it, and has failed to punish responsible employees.

In actual practice, federal prosecutors generally consider four factors when deciding whether to file criminal charges against an environmental violator: (a) the duration of the violation, (b) the degree of cooperation shown by the violator, (c) evidence of any intent to violate environmental law, and (d) the potential for deterrence. Specific situations that might draw criminal charges, rather than civil action, include

> the opportunity to deter the discharging or dumping of hazardous wastes without a permit; the knowing misuse of the regulatory apparatus, such as the deliberate failure to obtain necessary permits and file required reports; and a substantive violation of pollution laws which the offender conceals or about which he misleads the government. (Habicht, 1987, p. 10479)

Any of these acts "will virtually guarantee felony indictment and conviction" (p. 10485).

A national survey of 100 local prosecutor's offices in jurisdictions of 250,000 or more residents identified some significant considerations in the decision to criminally prosecute environmental offenses. The most crucial factors favoring criminal prosecution are the degree of harm posed by the offense and the criminal intent of the offender. The most significant factor opposing criminal prosecution is insufficient evidence or the inability to recognize appropriate evidence. Lack of resources was ranked lowest as a reason for rejecting criminal prosecution (National Institute of Justice, 1994).

The consensus among local prosecutors about standards for criminal prosecution is salutary but not totally reassuring. Their agreement masks serious potential for missed opportunities and inconsistent prosecution. For example, an offense's degree of harm should be an important concern in deciding to prosecute criminally. But the harmful effects of environmental offenses are often not felt or detected for years. Thus, the degree of harm, as a practical matter, is an unreliable factor in a prosecutor's immediate assessment about how to proceed (Hawes & Chu, 1987). In the absence of proximate and dramatic evidence of harm, the prosecutor may opt for civil action—or no action. To make matters worse, some of the evidentiary requirements for environmental prosecution are technical in nature. The strength of evidence can be compromised by the prosecutors' lack of experience or training in recognizing environmental criminality, investigators' inability to conduct immediate and proper searches, and lack of access to competent and timely laboratory testing services. These complications make uniform enforcement action unlikely, although local prosecutors tend to agree on what is important. Indeed,

Whether a violation is treated criminally, civilly, or administratively is more a function of what type of investigator learns of the violation first and in what judicial district the violation occurs, not the nature or environmental severity of the violation. (Gaynor et al., 1992, p. 4)

Weak Culpability

Ordinarily, for a crime to exist, there must be both a criminal act (actus reus) and a culpable state of mind (mens rea). Environmental crimes always make plain the criminal act such as pollution, contamination, and the transportation and storage of hazardous wastes without a permit. But the mental culpability—or mens rea—of the offender is not always so obvious. Although mens rea is a standard principle of Anglo-American law, the mens rea requirement has been seriously blurred in the prosecution of environmental crime. It is unlikely that the court would ever accept the notion that a criminal sanction can be imposed absent the proof of some degree of criminal intent (Harris et al., 1988). Except for the Refuse Act of 1899, knowledge is a required mental state for the existence of a criminal offense in all environmental statutes (Milne, 1988-1989). In practice, however, criminal intent has been interpreted in different ways, and the knowledge requirement has been cut back to the bone.

Mens rea can be present as specific intent, general intent, or strict liability arising from public welfare offenses. The absence of the first, leaving the field to the other two, spells the erosion of mens rea in environmental law (Kane, 1991). Specific intent, "the highest degree of intent, requires more than the intent to do the specific act that the law prohibits" (p. 314). Take the example of assault with the intent to commit murder. Specific intent requires that the offender must have meant to commit the assault and also have meant the victim's death as its result (Kane, 1991). In most environmental cases, it is difficult to establish criminal liability on the basis of such specific intent.

A crime of general intent, on the other hand, "merely requires that the act be done with a sufficient level of awareness" (Kane, 1991, p. 314). The knowledge requirement, broadly interpreted, is a form of general intent. Required knowledge is not of the statute that prohibits offenses and not of the illegal action taken by subordinates. Rather, it refers broadly to knowledge of the hazardous nature of the materials with which the firm is dealing and knowledge of the business as part of a highly regulated industry. This knowledge, furthermore, need not be reposited in one executive but can be the collective possession of the firm (Weidel et al., 1991).

Strict liability allows corporate officers to be held liable for the criminal violation of an environmental statute even when they did not intend the offense or participate in it. Strict liability is invoked in public welfare offenses because they can cause such widespread and fatal damage. Traditional mens rea places too heavy a burden on the justice system in these cases, and strict liability serves as a more potent deterrent against calamities, impressing firms who affect the public health and the environment to be extraordinarily careful and safe in their operations. The responsible corporate officer doctrine is considered an application of strict liability in environmental cases (Harig, 1992). A stricter view of mens rea, which emphasizes specific intent, has largely been abandoned. A polluter may be subject to criminal conviction when he or she should have known the law or when he or she holds a responsible position with a firm in which others commit offenses. As a result, "federal environmental laws no longer have culpability distinctions between civil and criminal offenses" (Gaynor et al., 1992, p. 29), and "criminal prosecution can be based on virtually any environmental violation, even if it is unintentional or it stems from the acts or omissions of a single individual" (Locke, 1991, p. 321). Moreover, weak culpability presents an occasion for prosecutorial discretion. The prosecutor's decision is based not necessarily on the principled and predictable application of the statutory scheme but rather on "inferred knowledge" or "presumed knowledge" (Harris et al., 1988, p. 236).

The revised standards for mens rea have been criticized as patently unjust (Saltzman, 1978) and hostile to a defendant's due process rights (Gaynor et al., 1992). The prosecution of individuals and corporations for environmental crimes in the absence of traditional mens rea, however, continues to be a trend. The potential for abuse here would be reduced if culpability were assessed more objectively by taking the following factors into account (Rebovich, 1996):

1. The level of supervision over activity that resulted in the violation
2. The steps or precautions previously taken to prevent a violation of this type
3. The frequency of past violations

4. The foreseeability of the violation
5. The degree of deliberateness
6. The nature of the offending agency (p. 93)

Attitudinal Obstacles

The attitudes of prosecutors, defendants, defense counsels, judges, and the public can be obstacles to environmental prosecution. A study of environmental prosecution in five county jurisdictions confirms this view (Hammett & Epstein, 1993a). Many prosecutors may initially resist getting involved in environmental cases because they lack prosecutorial experience with environmental violations, appropriate training, or the confidence to win the presumably complicated court battle. Defendants and their attorneys generally view environmental infractions as civil issues. To avoid a criminal label, they are willing to spend money to stall the start of the trial or to appeal the case back and forth for years. As a result of this delaying strategy, defendants may avoid the cost of compliance, lose hostile witnesses through death or disappearance, and watch evidence deteriorate and memories fade.

The public reaction to environmental crime and its prosecution is mixed. "While some environmental crime may be so devastating as to bring local residents into the streets protesting any delay in an offender's prosecution, criminal investigation of large local employers may elicit resounding demonstrations of public support for defendant companies" (Hammett & Epstein, 1993a, p. 50). Weak evidence of a demonstrable danger to public health, the fear of unemployment, and the willingness to take risks for economic progress may all explain the public's fickle view of environmental criminal prosecution (Hoban, 1987). Judges often perpetuate the administrative and regulatory bias toward handling environmental cases by heavily relying on the advice of regulatory agencies to set a monetary fine and by resisting prison sentences to save room for "hard-core" street criminals (Hammett & Epstein, 1993a). Prosecutors, who at the state and local level are often elected officials, work at the intersection of all these interests—defendant and counsel, judge, and public. Their decision to prosecute can be affected by any of them (Rebovich, 1996):

> Prosecutors can be besieged on one side by environmental groups demanding strict interpretation of the law and severe punishment in response to violations

against the environment and be pressured by business interests to temper such
legal action against the violators in an acknowledgment of the supposed
noncriminal nature of the offenses. (p. 91)

Prosecutors can call on discretion to balance such conflicts, but they are
always in danger of being corrupted.

The Problem of Parallel Proceedings

Parallel proceedings refer to concurrent civil or administrative proceedings and criminal prosecutions targeting the same violator for related
offenses. The combination of administrative, civil, and criminal sanctions in
environmental law has given rise to parallel enforcement proceedings. The
DOJ has endorsed parallel proceedings when one of the following occurs
(Marzulla & Roistacher, 1990):

1. There exists an imminent threat to public safety, health or the environment,
   demanding immediate civil injunctive relief.
2. The defendant's assets are in danger of being dissipated.
3. The statute of limitations is about to expire.
4. The civil and criminal actions are only marginally related. (pp. 4-5)

In recent years, prosecutors have more frequently brought parallel or succes-
sive criminal and civil enforcement actions against the same defendant,
basing both on the same conduct (Buchanan & Marous, 1992).

The limitations of administrative, civil, and criminal actions justify
parallel prosecution. Although administrative penalties facilitate remediation and deter environmental damage, they "are subject to statutory caps and
agencies' lack of contempt powers" (Duval, 1992, p. 538). Civil enforcement
can promptly protect and restore environmental quality because it requires
less burden of proof and ensures sufficient funds for recovery actions. But it
cannot provide the deterrence of a criminal conviction (Duval, 1992). The
criminal process lacks the immediate injunctive authority of civil and administrative proceedings. Parallel proceedings can override these limitations.
Administrative and civil penalties compensate for environmental damage,
and criminal prosecution channels social outrage while enhancing deterrence
(Arfmann, 1991; Buchanan & Marous, 1992). Recognizing these benefits of

parallel proceedings, Congress and state legislatures have authorized injunctive, remedial, and punitive sanctions for environmental violations.

Although parallel proceedings offer benefits to prosecutors, they also pose a variety of problems—constitutional conflicts, the risk of double jeopardy, the potential abuse or misuse of prosecutorial discretion (Buchanan & Marous, 1992; Hammett & Epstein, 1993a; Riesel, 1985). For example, double jeopardy protects a defendant against three abuses: a second prosecution for the same offense after acquittal, a second prosecution for the same offense after conviction, and multiple punishments for the same offense. For environmental prosecutors to honor double jeopardy, environmental cases in parallel proceedings should result only in sanctions that would be independently justified (Buchanan & Marous, 1992). Because many of the goals of a civil environmental case are remedial, as compared with the punitive objective of the criminal prosecution, separate prosecutions are needed to meet separate governmental interests. "There is no double jeopardy . . . when a defendant is civilly or criminally prosecuted by separate sovereign government entities even though both entities base their enforcement actions on the same conduct of the defendant" (p. 10).

A second danger of parallel proceedings is that "the prosecution may improperly disclose grand jury materials to civil regulators, or civil discovery may draw self-incriminating evidence for use in a parallel criminal case" (Duval, 1992, pp. 536-537). To avoid this miscarriage, prosecutors must coordinate investigations, exchange legitimate information, and protect the accused's rights (Duval, 1992).

In informal investigations such as "consensual witness interviews, permissive inspections, surveillance, and undercover operations prosecutors and civil attorneys may share evidence derived from these activities without impairing a violator's rights" (Duval, 1992, p. 545). Administrative inspections or document requests authorized by statutes as a part of administrative discovery may provide evidence for later civil or criminal proceedings. But "a criminal court may suppress evidence that law enforcement agents seized in an administrative search when they should have acted under a criminal search warrant" (p. 547). As a general rule, evidence obtained in civil discovery may be introduced in criminal actions. An exception is when "the government has brought a civil action solely to obtain evidence for its criminal prosecution or has failed to advise the defendant in its civil proceeding that it contemplates his criminal prosecution" (Riesel, 1985, p. 10077). A Fifth Amendment privilege against self-incrimination is available to individuals in civil discovery. Criminal investigation is permitted only with probable cause or a warrant. Evidence obtained from an illegal search and seizure is suppressed by the judge under the exclusionary rule. Nevertheless, "Information collected in an administrative or civil search under a lower standard of probable cause can be used in a criminal prosecution if the investigation was not conducted solely for the sake of criminal prosecution" (Duval, 1992, p. 569). Finally, although civil discovery is expansive, secrecy rules restrict grand jury discovery. Grand jury material has been prohibited in a parallel or subsequent civil proceeding since 1983 (Riesel, 1985).

Clearly, parallel proceedings are complex and difficult because a range of actions may occur simultaneously in both cases. The proceedings are extremely vulnerable to abuse. The EPA (1990) has explicitly disavowed parallel enforcement. The DOJ (1987) is also reluctant to initiate parallel proceedings. This option, however, should not be completely ignored. "Foreclosing concurrent civil and criminal proceedings without a full and impartial assessment of the costs and benefits in a particular case may sacrifice effective enforcement for a timorous reading of the requirements of fairness and efficiency" (Duval, 1992, p. 573).

Criminal Sanctions and Their Effects

Criminal Sanctions and Their Problems

Sanctions may be monetary or nonmonetary. Monetary sanctions consist of "federal criminal fines, restitution, administrative penalties, state criminal or civil fines, cleanup costs to be paid by the offender, voluntary restitution made known to the judge prior to sentencing, and court-ordered payments to victims or other third parties" (Cohen, 1992a, p. 83). Thus, some monetary sanctions arise from criminal judgments, whereas others result from civil or administrative proceedings. Nonmonetary sanctions for convicted corporations consist of corporate probation, community service, and public apologies. (You can't send a corporation to prison.). For convicted individuals, nonmonetary sanctions consist of incarceration, probation, and community service.

Although a corporate official may receive probation as part of the criminal sentence, the U.S. Court of Appeals has ruled that a sentence of probation for a corporate entity itself is excessive punishment. Because an organization cannot be imprisoned, the court reasoned, it also cannot be placed on probation (Nittoly, 1989). Nevertheless, 20% to 30% of convicted corporations are placed on probation in defiance of the ruling. Corporate probation has proved to be one of the most controversial issues confronting policymakers for environmental prosecution (Cohen, 1992a).

Community service is rarely used appropriately. The U.S. District Court of New Jersey sentenced two owners of a disposal firm to community service 1 day a week for 5 years picking up garbage at New Jersey military bases. This may serve as a precedent in environmental criminal prosecution but is not a norm in environmental cases. In some cases, community service consisted of convicted firms making financial donations to environmental programs (Cohen, 1992a). Issuing a public apology in a local newspaper for misdeeds has sometimes been a condition of probation (*Corporate Crime Reporter*, 1989).

Imprisonment carries the most powerful deterrent impact of any sanction. From 1985 through 1990, however, only about 30% of convicted environmental offenders, who were individuals, were incarcerated. The average length of the sentence was 6.75 months, substantially less than what the law allows (Cohen, 1992b). Given low incarceration rates and short sentences, the deterrence function of criminal sanction is weakened, perhaps trivialized. Moreover, because an organization as such cannot be incarcerated, any deterrent effect of imprisonment does not extend to corporate offenders. Finally, incarceration introduces two extra costs that must be weighed against any advantages it provides. The first is individual costs— "the direct disutility (or loss of income) from a jail sentence for the worker, which is a monotonically increasing function of the number of years spent in jail." The second is social costs, "including the costs of providing capital (prisons), labor (guards and support personnel), and raw materials and services (uniforms, food)" (Segerson & Tietenberg, 1992, p. 65). Under the economic theory of efficiency, incarceration does not maximize net social benefit, therefore, "as long as any specific level of deterrence achieved by incarceration could also be achieved by a fine, fines dominate" (p. 65).

Sentencing Guidelines and Their Impacts

Prior to 1987, defendants convicted of federal environmental crimes were sentenced according to the criminal penalty provisions of the statutes they violated. Since 1987, a judge may determine sentences under the federal sentencing guidelines (U.S. Sentencing Commission, 1990). Two important goals of the guidelines are these: first, removing unwarranted disparities to "ensure proportionality in sentencing among defendants found guilty of similar conduct," and, second, "removing the uncertainty that previously characterized the sentencing process" (Starr & Kelly, 1990, pp. 10096-10097). Under the guidelines, environmental offenses are divided into four categories: knowing endangerment of human life, offenses involving hazardous toxic substances, offenses involving other pollutants, and offenses against conservation and wildlife. A base penalty level is designated for each offense within each category. The penalty may be adjusted up or down, depending on the presence of other factors. Factors supporting an increase in the base penalty level include repeated discharging of pollutants, discharging without a permit, substantial actual or potential harm resulting from the offense, the highly toxic or dangerous nature and quality of the substance involved, a long duration of the offense, and a high risk associated with the offense. A decrease of the base penalty level could result from defendants' feeling of remorse, the violation being caused by negligence, or the violation involving only record keeping or reporting.

After the adjusted penalty level is determined, a sentencing table specifies the range of sentence for the particular offense. For example,

> The mandatory jail term for a person convicted of an ongoing, continuous or repetitive discharge, release or emission of a pollutant into the environment without a permit or in violation of a permit is 21-27 months. If the pollutant is hazardous, toxic, or a pesticide, this minimum is increased to 27-33 months. Further, if substantial cleanup expenditures are required, another 12-18 months is added to this range. (Cohen, 1992a, p. 99)

The sentence can be reduced by about 6 months, however, if the defendant accepts personal responsibility for his or her criminal conduct. A 6-month to 1-year reduction is also possible if the defendant was only a minor player in a criminal offense involving a large group of participants. Thus, under the guidelines, the traditional discretion judges have enjoyed in sentencing has been replaced with rigid mathematical calculations (Starr & Kelly, 1990).

The guidelines advocate determinate sentences. Parole is abolished to ensure that the sentence imposed by the court is the sentence the offender will serve. Probation, which was commonplace in the sentencing of environmental violators prior to the guidelines, is now restricted in use (Adler &

Lord, 1991). For example, probation can be awarded only when the minimum terms of imprisonment in the range specified by the sentencing table is zero months or when the defendants were convicted of offenses with penalty levels of 1 through 6. Furthermore, community confinement—as opposed to imprisonment in a distant facility—can be imposed only on defendants who are guilty of the crimes that carry penalty levels of 7 through 10. Finally, suspended sentences are not permitted. With all these rule changes, incarceration will become the rule, rather than the exception (Starr & Kelly, 1990).

The guidelines increase the average length of incarceration to about 30.7 months. By severely restricting probation, they also increase the incarceration rate (Cohen, 1992b). Consider the case of Guido and Hames Frezzo. They were convicted of six counts of violating the Clean Water Act and received jail sentences of 30 days each and fines totaling $50,000. Under the guidelines, the total offense level computes as 16, which translates to a sentencing range of 21 to 27 months of imprisonment (Starr & Kelly, 1990).

The guidelines send a clear message to both the judiciary and industry that environmental crimes must be recognized as a major problem and that criminal sentences must be taken seriously. The guidelines have two unfortunate defects, however. First, they do not establish special sentence ranges for convictions resulting from the responsible corporate officer doctrine or the principle of strict liability. Thus, "Corporate officers convicted under this doctrine will be sentenced the same way as an actor with actual knowledge" (Harig, 1992, p. 161). Second, the prospect of lengthier sentences may turn the government away from criminal prosecution. The government might file charges against only the most serious offender. Juries are likely to look sympathetically at defendants who will face imprisonment for crimes about which they had no actual knowledge. In addition, courts are reluctant to hand down prison terms to corporate officers (Harig, 1992). The high penalties of conviction may undermine, instead of promote, deterrence by discouraging criminal prosecution altogether (Adler & Lord, 1991; Cohen, 1992a).

Preventing Environmental Crime

The criminal sanction is an important tool to deter environmental crime. Nevertheless, it also carries potential to cause significant social harm. "Unlike traditional street crime that serves no socially useful purpose," many types of environmental crime, such as oil spills during transport, are "outgrowths of legitimate business activities" (Cohen, 1992a, p. 100). A total ban on these activities is obviously neither possible nor in society's interest. The danger is that although severe criminal punishment may influence corporations to adopt the safest and most careful practices, it may also push them to "undertake excessive and socially costly preventive activities to ensure they are never charged with a crime" (p. 101).

The theory of efficient sanction also argues that imprisonment is not always the best deterrent of corporate crime. It presumes that all sanctions, including imprisonment, have an equivalent monetary value (Posner, 1977, 1980). When collection costs are low and society receives a payment, the sanctions are efficient. Compared with a civil monetary sanction on an organization, imprisonment of individuals imposes high costs on society (prisons, guards, and the lost production of the prisoner, for example), and society receives no transfer funds comparable with the revenue from the fine. Therefore, only when fines do not ensure sufficient incentives does incarceration have a role to play (Polinsky & Shavell, 1993).

A simpler way of making a similar point is this. Criminal law is premised on coercion. Sometimes, some people must be made to obey. When they do not, sometimes they must forcibly be separated from society. But coercion is the most inefficient means of controlling undesirable behavior because of its staggering costs (Braithwaite, 1985). Because resources are always scarce, voluntary compliance is the best enforcement strategy (Frank & Lynch, 1992). Criminal sanctions are only one approach to preventing environmental crime. We argue that it should be used more frequently. But given these reservations, it should be used carefully.

Review Questions

1. What three factors explain the relatively meager number of federal prosecutors for criminal violations of environmental law?
2. What role do state attorneys general play in the criminal prosecution of environmental violators?
3. What factors contribute to successful criminal prosecutions by local prosecutors?
4. What new arguments have been advanced during the past decade to support or strengthen the concept of corporate criminal liability?

5. What does the "responsible corporate officer doctrine" hold, and how does it differ from "strict liability?"

6. What are the four main factors that contribute to the high level of prosecutorial discretion in criminal enforcement?

7. What are parallel proceedings, and what constitutional issues do they pose?

8. What types of criminal sanctions are available in criminal environmental cases, and which have been used sparingly?

9. What impact have the federal sentencing guidelines had on the sentencing of environmental criminal offenders?

CHAPTER 9

The Global Environmental Crisis

We inhabit a global village. That fate carries great promise as advances in transportation, communication, and commerce expand contacts, mutual interests, and understanding among diverse peoples. But it also poses a terrible threat to environmental survival. As economic production and consumption grow, the dangers to the environment engulf the entire world. The environmental effects of polluting, endangering species, and exhausting resources have become global. Environmental misbehavior has no respect for national or local boundaries: The misdeeds at one site ripple across the land to damage other places. The global village has its dark side. Our interdependence may destroy us, rather than save us. We may stand together, but we may fall together as well.

The nuclear meltdown at Chernobyl tainted the milk in Finland with radioactivity. Aerosols in the developed world weaken the ozone layer that protects the earth from the ultraviolet rays of the sun. The African rhinoceros is endangered by the Asian demand for its ground horn. Auto and industrial emissions in the United States and Western Europe contribute to global warming. Burning the Amazon rain forest in Brazil and overcutting timberland in Alaska and Siberia diminish the oxygen in the atmosphere.

Reversing the environmental crisis is no longer just a domestic struggle, requiring resolute antipollution measures by individual nations. The crisis is international in scope, and international law, which governs the relations between nations, must respond to it. From the global perspective, a central question is the role to be played by criminal enforcement and prosecution in efforts around the world to stem the prospects of environmental catastrophe.

Features of the Global Environmental Crisis

Global Warming

Since at least the late 1980s, accumulating scientific evidence has confirmed a trend of global warming. The average global temperature in the 1980s had climbed to approximately 59.4 degrees, compared with 58.2 degrees almost a century earlier. Of the 7 warmest years between 1850 and 1990, 6 have occurred after 1980, with the warmest year on record being 1990. The chances that this concentration of warm years is a random accident are extremely unlikely. In the second quarter of the next century, countries such as Australia, the United States, and China may experience temperature increases of 8 to 10 degrees as the greenhouse effect burgeons. In northern Africa and the Antarctic, the temperature rise could surpass 10 degrees (Flavin, 1991).

These changes could have catastrophic consequences. Freshwater supplies could be depleted. The geography of settlement could shift radically as currently desirable locales for living become inhospitable. Agriculture could be especially damaged by repeated droughts. Because trees can thrive only within narrow ranges of temperature and rainfall, forests might diminish. A temperature increase of 6 degrees, studies indicate, would raise the sea level approximately 3 feet, with disastrous consequences. Asian river deltas and floodplains, which sustain vital agriculture, would be inundated. Wetlands around the world, which spawn fish and other wildlife, would be overcome. And coastal cities from New Orleans to New York and Shanghai to Sydney would be at risk (Flavin, 1991).

Air Pollution

Air pollution is now a public health emergency of global dimensions. The United Nations estimates that one fifth of the world's population, including rural as well as urban dwellers, breathes badly polluted air. Although many Western nations have actually reduced emissions of sulfur dioxide and particulates, Eastern Europe and the countries of the former Soviet Union suffer from some of the highest air pollution levels in the world. Hasty industrialization, low energy efficiency, and reliance on heavily polluting fuels—especially high-sulfur coal—have placed Eastern-bloc nations far behind their Western industrialized counterparts in the fight against air pollution. The Hungarian government, for example, blames almost 6% of deaths in its country on air pollution (French, 1991).

Developing nations are no better off. Pollution regulation and technology lag far behind surging industrialization and energy consumption, choking air quality, especially in large cities. Breathing air in Bombay, India, is like smoking 10 cigarettes a day. In Beijing, China, respiratory illness is so routine that residents call it the "Beijing cough." Lead in approximately 70% of infants in Mexico City exceeds the safety levels prescribed by the United Nations World Health Organization to ensure healthy cognitive development (French, 1991). Shenyang, Tehran, and Seoul, all outside the West, have among the worst levels of sulfur dioxide for cities for which data are available (United Nations Environmental Program and the World Health Organization, 1988).

Clean air is a rare commodity around the globe. The most recent survey of the United Nation's Global Environmental Monitoring System estimates that more than half a billion urbanites around the world are exposed to toxic levels of sulfur dioxide. Residents in half the world's cities may breath dangerous amounts of carbon monoxide. One third of urban dwellers may have contact with unhealthy concentrations of lead (Switzer, 1994).

Water Pollution

Safe drinking water is unavailable to almost a third of the developing world's population. An even larger percentage lacks sanitation facilities. High rates of mortality and morbidity are the result (Porter & Brown, 1991). The landscape of the former Soviet Union and Eastern Europe are pockmarked with water disasters. The landlocked Aral Sea is evaporating as rainfall slows and rivers drain off water for agriculture. Life in the Baltic Sea is dying from decades, if not centuries, of agricultural, urban, and industrial effluents from its feeder rivers. The soil below St. Petersburg Harbor has a thousand times the normal levels of lead and cadmium (Switzer, 1994).

Several thousand military-industrial factories in Russia pollute the Volga River with approximately 10 billion cubic yards of effluent and waste a year (Pope, 1992). A gigantic paper plant with 36,000 workers releases chemical waste into Siberia's Lake Baikal, killing its fish (Switzer, 1994). A fire, and efforts to fight it, at the Swiss Sandos Chemical Company in 1986 released tons of biocides and other agricultural agents into the Rhine River, endangering water sources and killing fish and fowl in four other countries. The disaster reminded Europeans of their reliance on shared water supplies and waterways and the need for regional solutions to water pollution.

In Asia, contaminated surface water and exploding urban populations jeopardize drinking water. Hong Kong's beauty masks serious water pollution. Untreated sewage, livestock wastes, and heavy metals place water sources at risk. Industrial effluents go untreated, and chemical toxins are flushed down city drains. Japan leads Asia in pollution control, but increased population overloads the nation's sewer infrastructure. The heavy use of pesticides in Japanese agriculture leads to groundwater pollution (Vogel, 1990).

In Africa, adequate supplies of safe drinking water and sanitation facilities are lacking. As a consequence, water-related diseases such as guinea worm and schistosomiasis inflict millions of Africans (Switzer, 1994).

In many developing nations, water pollution is taken for granted. The benefits of clean water are not widely appreciated. Efforts to preserve the environment are meager. Expensive solutions to water pollution will remain unpopular in countries that are struggling to build their economies. For their part, many industrial countries, especially in Eastern Europe and the former Soviet Union, have tolerated unregulated toxic discharges, often directly into waterways. Environmental enforcement there has been sparse, legislation has been weak, and the media have been inattentive to pollution crises (Switzer, 1994).

Acid Rain

Pollution from acid rain ignores national boundaries. Power plants in the Ohio Valley cause acid rainfall in Canada. High-sulfur coal emissions from northern Czechoslovakia, eastern Germany, and northern Poland—the so-called dirty triangle—generate acid rain downwind in regions to the east, where forests are dying (McCormick, 1985; Thompson, 1991). Russian military factories in the Kola Peninsula spew 700 tons of sulfur dioxide across the border into Finland each year, ravaging hundreds of square miles of forest (Sanders, 1991).

Toxic Waste Dumping

In 1988, a barge dumped 3,000 tons of black sediment on the beaches of Haiti. Armed with a permit to discharge fertilizer, the barge was actually disposing of toxic ash from an incinerator in Philadelphia. The incident dramatized how waste management was becoming internationalized. Industries and governments in nations with strict rules for hazardous waste disposal were reducing their costs by exporting waste to cash-starved countries in the Caribbean, South America, Africa, and the Pacific. Developing nations, desperate for foreign exchange, are frequently tempted to serve as dumping grounds for foreign waste, although they lack the technology to safely dispose of it. Waste producers in industrialized nations often are confronted with irresistible financial incentives to export their "product." The cost of hazardous waste disposal in the United States was estimated by the EPA at $250 to $350 a ton. The fee to dump in developing nations is as low as $40 a ton (Lawrence & Wynne, 1989; Switzer, 1994).

Although Western nations are redoubling their commitment to recycling hazardous waste and reducing its generation at the source, the export of toxic wastes will continue to grow in the future. Developed nations are not bringing their own disposal facilities on line quickly enough to meet demand. Nations of the European Economic Community, for example, have the capacity to safely process 10 million tons of hazardous waste a year, but they produce more than 30 tons a year (Axelrod, 1994; European Environmental Bureau, 1989). If environmental standards become stricter in industrialized nations, more waste will be labeled as hazardous and further burden lagging facilities (Koppen, 1988). Efforts by industrialized nations to curtail the burning and dumping of hazardous waste at sea will also strain disposal capacity on land. Nine European nations agreed, for example, to decrease the disposal of mercury, lead, cadmium, and dioxins into the North Sea by 70% by 1995. This came at a time when European countries had already reduced North Sea dumping by several hundred thousand tons a year (Axelrod, 1994). Newly industrialized nations such as India, Malaysia, Korea, Mexico, Thailand, Indonesia, and the Philippines produce vast new amounts of hazardous waste but lack the facilities to dispose of them properly.

International Environmental Law

A Brief History of International Environmental Law

At the beginning of this century, international environmental law was meager and governed by the principles of unrestrained national sovereignty over natural resources and complete freedom of the high seas. The Trial Smelter Arbitration between the United States and Canada presented a rare and precedent-setting case of international environmental adjudication during this period. This agreement confirmed the principle of responsibility for transboundary environmental damage: A state is liable for environmental destruction in other countries if it resulted from action inside its own borders.

By the 1940s, conservation and preservation were the key themes in managing natural resources. These emphases spurred agreements to guard wildlife and flora. International treaties to limit whaling, control fishing, and protect birds were also hammered out. In the next two decades, treaties to assign responsibility for damage from nuclear contamination and oil spills were also signed. By the late 1960s, additional conventions on oil pollution were put into effect (Weiss, 1992).

The contemporary era of international environmental law dates to the 1970s, coinciding with the rise of the environmental movement in Western industrialized nations. Since 1970, more than 870 international agreements address at least one aspect of the environment. The scope of these multinational agreements has broadened enormously:

> from preservation of designated species to conservation of ecosystems; from control of direct emissions into lakes to comprehensive river-basin system regimes; from agreements that take effect only at national borders to ones that constrain activities and resource use within national borders, such as those for world heritages and wetlands. (Weiss, 1992, p. 9)

During the past decade, international agreements have covered a variety of issues including protection of the ozone layer, reduction of sulfur emissions, preservation of forests against atmospheric pollution, prevention of ocean dumping in the South Pacific, control of nitrogen oxide emissions, maintenance of global climate, preserving the marine environment of the Caribbean, establishing practices for the safe international movement of radioactive waste, guarding the Northeast Atlantic against pollution by hydrocarbons, and protecting the environments of the Arctic and Antarctica. Bilateral agreements have also kept pace during this era. The United States, for example, has bilateral understandings with Canada and Mexico on the transport of hazardous wastes and with Mexico on transboundary air pollution. These agreements are tougher, wider-ranging, and more sophisticated than international jurists would have thought possible only a decade ago.

The Nature and Problems of International Environmental Law

Treaties have been the chief source of international law on the environment. These written agreements obligate only those states that have consented to them. Customary international law grows from prevailing practice and precedent-setting cases. "Soft law" consists of recommendations, resolutions, and declarations, often passed at international conferences, that urge conduct on states but that lack enforcement powers to require compliance or sanctions to penalize violators (Kiss, 1992; McLoughlin & Bellinger, 1993). Some treaties obligate contracting states to undertake action without specifying its precise nature. These treaty provisions fall between "soft" and "hard" obligations; specific standards are not enforceable, but some ameliorating action, however small, is guaranteed (Kiss, 1992).

The most fundamental principle of international environmental law is that a state is responsible for the environmental harm that activity on its own territory causes another state. This principle is "soft law" but stills carries weight because it is embodied as Principle 21 in the Stockholm Declaration of 1972, one of the cornerstones of international environmental law. A second basic principle is the duty of nations to cooperate with each other for the preservation of the environment. Cooperation has come to include the notification of affected countries about environmental accidents and prior consultation with victim states about new or increased pollution.

International environmental law is an imperfect system for protecting the environment. The law is extensive in some areas but sparse in others, depending entirely on the interest of nations. For example, 60 multinational agreements cover the marine environment, whereas only a few regulate atmospheric pollution. Treaties bind only those states that voluntarily agree to them. They often slash standards to the lowest common denominator to attract adherents. Ratification may proceed slowly, and enforcement may prove difficult. In the end, compliance depends most of all on the good faith of the signatories (Soros, 1994). Finally, the principle of one state's repairing the environmental harm its actions have caused another state is often difficult to implement. The link between environmental harm and its cause may be murky. Assessing the extent of environmental damage may prove elusive, especially when its full and final effects are delayed for years. Despite these obstacles, strides have been taken in regulating the environment on a regional and global scale.

Environmental Control Around the Globe

The European Community

The European Community (EC) is the most advanced regional organization in the world, committed to full economic integration, a single currency and monetary system, and unrestricted travel between member nations. The EC has pioneered strict environmental regulations. In theory, the EC puts environmental protection on an equal footing with economic development (Axelrod, 1994).

The EC is committed to a broad legislative agenda, which member nations are supposed to adopt. First, carbon dioxide emissions are to be steadied at 1990 levels by the year 2000. Countries may levy a carbon tax to decrease reliance on high-polluting fuels, encourage energy efficiency, and stimulate the use of alternative sources of energy. A tax on oil started at $1 per barrel in 1993 and could rise as high as $10 a barrel by 2000 (Axelrod, 1994; Montgomery, 1991). Second, as EC countries have eased transborder travel, they have strengthened monitoring and other controls over hazardous waste to prevent its unrestricted movement. Third, by early in the 21st century, 90% of packaging, which accounts for more than 50 tons of waste per year in the EC, would be recovered, mainly through recycling. Fourth, "ecolabeling" was adopted in 1992 to identify and promote products that reduced environmental harm through all phases of their life cycle. Finally, EC members have undertaken a number of initiatives to improve air quality, from incentives for burning low-sulfur fuels and environmentally sensitive factory siting to strict auto emissions standards (Axelrod, 1994; Liberatore & Lewanski, 1990; Switzer, 1994).

Air Quality

Eastern Europe, which has harbored the world's worst air pollution from industrial sources, has recently begun major programs to improve air quality. The East European Environmental Center was dedicated in 1990 in Budapest, Hungary, with assistance from the United States, to design programs that would improve air and water quality. Joint ventures with world auto manufacturers are producing less-polluting cars to replace Eastern European models such as the Trabant, which was notorious for its dirty emissions. Poland is reducing its heavy use of high-sulfur coal, and Katowice, once dubiously honored as Eastern Europe's most polluted metropolis, is becoming a model clean city. In China, where population growth continually outpaces pollution reforms, some progress has been made in substituting gas for coal-burning stoves (Switzer, 1994).

Marine Protection

In the 1950s and 1960s, international agreements on the marine environment dealt largely with oil spills. But beginning mainly in the 1970s, they broadened their focus to cover many issues that gravely affected the oceans. A milestone agreement was the MARPOL, the Marine Pollution Convention of 1973, which restricted the dumping of a variety of pollutants from land and at sea. About the same time, the London Dumping Convention curbed the disposal of toxic—most significantly, radioactive—waste at sea. Since the mid-1970s, the United Nations has sponsored the Regional Seas Program to preserve clean oceans around the world. It first sponsored an action plan to combat pollution in the Mediterranean Sea, where contamination was reaching critical levels (Haas, 1990; Switzer, 1994).

Reducing Acid Rain

In Europe, efforts to combat acid rain have been under way since the late 1970s and have accelerated more recently. The United Nations' Economic Commission for Europe passed the Convention on Long-Range Transboundary Air Pollution in 1979. Although its provisions are not enforceable, it has served as a framework for designing a regional plan to reduce acid rain. The convention was revised in 1994 to include a sulfur protocol that would dramatically reduce sulfur dioxide emissions in Europe and North America by 2000. In 1985, 30 nations signed a protocol in Helsinki to reduce sulfur emissions by 30% by 1993. Some European nations withheld their approval of the accord, most notably, the United Kingdom, but the emission goals were met anyway (LaBastille, 1986; Pearce, 1992; Switzer, 1994).

Control of Waste Trading

In 1985, the Cairo Guidelines implemented a United Nations promise from a decade earlier to regulate toxic waste trading between nations. Guidelines were established to notify and gain prior consent from receiving countries. The ability of receiving nations to dispose of the waste properly had to at least match that of the sending country. Under pressure from African nations, which protested against "waste colonialism," the United Nations issued stricter regulations in 1987 for waste trading. In 1989, waste trading was restricted further when the EC approved the Lome Convention with 68 nations of Africa, the Caribbean, and the Pacific. The accord bans the transport of all hazardous waste, including radioactive materials, from the EC to these countries. A more broadly based agreement, the Basel Convention, allows for the shipment of hazardous wastes between participating countries but only with informed consent. In 1991, 12 African nations banned the import of hazardous wastes altogether (Porter & Brown, 1991; Shearer, 1993; Switzer, 1994).

A Realistic View of Protecting the Global Environment

The advanced industrialized countries of North America, Europe, and the Pacific Rim have pressed the hardest for the international regulation of the environment. Their sense of urgency derives from longer familiarity with the environmental devastation of industrialization. Their research underscores the gravity of threats to the environment, some of which might otherwise go unnoticed. They can afford to spend money on cleaning up the environment. In addition, their open societies and democratic politics encourage citizens to become environmental activists.

In the 1970s, the developing countries, in contrast, were more reserved—even suspicious—about regulating the environment on an international scale. They were likely to endorse the quickest road to economic vitality. They sometimes viewed the call for regulation as a plot by the industrialized West to hold them back, and they sometimes argued in favor of the same opportunity to damage the environment that the industrialized nations exercised in their rise to prosperity. By the 1980s, however, the developing nations realized that water pollution, soil loss, deforestation, the expansion of desert, and other environmental crises impaired their prospects for economic growth. The gap between the views of the industrialized and developing worlds closed (Finkle & Crane, 1985; Hardin, 1974; Soros, 1994).

Fighting Environmental Crime in Other Nations

We turn, finally, to examine the representative experiences of three nations—Great Britain, Australia, and China—in fighting environmental crime.

Great Britain

Great Britain was among the first European nations to regulate the environmental effects of industrial production. In 1863, it enacted the Alkali Acts, which placed controls on 95% of emissions from alkali plants. In this century, the Clean Air Act empowered local authorities to regulate "smoke control areas." Pollution inversions over London in 1972 and 1974, which temporarily closed Heathrow Airport, prompted new legislation to reduce the sulfur content of fuel oils, the main culprits in the episodes (Elsom, 1987; Switzer, 1994).

Responsibility for the environment is divided among a variety of local and national regulatory agencies. The result is a fragmented and uncoordinated assault on environmental violations. The secretary of state for the environment formulates national strategy for the environment. Policies governing clean air, water, solid wastes, and noise are the responsibility of the Department of the Environment, although the Department of Trade is charged with monitoring oil pollution at sea. The Department of Transport oversees pollution on roads and waterways, whereas the Department of Agriculture, Fisheries, and Food regulates pesticides and safeguards fisheries (Holdgate, 1979; Moore, 1986).

The bulk of enforcement and prosecution for hazardous waste offenses is conducted by local Waste Regulation Authorities, which also license waste disposers and devise disposal plans for their areas. These local agencies receive uneven funding and adhere to inconsistent enforcement standards. Pollution cases are usually resolved without prosecuting the offender and in a private setting, beyond public scrutiny. The police do not undertake criminal investigations of major environmental offenses but leave this task to the regulatory authorities. But they may be peripherally involved with environmental violations, assisting the specialized agencies in protecting life and property at the pollution scene (McKenna, 1993).

National environmental standards are uncommon in Great Britain. Instead, emission and discharge limits are established for each offender in light of local circumstances. Great Britain is less vigorous than other European countries, the United States, and Canada in investigating and prosecuting environmental crimes. Environmental regulations are generally not as strict as those in North America. As a member of the EC, Great Britain must address environmental crises in a larger regional context, but, traditionally suspicious of integration with continental Europe, it has sometimes been slow to implement the environmental standards of the EC (Moore, 1986; Pearce & Caufield, 1981; Swaigen, 1981).

Australia

Australia's entry into environmental regulation is recent and restrained, dating from the mid-1970s. At the federal level, more than three dozen statutes cover a variety of environmental issues including protection of the ozone layer of the atmosphere, discharge of oil by ships at sea, the export and import of hazardous wastes, the use of industrial chemicals in manufacturing, and safeguards for the transport and disposal of nuclear material (Norberry, 1993). More than 300 statutes regulate the environment in Australia's six states and two territories. At this level, two models of legislation predominate: one, practiced in New South Wales, South Australia, Queensland, and the Australian Capital Territory, where statutes specialize in particular aspects of environmental regulation such as air pollution or waste management; and the other, used in Victoria, Western Australia, and Tasmania, where an array of environmental concerns are consolidated into one comprehensive act (Norberry, 1993). Regardless of which model is used, the same criteria for defining pollution violations permeate the law. Violations occur when pollutants are discharged without a required license, contrary to license conditions, in breach of prescribed emission standards, or without using the best available means (Bates, 1992).

For the most part, Australia imposes administrative and civil sanctions—bureaucratic remedies and fines—for environmental violations. Criminal penalties—mainly imprisonment—are appearing, however, in a small but growing number of laws. For example, the Environmental Offenses and Penalties Act of 1989 in New South Whales exacts a maximum criminal fine of $1 million on corporate violators and up to 7 years of imprisonment for individuals. The Environmental Protection Act of 1986 in Western Australia can impose a maximum sentence of 6 months in jail on pollution violators. The Clean Waters Act in Queensland contains an option of 12 months of imprisonment for second-time offenders. Nevertheless, incarceration was avoided altogether as a sentence in an actual case until the 1990s (Norberry, 1993). Environmental regulators emphasize cooperative arrangements, negotiation, and education with environmental violators. Nonetheless, prosecution is an important enforcement tool, especially for large or repeated violations. Prosecutors favor civil prosecution, with criminal prosecution reserved for the most egregious cases (Chappell & Norberry, 1990).

China

As China, harboring one fifth of the world's population, enjoys spectacular economic growth, it uses up natural resources at an astonishing pace. At current rates of growth, China's coal consumption, for example, will double in less than 20 years. Pollution and other forms of environmental degradation also multiply accordingly. China's predicament is housing a huge population while owning a small inventory of the world's resources. It holds 22% of the world's population but possesses only 7% of its freshwater and farmland, 3% of its forests, and 2% of its oil (Ryan & Flavin, 1995).

Water shortages, which plague northern China especially, are aggravated by pollution that contaminates freshwater supplies. Only one fifth of industrial and residential wastewater is treated in even rudimentary fashion (People's Republic of China National Environmental Protection Agency and State Planning Commission, 1994). Amid a nationwide construction boom, deforestation has intensified. Cutting outstrips planting trees. The pressure to fell trees illegally mounts. The Ministry of Forestry estimates that forests twice the size of Luxembourg are illegally cut each year (Ryan & Flavin, 1995).

China is home to perhaps the world's worst air pollution. As energy needs explode, reliance on low-quality, high-sulfur coal continues. Roughly three fourths of China's energy demands—compared with a quarter in the United States—are met by coal. China is the world's leading consumer of coal, a rank it will retain into the foreseeable future (Demonds, 1994). China has been unable to invest in the simplest pollution control equipment. Most coal stokes small factory boilers, household stoves, and space heaters, whose emissions are difficult to control (Sinton, 1992). Air pollution is taking another turn for the worse as automobiles become more prevalent. The number of autos in China skyrocketed from 613,000 in 1970 to 5.8 million in 1990. More ominously, the government anticipates production in China of 3 million cars annually by 2000 (Tyler, 1994). Cities in northern China experience some of the highest sulfur and particulate levels in the world. These pollutants surpass standards of the United Nations World Health Organization everywhere in the country. Not surprisingly, lung diseases are the leading cause of death in China (French, 1990). Acid rain from Chinese coal has been detected in Japan and South Korea. Losses to crops, forests, and buildings from acid rain in China are approximately $2.8 billion per year.

Environmental protection was not an aim of the Chinese government until the 1970s. After participating in the Stockholm Conference on the Human Environment in 1972, a commitment to environmental regulation in China gradually evolved. The first, albeit experimental, law on environmental protection was passed in 1979 (Zhou, 1992). A comprehensive environmental protection act was promulgated in 1989. Additional laws governing air and water pollution and protection of the marine environment have also been enacted (Zou & Zhang, 1993).

The comprehensive environmental protection law of 1989 provides for the criminal punishment of environmental offenders in certain instances. Criminal sanctions may be applied in the event of pollution accidents that cause heavy property losses, serious injury, or death. Offenders who seriously damage natural resources are also subject to criminal penalties. Clean air and water legislation establishes criminal penalties as well. Offenders who cause accidents with explosive, inflammable, radioactive, poisonous, or corrosive materials may receive imprisonment of up to 7 years, depending on the severity of the incident. Government officials who are responsible for serious environmental harm may be incarcerated for up to 5 years. Despite these criminal options, administrative and civil sanctions prevail in practice (Zou & Zhang, 1993).

Conclusion

Environmental crime is not simply a domestic problem but also an international one. As developing countries "develop"—as their economies prosper—the world's environment will suffer. This has been the paradox of development: As the lives of more people improve, the environment worsens. Industrial expansion and consumer growth in the developing world will generate pollution just as they have historically in the West. New technology and energy sources may some day break this link between modernizing the economy and contaminating the earth. But in the short and medium term, nothing offers a sure solution. The small but steady gains one might envision toward "clean" development could easily be nullified by the polluting effects and resource depletion from sheer population growth.

"The fundamental challenge for international [environmental] law is to handle problems which exist irrespective of frontiers in a system of nation states that takes territorial sovereignty as one of its most sacred legal tenets" (Plater, Abrams, & Goldfarb, 1992, p. 997). In the end, self-interested, domestic action by individual nations to more strictly regulate the environment will have the greatest impact on reducing pollution around the world. But as this chapter has emphasized, more than resolute antipollution measures by individual nations is required. International law and agreements must play a key role in extending environmental regulation around the globe. If international environmental law is truly to succeed, the already industrialized nations must offer convincing incentives to developing nations to avoid sacrificing environmental protection for the quickest road to economic vitality.

Criminal enforcement and prosecution of environmental offenders will play a modest but growing role in the domestic regulation of the environment by individual nations. Some environmental criminal law has already been adopted by an overwhelming majority of the nations of the world. Criminal environmental enforcement and prosecution are practiced in some measure by every industrialized nation. As the case histories of Great Britain, Australia, and China indicate, criminal sanctions play an important if uneven role in environmental protection in countries other than the United States. One could also cite the environmental criminal law in countries such as South Korea, Malaysia, Costa Rica, India, Brazil, Hungary, and Israel.

Nevertheless, criminal environmental law is likely to remain a tool of individual nations. It is unlikely to be an instrument of international treaties and agreements. Nation-states are extremely reluctant for any reason to subject themselves, their enterprises, or their citizens to criminal prosecution by international tribunals or to the stigma of criminal sanctions. Environmental transgressions provide no exception to this iron rule. "Because jealous guarding of sovereignty is such a fundamental principle of international legal policy each state hesitates to the point of stalemate in yielding authority to higher levels of international authority" (Plater et al., 1992, p. 1012). State *criminal* liability is not an accepted tenet of international law. Consequently, international environmental agreements will continue to focus on notification, emergency assistance, compensation, and remediation.

Review Questions

1. What are some of the chief features of the global environmental crisis?
2. What are the two basic principles of international environmental law?
3. What makes international environmental law weak and ineffective?
4. What practice or policy gives hope of an improved environment in each of the following areas: air quality, marine protection, acid rain, and waste trading?
5. What is the most notable achievement in fighting environmental crime in Great Britain, Australia, and China?

References

Abadinsky, H. (1990). *Organized crime* (3rd ed.). Chicago: Nelson-Hall.

Abas, B. (1989, December). Rocky Flats: A mistake from day one. *Bulletin of the Atomic Scientists, 45,* 15-24.

Abrams, N. (1982). Criminal liability of corporate officers for strict liability offenses: A comment on Dotterweich and Park. *UCLA Law Review, 28,* 463-477.

Adler, R. W., & Lord, C. (1991). Environmental crimes: Raising the stakes. *George Washington Law Review, 59*(4), 781-861.

Albanese, J. (1984). Love Canal six years later: The legal legacy. *Federal Probation, 48*(2), 53-58.

Albanese, J. S., & Pursley, R. D. (1993). *Crime in America: Some existing and emerging issues.* Englewood Cliffs, NJ: Prentice Hall.

Alibrani, T. (1993, October). Surfer takes on the navy. *Progressive, 57*(10), 17.

Allan, R. (1987). Criminal sanctions under federal and state environmental statutes. *Ecology Law Quarterly, 9*(4), 117-179.

Arbuckle, G. (1993a). Liabilities and enforcement. In G. Arbuckle et al. (Eds.), *Environmental law handbook* (pp. 42-59). Rockville, MD: Government Institutes.

Arbuckle, G. (1993b). Water pollution control. In G. Arbuckle et al. (Eds.), *Environmental law handbook* (pp. 151-220). Rockville, MD: Government Institutes.

Arfmann, D. L. (1991). The double jeopardy problem inherent in RCRA enforcement: An overview and possible solutions. *Environmental Law Reporter, 21*(12), 10711-10717.

Aron, N. (1989). *Liberty and justice for all: Public interest law in the 1980s and beyond.* Boulder, CO: Westview.

Arthur D. Little, Inc. (1991, July). *Environmental damage rated as most serious among business crimes: Corporate executives should be held liable survey shows* [Press release]. Boston: Author.

Asinoff, R. (1986). Corporations must hold responsible for environmental disasters. In J. Bach & L. Hall (Eds.), *The environmental crisis: Opposing viewpoints* (pp. 26-34). San Diego, CA: Greenhaven.

Associated Press. (1989, October 15). Judge issues final clearance in Fernald lawsuit. *Tri-City Herald,* p. D-8.

Axelrod, R. S. (1994). Environmental policy and management in the European Community. In N. J. Vig & M. E. Kraft (Eds.), *Environmental policy in the 1990s: Toward a new agenda* (2nd ed., pp. 253-273). Washington, DC: Congressional Quarterly.

Bailes, K. E. (Ed.). (1985). *Environmental history.* Lanham, MD: University Press of America.

Barak, G. (1991). *Crimes by the capitalist state: An introduction to state criminality.* Albany: State University of New York Press.

Barrett, J. F., & Clarke, V. M. (1991). Perspectives on the knowledge requirement of section 6928(d) of RCRA after United States v. Dee. *George Washington Law Review, 59*(4), 862-888.

Barton, A. (1969). *Communities in disaster.* Garden City, NY: Doubleday.

Bates, G. (1992). *Environmental law in Australia* (3rd ed.). Sydney, Australia: Butterworths.

Begley, S. (1988, August 29). A long summer of smog. *Newsweek, 111,* 46-48.

Bennett, S. C. (1990). Developments in the movement against corporate crime. *New York University Law Review, 65,* 871-890.

Berry, J. (1988, October 28). Chemicals and cancer. *People's Daily World,* p. 3.

Black's law dictionary. (1990). Anaheim, CA: West.

Blau, P. M. (1970). A formal theory of differentiation in organizations. *American Sociological Review, 35,* 201-218.

Block, A. A., & Scarpitti, F. R. (1985). *Poisoning for profit: The Mafia and toxic waste in America.* New York: William Morrow.

Blumenthal, R. (1983, June 5). Illegal dumping of toxins laid to organized crime. *New York Times,* pp. A1, B44.

Bowman, A. O. (1984). Intergovernmental and intersectional tensions in environmental policy implementation: The case of hazardous waste. *Policy Studies Review, 4*(2), 230-244.

Bowman, A. O. (1985). Hazardous waste management: An emerging policy area within an emerging federalism. *Publius: The Journal of Federalism, 15,* 131-144.

Box, S. (1983). *Power, crime and mystification.* London: Tavistock.

Braithwaite, J. (1985). *To punish or persuade: Enforcement of coal mine safety.* Albany: State University of New York Press.

Braithwaite, J., & Fisse, B. (1990). On the plausibility of corporate crime theory. *Advances in Criminological Theory, 2,* 15-38.

Breen, B. (1985). Federal supremacy and sovereign immunity waivers in federal environmental laws. *Environmental Law Reporter, 15,* 10326-10332.

Brewer, W. M. S. (1995, May). Traditional policing and environmental enforcement. *FBI Law Enforcement Bulletin, 64,* 6-13.

Brook, D. (1994). US factories in Mexico cause toxic pollution. In C. Cozic (Ed.), *Pollution* (pp. 79-84). San Diego, CA: Greenhaven.

Brown, M. H. (1981). *Laying waste: The poisoning of America by toxic chemicals.* New York: Washington Square Press.

Brownell, W. (1993). Clean Air Act. In G. Arbuckle et al. (Eds.), *Environmental law handbook* (pp. 120-150). Rockville, MD: Government Institutes.

Buchanan, S. C., & Marous, J. M. (1992, April). Recent expansions of the double jeopardy clause should not present insurmountable problems for environmental prosecutors. *National Environmental Enforcement Journal, 7,* 3-18.

Bynum, T. (1987). Controversies in the study of organized crime. In T. Bynum (Ed.), *Organized crime in America: Concepts and controversies* (pp. 3-11). Nonsey, NY: Criminal Justice Press.

Cabrera, N. J. (1995). Control and prevention of crime committed by state-supported educational institutions. In J. R. Ross (Ed.), *Controlling state crime: An introduction* (pp. 163-206). New York: Garland.

Cahn, R., & Cahn, P. (1985). The environmental movement since 1970. *EPA Journal, 11*(9), 35.

Calhoun, M. L. (1995, September 15). Cleaning up the military's toxic legacy. *USA Today,* p. 60.

Calve, J. P. (1991). Environmental crimes: Upping the ante for noncompliance with environmental law. *Military Law Review, 133,* 249-278.

Carson, R. (1962). *Silent spring.* Greenwich, CT: Fawcett.

Cartusciello, N. S., & Hutchins, P. (1994). *Environmental crime statistics: FY 83 though FY 94.* Unpublished paper, released by U.S. Department of Justice, Environmental Crimes Section, Washington, DC.

Case, D. (1993). Resource Conservation and Recovery Act. In G. Arbuckle et al. (Eds.), *Environmental law handbook* (pp. 60-93). Rockville, MD: Government Institutes.

Chambliss, W. (1989). State-organized crime. *Criminology, 27,* 183-208.

Chambliss, W., & Seidman, S. (1982). *Law, order and power.* Reading, MA: Addison-Wesley.

Chappel, D., & Norberry, J. (1990). Deterring polluters: The search for effective strategies. *Univeristy of New South Wales Law Journal, 13,* 97-117.

Claybrook, J. (Ed.). (1984). *Retreat from safety: Reagan's attack on America's health.* New York: Pantheon.

Clinard, M. (1990). *Corporate corruption: The abuse of power.* New York: Praeger.

Clinard, M., & Quinney, R. (1973). *Criminal behavior systems: A typology* (2nd ed.). New York: Holt, Rinehart & Winston.

Clinard, M., & Yeager, P. (1978). Corporate crime: Issues in research. *Criminology, 16,* 255-275.

Clinard, M., & Yeager, P. (1979). *Illegal corporate behaviors.* Washington, DC: U.S. Law Enforcement Assistance Administration.

Clinard, M., & Yeager, P. (1980). *Corporate crime.* New York: Free Press.

Cohen, M. (1992a). Criminal penalties. In T. H. Tietenberg (Ed.), *Innovation in environmental policy: Economic and legal aspects of recent developments in environmental enforcement and liability* (pp. 75-108). Aldershot, UK: Edward Elgar.

Cohen, M. (1992b). Environmental crime and punishment: Legal/economic theory and empirical evidence on enforcement of federal environmental statutes. *Journal of Criminal Law and Criminology, 82*(4), 1054-1108.

Coleman, J. (1994). *The criminal elite: The sociology of white-collar crime.* New York: St. Martin's.

Commoner, B. (1990). *Making peace with the planet.* New York: Pantheon.

Conklin, J. (1977). *Illegal but not criminal: Business crime in America.* Englewood Cliffs, NJ: Prentice Hall.

Corporate Crime Reporter. (1989, August). (Vol. 3, p. 16).

Couch, S., & Kroll-Smith, S. J. (1985). The chronic technical disaster: Toward a social scientific perspective. *Social Science Quarterly, 66,* 564-575.

Council on Environmental Quality. (1981). *Environmental quality.* Washington, DC: Government Printing Office.

Crawford, C. (1994). Large corporations are serious polluters. In C. Cozic (Ed.), *Pollution* (pp. 73-78). San Diego, CA: Greenhaven.

Cressey, D. (1969). *Theft of the nation.* New York: Harper & Row.

Cressey, D. (1989). Poverty of theory in corporate crime research. *Advances in Criminological Theory, 1,* 31-55.

Crotty, P. M. (1987). The new federalism game: Primacy implementation of environmental policy. *Publius: The Journal of Federalism, 17,* 53-67.

Curtis, D., & Walsh, B. (1991). *Environmental quality: 22nd annual report.* Washington, DC: Government Printing Office.

Dan, C. (1990). Pressure builds in nuclear waste tank. *New Scientist, 128,* 30.

Davis, C. E., & Lester, J. P. (1989). Federalism and environmental policy. In J. Lester (Ed.), *Environmental politics and policy: Theories and evidence* (pp. 57-84). Durham, NC: Duke University Press.

Day, D. (1989). *The environmental war.* New York: Ballantine.

DeBonis, J. (1991). The Forest Service inside out. *Wildlife Conservation, 94*(3), 88-89.

DeCicco, J., & Bonanno, E. (1988). A comparative analysis of the criminal environmental laws of the fifty states: The need for statutory uniformity as a catalyst for effective enforcement of existing and proposed laws. *Criminal Justice Quarterly, 9*(4), 216-233.

Demonds, R. L. (1994). *Patterns of China's lost harmony: A survey of the country's environmental degradation and protection.* New York: Routledge.

DiMento, J. F. (1993, January). Criminal enforcement of environmental law. *Annals of the American Association of Political and Social Sciences, 525,* 134-136.

DiSilvestro, R. L. (1991). There is an environmental crisis. In N. Bernards (Ed.), *The environmental crisis: Opposing viewpoints* (pp. 17-24). San Diego, CA: Greenhaven.

Doerr, B. H. (1985). Prosecuting corporate polluters: The sparing use of criminal sanctions. *University of Detroit Law Review, 62,* 659-676.

Douglas, J., & Johnson, J. M. (Eds.). (1977). *Official deviance.* Philadelphia: J. B. Lippincott.

Dowie, M., & Mother Jones. (1987). The dumping of hazardous products on foreign markets. In S. Hills (Ed.), *Corporate violence: Injury and death for profit* (pp. 47-58). Savage, MD: Rowman & Littlefield.

Doyle, K. (1993). Cleaning up federal facilities: Controversy over an environmental peace dividend. *Environment Reporter, 23*(47), 2659-2669.

Dump site toxic chemicals carried in storm sewers. (1976, November 4). *Niagara Gazette,* p. 1.

Dunlap, R. E. (1989). Public opinion and environmental policy. In J. Lester (Ed.), *Environmental politics and policy: Theories and evidence* (pp. 87-134). Durham, NC: Duke University Press.

Dunlap, R. E., & Dillman, D. A. (1976). Decline in public support for environmental protection: Evidence from a 1970-74 panel study. *Rural Sociology, 41,* 382-390.

Dunlap, R. E., & Van Liere, K. (1978). The new environmental paradigm. *Journal of Environmental Education, 9,* 10-19.

Duval, N. M. (1992). Towards fair and effective environmental enforcement: Coordinating investigations and information exchange in proceedings. *Harvard Environmental Law Review, 16,* 535-573.

Earth First. (1992a). Can the USFS be reformed? *Radical Environmental Journal, 7*(5), 1.

Earth First. (1992b). Land of many abuses: A citizen's guide to the US Forest Service. *Radical Environmental Journal, 7*(5), 2.

Easterbrook, F. H., & Fischel, D. R. (1985). Limited liability and the corporation. *University of Chicago Law Review, 52,* 89-117.

Edelstein, M. R. (1988). *Contaminated communities: The social and psychological impacts of residential toxic exposure.* Denver, CO: Westview.

Edwards, S. M. (1996). Environmental criminal enforcement: Efforts by the states. In S. Edwards, T. Edwards, & C. Fields (Eds.), *Environmental crime and criminality: Theoretical and practical issues* (pp. 205-244). New York: Garland.

Elsom, D. (1987). *Atmospheric pollution.* New York: Basil Blackwell.

Epstein, J., & Hammett, T. M. (1995, January). *Law enforcement response to environmental crime.* Washington, DC: National Institute of Justice.

Epstein, S. S., Brown, L. O., & Pope, C. (1982). *Hazardous waste in America.* San Francisco: Sierra Club Books.

Erickson, J. (1992). *World out of balance: Our polluted planet.* Blue Ridge Summit, PA: TAB Books.

Erickson, K. (1976). *Everything in its path.* New York: Simon & Schuster.

European Environmental Bureau. (1989). Managing hazardous wastes: The unmet challenge. In *Toxic terror: Dumping of hazardous wastes in the Third World* (pp. 126-128). Geneva, Switzerland: Third World Network.

Everest, L. (1988). *Behind the poison cloud: Union Carbide's Bhopal massacre.* Chicago: Banner.

Falk, R. (1988). The special challenge of our time: Cultural norms relating to nuclearism. In A. Westing (Ed.), *Cultural norms, war and the environment* (pp. 53-63). New York: Oxford University Press.

Farrell, R., & Swigert, V. (1985). The corporation in criminology: New direction for research. *Journal of Research in Crime and Delinquency, 22,* 83-94.

Finger, M. (1991). The military, the nation state and the environment. *The Ecologist, 21*(5), 220-225.

Finkle, J. L., & Crane, B. B. (1985, March). Ideology and politics at Mexico City: The United States at the 1984 International Conference on Population. *Population and Development Review, 11,* 1-28.

Finney, J. W. (1974, February, 22). Vietnam defoliants study sees effect of 100 years. *New York Times,* pp. A1, A4.

Fishlock, D. (1994). The dirtiest place on earth. *New Scientist, 141,* 34-37.

Flavin, C. (1991). The heat is on. In L. R. Brown (Ed.), *The Worldwatch reader on global environmental issues* (pp. 75-96). New York: Norton.

Forest Service stops whistle blowers. (1992). *Environment, 34*(8), 23-24.

Frank, N. (1987). Murder in the workplace. In S. Hills (Ed.), *Corporate violence: Injury and death for profit* (pp. 103-105). Savage, MD: Rowman & Littlefield.

Frank, N. (1993, January). Maiming and killing: Occupational health crimes. *Annals of the American Academy of Political and Social Science, 525,* 107-118.

Frank, N., & Lynch, M. (1992). *Corporate crime, corporate violence: A primer.* Albany, NY: Harrow & Heston.

French, H. F. (1990). *Changing the air: A global agenda.* Washington, DC: Worldwatch Institute.

French, H. F. (1991). You are what you breathe. In L. R. Brown (Ed.), *The Worldwatch reader on global environmental issues* (pp. 97-111). New York: Norton.

Friedrichs, D. O. (1995a). State crime or governmental crime: Making sense of the conceptual confusion. In J. I. Ross (Ed.), *Controlling state crime: An introduction* (pp. 53-80). New York: Garland.

Friedrichs, D. O. (1995b). *Trusted criminals: White collar crime in contemporary society.* Belmont, CA: Wadsworth.

Fromm, E. M. (1990). Commanding respect: Criminal sanctions for environmental crimes. *St. Mary's Law Journal, 21,* 821-863.

Gabor, T. (1994). *Everybody does it! Crime by the public.* Toronto, Ontario, Canada: University of Toronto Press.

Gallagher, C. (1993). *American ground zero: The secret nuclear war.* Cambridge: MIT Press.

Gates, D. F., & Pearson, B. J. (1991). Hazardous materials: Incident response training for law enforcement. *Police Chief, 9,* 15-18.

Gaynor, K. A., Remer, J. C, & Martman, T. R. (1992). Environmental criminal prosecution: Simple fixes for a flawed system. *Villanova Environmental Law Journal, 3*(1), 1-31.

Geis, G. (1979). Avocational crime. In D. Glaser (Ed.), *Handbook of criminology* (pp. 272-298). New York: Rand McNally.

Geis, G., & Meier, R. (1977). *White collar crime: The offenses in business, politics and the professions.* New York: Free Press.

Gerber, M. (1992). *On the home front: The Cold War legacy of the Hanford Nuclear Site.* Lincoln: University of Nebraska Press.

Gibbons, D. C. (1983). Mundane crime. *Crime & Delinquency, 29,* 213-238.

Gibbs, L. M. (1982). *Love Canal: My story.* Albany: State University of New York Press.

Gillroy, J. M., & Shapiro, R. Y. (1986). The polls: Environmental protection. *Public Opinion Quarterly, 50,* 270-279.

Glick, H. R. (1988). *Courts, politics, and justice* (2nd ed.). New York: McGraw-Hill.

Goewey, D. W. (1987). Assuring federal facility compliance with RCRA and other environmental statutes: An administrative proposal. *William & Mary Law Review, 28,* 513-552.

Gore, A. (1993). *Earth in the balance: Ecology and the human spirit.* New York: Plume.

Gough, M. (1986). *Dioxin, Agent Orange: The facts.* New York: Plenum.

Gould, R. (1985). *Going sour: Science and politics of acid rain.* Cambridge, MA: Birkhauster Boston.

Gourlay, K. A. (1992). *World of waste: Dilemmas of industrial development.* Atlantic Highlands, NJ: Zed Books.

Green, M. (1972). *The closed enterprise system.* New York: Grossman.

Green, M., & Berry, J. (1985). White collar crime is big business: Corporate crime: I. *The Nation, 6,* 240.

Greenpeace International. (1988). International trade in toxic wastes: Policy and data analysis. *Third World Quarterly, 9,* 39-52.

Gross, E. (1978). Organized crime: A theoretical perspective. In N. Denzin (Ed.), *Studies in symbolic interaction* (pp. 55-85). Greenwich, CT: JAI.

Gross, E. (1980). Organizational structure and organizational crime. In G. Geis & E. Stotland (Eds.), *White collar crime: Theories and research* (pp. 52-67). Beverly Hills, CA: Sage.

Grossman, J. B., & Grossman, M. H. (Eds.). (1971). Introduction. In *Law and change in modern America* (pp. 1-10). Pacific Palisades, CA: Goodyear.

Haas, P. M. (1990). *Saving the Mediterranean: The politics of international environmental cooperation.* New York: Columbia University Press.

Habicht, H. F. (1987). The federal perspective on environmental criminal enforcement: How to remain on the civil side. *Environmental Law Reporter, 17*(12), 10478-10485.

Hagan, F. (1983). The organized crime continuum: A further specification of a new conceptual model. *Criminal Justice Review, 8,* 52-57.

Hagan, F. (1994). *Introduction to criminology.* Chicago: Nelson-Hall.

Hall, R. H. (1982). *Organizations: Structure and process* (3rd ed.). Englewood Cliffs, NJ: Prentice Hall.

Hammett, T., & Epstein, J. (1993a). *Local prosecution of environmental crime.* Washington, DC: National Institute of Justice.

Hammett, T., & Epstein, J. (1993b, August). *Prosecuting environmental crime: Los Angeles County* (Program focus). Washington, DC: National Institute of Justice.

Hammitt, J. K., & Reuter, P. (1988). *Measuring and deterring illegal disposal of hazardous waste: A preliminary assessment.* Santa Monica, CA: RAND.

Hardin, G. (1974, October). Living on a lifeboat. *Bioscience, 24,* 561-568.

Harig, L. A. (1992). Ignorance is not bliss: Responsible corporate officers convicted of environmental crimes and the federal sentencing guidelines. *Duke Law Journal, 42,* 145-165.

Harris, C., Cavanaugh, P., & Zisk, R. (1988). Criminal liability for violations of federal hazardous waste law: The "knowledge" of corporations and their executives. *Wake Forest Law Review, 23*(2), 203-236.

Haskell, E., & Price, V. S. (1973). *State environmental management: Case studies of nine states.* New York: Praeger.

Hawes, A., & Chu, F. Y. (1987, October). Proximate cause in toxic-tort cases: There are many steps to proving chemically induced illnesses. *Trial, 23,* 68-72.

Hedman, S. (1991). Expressive functions of criminal sanctions in environmental law. *George Washington Law Review, 59*(4), 889-899.

Henry, S. (1991). The informal economy: A crime of omission. In G. Barak (Ed.), *Crimes by the capitalist state: An introduction to state criminality* (pp. 253-272). Albany: State University of New York Press.

Heritage Foundation. (1991). Government intervention cannot protect the environment. In N. Bernards (Ed.), *The environmental crisis: Opposing viewpoints* (pp. 239-245). San Diego, CA: Greenhaven.

Herm, S. (1991). Criminal enforcement of environmental laws on federal facilities. *George Washington Law Review, 59*(4), 938-967.

Hippard, J. J. (1973). The unconstitutionality of criminal liability without fault: An argument for a constitutional doctrine of mens rea. *Houston Law Review, 10,* 1039-1058.

Hirschhorn, J. (1988). Cutting production of hazardous waste. *Technology Review, 91*(3), 52-61.

Hirschi, T. (1969). *Causes of delinquency.* Berkeley: University of California Press.

Hoban, T. M. (1987). *Green justice: The environment and the courts.* Boulder, CO: Westview.

Holdgate, M. W. (1979). *A perspective on environmental pollution.* Cambridge, UK: Cambridge University Press.

Hornblower, M. (1980, February 25). US firms export products banned here as health risks. *Washington Post,* pp. A1, A16.

Hoyle, R. (1993). *Gale environmental almanac.* Detroit, MI: Gale Research.

Howells, G. (1990). *Acid rain and acid waters.* New York: Ellis & Howard.

Hutchins, P. (1991). *Environmental criminal statistics FY83 through FY90* [Internal memorandum]. Washington, DC: U.S. Department of Justice, Environmental Crimes Section.

Hynes, P. H. (1989). *The recurring silent spring.* New York: Pergamon.

Ianni, F. (1973). *Ethnic succession in organized crime.* Washington, DC: Government Printing Office.

Jackall, R. (1988). *Moral mazes.* New York: Oxford University Press.

Jacob, H. (1984). *Justice in America: Courts, lawyers and judicial process* (4th ed.). Boston: Little, Brown.

Jamieson, K. (1994). *The organization of corporate crime: Dynamics of antitrust violation.* Thousand Oaks, CA: Sage.

Janis, I. (1971). *Stress and frustration.* New York: Harcourt, Brace & Jovanovich.

Jessup, D. H. (1990). *Guide to state environmental programs* (2nd ed.). Washington, DC: Bureau of National Affairs.

Johnson, C. J. (1988, December 18). Rocky Flats: Death Inc. *New York Times,* p. A3.

Johnstone, L. C. (1971). Ecocide and the Geneva protocol. *Foreign Affairs, 49,* 711-720.

Judge halts all clearcutting on Texas National Forest. (1993). *Save America's Forests, 4*(2), 1.

Kadish, S. H. (1968). Some observations on the use of criminal sanctions in enforcing economic regulations. In G. Geis (Ed.), *White collar criminal: The offender in business and the professions* (pp. 388-409). New York: Atherton.

Kane, L. S. (1991). How can we stop corporate environmental pollution: Corporate officer liability. *New England Law Review, 26,* 293-317.

Karplus, W. J. (1992). *The heavens are falling: The scientific prediction of catastrophes in our time.* New York: American Interface Corporation.

Kauzlarich, D., & Kramer, R. C. (1993). State-corporate crime in the US nuclear weapons production complex. *Journal of Human Justice, 5*(1), 4-28.

Kelly, B. C. (1981). Kepone. In R. Nader, R. Brownstein, & J. Richard (Eds.), *Who's poisoning America: Corporate polluters and their victims* (pp. 85-127). San Francisco: Sierra Club Books.

Kemp, D. (1990). *Global environmental issues: A criminological approach.* London: Routledge.

Kiss, A. (1992). The implications of global change for the international legal system. In E. B. Weiss (Ed.), *Environmental change and international law: New challenges and dimensions* (pp. 313-339). Tokyo: United Nations Press.

Koppen, I. J. (1988). *The European Community's environmental policy* (European University Institute Working Paper No. 88/328). Florence, Italy: European University Institute.

Kraft, M. E., & Vig, N. J. (1990). Environmental policy from the seventies to the nineties: Continuity and change. In N. J. Vig & M. E. Kraft (Eds.), *Environmental policy in the 1990s* (pp. 3-32). Washington, DC: Congressional Quarterly.

Kramer, R. C., & Michalowski, R. J. (1990, November). *State-corporate crime.* Paper presented at the annual meeting of the American Society of Criminology, Baltimore.

Kuruc, M. (1985). Putting polluters in jail: The imposition of criminal sanctions on corporate defendants under environmental statutes. *Land and Water Review, 20,* 98-108.

Kurzman, D. (1987). *A killing wind.* New York: McGraw-Hill.

LaBastille, A. (1986, May-June). The international acid test. *Sierra, 8,* 51-52.

Ladd, E., & Bowman, K. (1995). *Attitudes toward the environment: Twenty-five years after Earth Day.* Washington, DC: AEI.

Lamperti, J. (1984). Government and the atom. In J. Dennis (Ed.), *The nuclear almanac: Confronting the atom in war and peace* (pp. 67-70). Reading, MA: Addison-Wesley.

Lawrence, D., & Wynne, B. (1989). Transporting waste in the European Community: A free market? *Environment, 30*(6), 14.

Lazarus, R. (1994). Assimilating environmental protection into legal rules and the problem with environmental crime. *Loyola of Los Angeles Law Review, 27,* 867-891.

LeBlanc, M., & Frechett, M. (1989). *Male criminal activity from childhood through youth: Multilevel and developmental perspectives.* New York: Springer-Verlag.

Lee, R. (1993). Comprehensive environmental response, compensation, and liability act. In G. Arbuckle et al. (Eds.), *Environmental law handbook* (pp. 267-320). Rockville, MD: Government Institutes.

Leonard, A. (1994). The plastic industry pollutes Third World countries. In C. Cozic (Ed.), *Pollution* (pp. 85-91). San Diego, CA: Greenhaven.

Levenson, L. L. (1993). Good faith defenses: Reshaping strict liability crimes. *Cornell Law Review, 78,* 401-469.

Lewis, J. (1985). The birth of EPA. *EPA Journal, 11*(9), 4-5.

Liberatore, A., & Lewanski, R. (1990). The evolution of Italian environmental policy. *Environment, 32*(5), 2.

Locke, R. C. (1991). Environmental crimes: The absence of intent and the complexities of compliance. *Columbia Journal of Environmental Law, 16,* 311-331.

Lowry, W. (1992). *The dimensions of federalism: State governments and pollution control policies.* Durham, NC: Duke University Press.

Lynch, M. J. (1990). The greening of criminology: A perspective on the 1990s. *Criminologist, 2*(30), 11-12.

Maioli, T. M., & Staub, M. A. (1988). The utilization of traditional investigative methods in the investigation of hazardous waste crimes. *Federal Environmental Enforcement Journal, 4,* 4-7.

Maltz, M. (1985). Toward defining organized crime. *Crime & Delinquency, 22,* 338-346.

Managing hazardous wastes produced by small quantity generators. (1987). Division of Environmental Studies, University of California, Davis, in cooperation with Senate Office of Research. Davis, CA: Author.

Marino, R. J. (1982). *Case history of a toxic waste dumper: The manipulation of the state department of environmental conservation and the consequences of non-enforcement: New York State Senate Report.* Albany: New York State Senate.

Marshall, C. (1987). An excuse for workplace hazards. *The Nation, 25,* 532.

Marzulla, R. J., & Kappel, G. (1991). Nowhere to turn, nowhere to hide: Criminal liability for violations of environmental statutes in the 1990s. *Columbia Journal of Environmental Law, 16,* 201-225.

Marzulla, R. J., & Roistacher, C. H. (1990). Parallel civil and criminal proceedings: Environmental double exposure? *White-Collar Crime Reporter, 4*(3), 1-10.

Matulewich, V. A. (1991, April). Environmental crimes prosecution: A law enforcement partnership. *FBI Law Enforcement Bulletin, 60,* 20-25.

McCarthy, J. E., & Reisch, M. E. A. (1987, January). *Hazardous waste fact book.* Washington, DC: Congressional Research Service.

McCormick, J. (1985). *Acid earth: The global threat of acid pollution.* Washington, DC: International Institute for Environment and Development.

McKenna, S. (1993). The environment, crime and the police. *Police Journal, 66*(1), 95-103.

McKibben, G. (1992, April 22). Is jail in the future for corporate polluters? *Boston Globe,* p. A1.

McLoughlin, J., & Bellinger, E. G. (1993). *Environmental pollution control: An introduction of principles and the practice of administration.* London: Graham & Trotman/Marinus Nijhoff.

McMurray, R. I., & Ramsey, S. D. (1986). Environmental crime: The use of criminal sanctions in enforcing environmental laws. *Loyola of Los Angeles Law Review, 19,* 2233-2269.

Meier, B. (1985, January 7). Dirty job: Against heavy odds, EPA tries to convict polluters and dumpers. *Wall Street Journal,* pp. 1, 18.

Merton, R. (1938). Social structure and anomie. *American Sociological Review, 3,* 672-682.

Miller, M. (1993). Federal regulation of pesticides. In G. Arbuckle et al. (Eds.), *Environmental law handbook* (pp. 412-453). Rockville, MD: Government Institutes.

Miller, T. G. (1992). *Living in the environment: An introduction to environmental science* (7th ed.). Belmont, CA: Wadsworth.

Milne, R. A. (1988-1989). The mens rea requirements of the federal environmental statutes: Strict criminal liability in substance but not form. *Buffalo Law Review, 37*(1), 307-336.

Minister, M. K. (1994). Federal facilities and the deterrence failure of environmental laws: The case for criminal prosecution of federal employees. *Harvard Environmental Law Review, 18,* 137-183.

Mitchell, R. C. (1980). Public opinion on environmental issues. In Council on Environmental Quality (Ed.), *11th annual report of the CEQ* (pp. 7-15). Washington, DC: Government Printing Office.

Mokhiber, R., & Shen, L. (1981). Love Canal. In R. Nader, R. Brownstein, & J. Richard (Eds.), *Who's poisoning America: Corporate polluters and their victims in the chemical age* (pp. 268-310). San Francisco: Sierra Club Books.

Molina, L. F. (1995). Can states commit crimes? The limits of formal international law. In J. I. Ross (Ed.), *Controlling state crime: An introduction* (pp. 349-418). New York: Garland.

Montgomery, P. L. (1991, September 26). Heavy energy tax is proposed to curb emissions in Europe. *New York Times,* p. A6.

Moore, J. W. (1986). *The changing environment.* New York: Springer-Verlag.

Morton, J. (1990). The truth about the cancer epidemic. *Against the Current, 5*(3), 19-23.

Mueller, G. O. (1996). An essay on environmental criminality. In S. Edwards, T. Edwards, & C. Fields (Eds.), *Environmental crime and criminality: Theoretical and practical issues* (pp. 3-34). New York: Garland.

Mumford, L. (1963). *Techniques and civilization.* New York: Harcourt, Brace and World.

Mustokoff, M. (1981). *Hazardous waste violations: A guide to their detection, investigation and prosecution.* Washington, DC: U.S. Department of Justice.

Nader, R. (1965). *Unsafe at any speed: The designed-in dangers of the American automobiles.* New York: Grossman.

Nader, R. (1973). *The consumer and corporate accountability.* New York: Harcourt Brace Jovanovich.

National Academy of Sciences. (1987). *Safety issues at the defense production reactors: A report to the Department of Energy.* Washington, DC: National Academy Press.

National Advisory Committee on Oceans and Atmosphere. (1984). *Nuclear waste management and use of the sea.* Washington, DC: Government Printing Office.

National Institute of Justice. (1994). *Environmental crime prosecution: Results of a national survey.* Washington, DC: Government Printing Office.

Needleman, M. L., & Needleman, C. (1979). Organizational crime: Two models of criminogenesis. *Sociological Quarterly, 20,* 517-528.

Nelkin, D., & Brown, M. S. (1984). *Workers at risk: Voices from the workplace.* Chicago: University of Chicago Press.

Nettler, G. (1982). *Lying, cheating, and stealing.* Cincinnati, OH: Anderson.

New Jersey Superior Court. (1980). *State of New Jersey v. Duane Marine Salvage Corporation* [Indictment No. 71-80-4].

Newton, L., & Dillingham, C. (1994). *Watersheds: Classic cases in environmental ethics.* Belmont, CA: Wadsworth.

New York State Senate Select Committee on Crime. (1980, July 8). *In the matter of a public hearing on organized crime and toxic waste,* 96th Cong., 2d Sess. (testimony of John Fine).

Nittoly, P. G. (1989). Current trends in the prosecution of environmental offenses. *Toxic Law Reporter, 3*(34), 1032-1039.

Nittoly, P. G. (1991). Environmental criminal cases: The dawn of a new era. *Seton Hall Law Review, 21,* 1125-1152.

Nixon, R. (1992). *The local prosecution of environmental crime.* Washington, DC: American Prosecutors Research Institute.

No evidence on toxic residues—NCHD. (1977, May 3). *Niagara Gazette,* p. 3.

Norberry, J. (1993). Australia. In A. Alvazzi del Frate & J. Norberry (Eds.), *Environmental crime, sanctioning strategies and sustainable development* (pp. 27-103). Rome: Canberra.

Null, G. (1990). *Clearer, cleaner, safer, greener.* New York: Villard.

O'Brien, M. A. (1991, April). The environmental protection forum. *FBI Law Enforcement Bulletin, 60,* 9-13.

Orme, T. (1992, Summer). Superfund: Is it bulldozing our public health dollars? *Priorities for Long Life & Good Health, 21,* 6-9.

Park, C. (1987). *Acid rain: Rhetoric and reality.* New York: Methuen.

Pearce, F. (1992). Will Britain fail the acid test? *New Scientist, 136,* 11.

Pearce, F., & Caufield, C. (1981). Toxic wastes: The political connections. *New Scientist, 90,* 408-410.

Pearsall, J. D. (1994). *Local agency criminal environmental investigations: A place to start.* Palm Beach County, FL: Environmental Crimes Investigations.

People's Republic of China National Environmental Protection Agency and State Planning Commission. (1994). *National environmental action plan 1991-2000.* Beijing, China: NEPA.

Perez-Pena, R. (1993, September 21). Landfill operators charged in dumping scheme. *New York Times,* p. B6.

Petrakis, G. J. (1992). *The new face of organized crime.* Dubuque, IA: Kendall/Hunt.

Petulla, J. (1987). *Environmental protection in the US: Industry, agencies, and environmentalists.* San Francisco: San Francisco Study Center.

Plater, Z., Abrams, R., & Goldfarb, W. (1992). *Environmental law and policy: Nature, law, and society.* St. Paul, MN: West.

Police Practice. (1991, April). CHP's hazardous waste investigative unit. *FBI Law Enforcement Bulletin, 60,* 12-13.

Polinsky, A. M., & Shavell, S. (1993). Should employees be subject to fines and imprisonment given the existence of corporate liability? *International Review of Law and Economics, 13*(3), 239-258.

Pollock, M. S. (1992). Local prosecution of environmental crime. *Environmental Law, 22*(4), 1405-1411.

Pope, V. (1992, April 13). Poisoning Russia's river of plenty. *U.S. News & World Report, 112,* 49-51.

Porter, G., & Brown, J. W. (1991). *Global environmental politics.* Boulder, CO: Westview.

Posner, R. A. (1977). *Economic analysis of law* (2nd ed.). Boston: Little, Brown.

Posner, R. A. (1980). Retribution and related concepts of punishment. *Journal of Legal Studies, 9*(1), 71-92.

Pugh, D. S. (1984). The measurement of organization structures: Does context determine form? In D. Pugh (Ed.), *Organizational theory* (2nd ed., pp. 67-86). New York: Penguin.

Rapp, D. (1990). Special report. *Congressional Quarterly, 1,* 20-35.

Raucher, S. (1992). Raising the stakes for environmental polluters: The Exxon Valdez criminal prosecution. *Ecology Law Quarterly, 19*(1), 146-185.

Rebhan, H. (1980, March 6). Labor battles hazard export. *Multinational Monitor, 1,* 6-7.

Rebovich, D. (1986). *Understanding hazardous waste crime: A multistate examination of offense and offender characteristics in the Northeast.* Washington, DC: Northeast Hazardous Waste Project.

Rebovich, D. (1992). *Dangerous ground: The world of hazardous waste crime.* New Brunswick, NJ: Transaction Publishing.

Rebovich, D. (1996). Prosecutorial decision making and the environmental prosecutor: Reaching a crossroads for public protection. In S. Edwards, T. Edwards, & C. Fields (Eds.), *Environmental crime and criminality: Theoretical and practical issues* (pp. 77-98). New York: Garland.

Regenstein, L. (1982). *America the poisoned.* Washington, DC: Acropolis.

Reicher, D. W., & Scher, S. J. (1988, January-February). Laying waste to the environment. *Bulletin of the Atomic Scientists, 44,* 29-31.

Reiman, J. (1979). *The rich get richer and the poor get prison: Ideology, class, and criminal justice.* New York: Free Press.

Renner, M. (1980). The health costs of pollution. *Current, 5,* 2-3.

Riesel, D. (1985). Criminal prosecution and defense of environmental wrongs. *Environmental Law Reporter, 15*(3), 10065-10081.

Ringquist, E. (1993). *Environmental protection at the state level: Politics and program in controlling pollution.* Armonk, NY: M. E. Sharpe.

Robinson, D. F. (1990, November-December). 1990 EPA: New era for the nation's forests? *American Forests, 46.*

Rosenbaum, W. A. (1991). *Environmental politics and policy* (2nd ed.). Washington, DC: Congressional Quarterly.

Rosenbaum, W. A. (1994). The clenched fist and the open hand: Into the 1990s at EPA. In N. J. Vig & M. E. Kraft (Eds.), *Environmental policy in the 1990s: Toward a new agenda* (2nd ed., pp. 121-143). Washington, DC: Congressional Quarterly.

Ross, D. (1996). A review of EPA criminal, civil, and administrative enforcement data: Are the efforts measurable deterrents to environmental criminals? In S. Edwards, T. Edwards, & C. Fields (Eds.), *Environmental crime and criminality: Theoretical and practical issues* (pp. 55-75). New York: Garland.

Ross, J. I. (Ed.). (1995). *Controlling state crime: An introduction.* New York: Garland.

Ross, L. H. (1961). Traffic law violations: A folk crime. *Social Problems, 8,* 231-241.

Ross, L. H. (1983). Folk crime revisited. *Criminology, 11*(1), 71-85.

Russell, L., & Meiorin, Z. (1985). *The disposal of hazardous waste by small quantity generators: Magnitude of the problem.* Oakland, CA: Association of Bay Area Governments.

Ryan, M., & Flavin, C. (1995). Facing China's limits. In *State of the world: A Worldwatch Institute report on progress toward a sustainable society* (pp. 113-131). New York: Norton.

Ryan, W. (1971). *Blaming the victim.* New York: Vintage.

Saltzman, A. (1978). Strict criminal reliability and the United States Constitution: Substantive criminal law due process. *Wayne Law Review, 24*(5), 1571-1640.

Sanders, G. (1991, May-June). No friends to the fir. *Sierra, 13,* 36-39.

Sarokin, D. J., Muir, W. R., Miller, C. G., & Sperber, S. (1985). *Cutting chemical wastes: What 29 organic chemical plants are doing to reduce hazardous wastes.* New York: Inform.

Savas, E. S. (1977). *The organization and efficiency of solid waste collection.* Lexington, MA: D. C. Heath.

Scarpitti, F., & Block, A. (1987). America's toxic waste racket: Dimensions of the environmental crisis. In T. Bynum (Ed.), *Organized crime in America: Concepts and controversies* (pp. 115-128). New York: Criminal Justice Press.

Schmalleger, F. (1995). *Criminal justice today: An introductory text for the 21st century.* Englewood Cliffs, NJ: Prentice Hall.

Schnaiberg, A., & Gould, K. (1994). *Environment and society: The enduring conflict.* New York: St. Martin's.

Schoenbaum, T. J., & Rosenberg, R. H. (1991). *Environmental policy law: Problems, cases, and readings* (2nd ed.). Westbury, NY: Foundation Press.

Scholz, J. T. (1984). Cooperation, deterrence, and the ecology of regulatory enforcement. *Law and Society Review, 18*(2), 179-224.

Schuck, P. H. (1987). *Agent Orange on trial.* Cambridge, MA: Belknap.

Scott, R. W. (1975). Organizational structure. *Annual Review of Sociology, 1,* 1-20.

Segerson, K., & Tietenberg, T. H. (1992). Defining efficient sanctions. In T. H. Tietenberg (Ed.), *Innovation in environmental policy: Economic and legal aspects of recent developments in environmental enforcement and liability* (pp. 53-73). Aldershot, UK: Edward Elgar.

Selmi, D. P. (1986). Enforcing environmental laws: A look at the state civil penalty statutes. *Loyola of Los Angeles Law Review, 19,* 1279-1340.

Seymour, J. F. (1989). Civil and criminal liability of corporate officers under federal environmental laws. *Environmental Reporter, 20*(6), 337-348.

Shapiro, S. (1976, February). *A background paper on white collar crime.* Paper presented at the faculty seminar on white collar crime, Yale Law School, New Haven, CN.

Sharkansky, I. (1995). A state action may be nasty but is not likely to be a crime. In J. I. Ross (Ed.), *Controlling state crime: An introduction* (pp. 35-52). New York: Garland.

Shearer, R. H. (1993). Comparative analysis of the Basel and Bamako conventions on hazardous waste. *Environmental Law, 23*(1), 141-167.

Shover, N., & Bryant, K. (1993). Theoretical explanations of corporate crime. In M. Blankenship (Ed.), *Understanding corporate criminality* (pp. 141-176). New York: Garland.

Shulman, S. (1992). *The threat at home: Confronting the toxic legacy of the U.S. military.* Boston: Beacon.

Silverman, M., Lee, P., & Lydecker, M. (1982). *Prescription for death: The drugging of the Third World.* Berkeley: University of California Press.

Simon, D. R., & Eitzen, D. S. (1993). *Elite deviance* (4th ed.). Boston: Allyn & Bacon.

Sinton, J. E. (1992). *China energy data book.* Berkeley, CA: Lawrence Berkeley Laboratory.

Situ, Y. (1997). *Public transgression of environmental law: A preliminary study.* Unpublished manuscript.

Sloan, T. (1993). *Ciba-Geigy: Toms River Chemical.* Unpublished manuscript.

Smith, D. C. (1980). Paragons, pariahs and pirates: A spectrum-based theory of enterprise. *Crime & Delinquency, 26*(3), 358-386.

Snider, L. (1993). *Bad business: Corporate crime in Canada.* Toronto, Ontario: Nelson Canada.

Soros, M. S. (1994). From Stockholm to Rio: The evolution of global environmental governance. In N. J. Vig & M. E. Kraft (Eds.), *Environmental policy in the 1990s: Toward a new agenda* (2nd ed., pp. 299-322). Washington, DC: Congressional Quarterly.

Speer, R. D., & Bullanowski, G. A. (1984). *Speer's digest of toxic substances state law: 1983-84.* Boulder, CO: Strategic Assessments.

Starheim, F. J., & Steen, D. W. (1989). Acid rain: Public policy and environmental protection. In D. McKee (Ed.), *Energy, the environment, and public policy: Issues for the 1990s* (pp. 89-102). New York: Praeger.

Starr, J. W. (1986). Countering environmental crimes. *Environmental Affairs, 13,* 379-395.

Starr, J. W. (1991). Turbulent times at Justice and EPA: The origins of environmental criminal prosecutions and the work that remains. *George Washington Law Review, 59*(4), 900-915.

Starr, J. W., & Kelly, T. J. (1990). Environmental crimes and the sentencing guidelines: The time has come . . . and it is hard time. *Environmental Law Reporter, 20*(3), 10096-10104.

Steele, K. D. (1989, October). Hanford: America's nuclear graveyard. *Bulletin of the Atomic Scientists, 45,* 15-19.

Steinberg, M. W. (1990). Can EPA sue other federal agencies? *Ecology Law Quarterly, 17*(2), 317-325.

Stever, D. W. (1987). Perspectives on the problem of federal facility liability for environmental contamination. *Environmental Law Reporter, 17*(4), 10114-10128.

Stewart, R. (1991, January 8). [Address]. Presented at the 1991 Environmental Law Enforcement Conference, New Orleans, LA.

Stone, C. D. (1987). A slap on the wrist for the Capone mob. In S. Hills (Ed.), *Corporate violence: Injury and death for profit* (pp. 121-132). Savage, MD: Rowman & Littlefield.

Stretton, H. (1976). *Capitalism, socialism and the environment.* Cambridge, UK: Cambridge University Press.

Strock, J. (1991). Environmental criminal enforcement priorities for the 1990s. *George Washington Law Review, 59*(4), 916-937.

Sullivan, T. (1993). Basics of environmental law. In G. Arbuckle et al. (Eds.), *Environmental law handbook* (pp. 1-41). Rockville, MD: Government Institutes.

Sutherland, E. (1940, February). White collar criminality. *American Sociological Review, 5,* 1-12.

Sutherland, E. (1949). *White-collar crime.* New York: Holt, Rinehart & Winston.

Sutherland, E. (1973). Development of the theory. In K. Schuessler (Ed.), *On analyzing crime* (pp. 13-29). Chicago: University of Chicago Press.

Swaigen, J. (1981). *Environmental rights in Canada.* Toronto, Ontario, Canada: Butterworths.

Switzer, J. V. (1994). *Environmental politics: Domestic and global dimensions.* New York: St. Martin's.

Sykes, G., & Matza, D. (1957). Techniques of neutralization: A theory of delinquency. *American Sociological Review, 22,* 667-670.

Szasz, A. (1986). Corporations, organized crime, and the disposal of hazardous waste: An examination of the making of a criminogenic regulatory structure. *Criminology, 24*(1), 1-27.

Tallmer, M. (1987). Chemical dumping as a way of corporate life. In S. Hills (Ed.), *Corporate violence: Injury and death for profit* (pp. 111-120). Savage, MD: Rowman & Littlefield.

Thompson, J. (1991, June). Eastern Europe's dark dawn. *National Geographic, 148,* 36-68.

Thornburgh, D. (1991). Criminal enforcement of environmental laws: A national priority. *George Washington Law Review, 59*(4), 775-780.

Tietenberg, T. H. (Ed.). (1992). *Innovation in environmental policy: Economic and legal aspects of recent developments in environmental enforcement and liability.* Aldershot, UK: Edward Elgar.

Tracy, P. E., Wolfgang, M. E., & Figlio, R. M. (1990). *Delinquency careers in two birth cohorts.* New York: Plenum.

Tyler, P. (1994, September 22). China planning people's car to put masses behind wheel. *New York Times,* p. A1.

United Nations Environmental Program and the World Health Organization. (1988). *Assessment of urban air quality.* Nairobi, Kenya: Global Environmental Monitoring System.

United Nations General Assembly. (1976). *Resolution adopted by the General Assembly: Convention on the prohibition of military and any other hostile use of environmental modification techniques* (A/RES/31/72).

U.S. Arms Control and Disarmament Agency. (1990). *Arms control and disarmament agreements: Texts and histories of the negotiations.* Washington, DC: Author.

U.S. Bureau of the Census. (1992). *Statistical abstract of the United States.* Washington, DC: Government Printing Office.

U.S. Congress. (1988). *Nuclear health and safety: Summary of major problems at DOE's Rocky Flats plants.* Washington, DC: Government Printing Office.

U.S. Congress, Senate Committee on Foreign Relations. (1978). *Environmental modification treaty: Hearing before the Committee of Foreign Relations,* 95th Cong., 2d Sess. Washington, DC: Government Printing Office.

U.S. Congress, Senate Subcommittee of the Committee on Governmental Affairs. (1985). *Hearing on the management and operations of the U.S. Department of Energy's Fernald, Ohio, Feed Materials Production Center,* 99th Cong., 1st Sess. Washington, DC: Government Printing Office.

U.S. Department of Agriculture. (1992). Counting false forests? *Environment, 34,* 21.

U.S. Department of Justice. (1987). Guidelines for civil and criminal parallel proceedings. *Environmental Law Reporter, 18*(11), 35153-35161.

U.S. Department of Justice. (1991). *Factors in decisions on criminal prosecutions for environmental violations in the context of significant voluntary compliance or disclosure efforts by the violator.* Washington, DC: Governmental Printing Office.

U.S. Department of Justice. (1993). *Statistical report: Fiscal year 1993, Environmental and Natural Resources Division.* Washington, DC: Government Printing Office.

U.S. Department of the Army. (1971). *Tactical employment of herbicides*. Washington, DC: Government Printing Office.

U.S. Environmental Protection Agency. (1982). *Proposed national priorities list: As provided for in section 105 (8) (13) of CERCLA*. Washington, DC: Author.

U.S. Environmental Protection Agency. (1984). *Environmental Protection Agency civil penalty policy*. Washington, DC: Government Printing Office.

U.S. Environmental Protection Agency. (1985a). *Functions and general operating procedures for the criminal enforcement program*. Washington, DC: Government Printing Office.

U.S. Environmental Protection Agency. (1985b). *Study of literature concerning the roles of penalties in regulatory enforcement*. Washington, DC: Government Printing Office.

U.S. Environmental Protection Agency. (1990). *Environmental criminal enforcement: A law enforcement officer's guide*. Washington, DC: Author.

U.S. Environmental Protection Agency. (1992). *Enforcement accomplishment report fiscal year 1991*. Washington, DC: Government Printing Office.

U.S. Environmental Protection Agency. (1994). *Introduction to environmental law enforcement: A guide for local law enforcement*. Washington, DC: Northeast Environmental Enforcement Project.

U.S. Environmental Protection Agency, Office of Solid Waste and Emergency Response. (1990). *The nation's hazardous waste management program at crossroads: The RCRA implementation study*. Washington, DC: Author.

U.S. General Accounting Office. (1986). *Nuclear energy: Environmental issues at DOE's nuclear defense facilities*. Washington, DC: Government Printing Office.

U.S. House of Representatives. (1979). *Involuntary exposure to Agent Orange and other toxic spraying: Hearing before the Subcommittee on Oversight and Investigations*, 96th Cong., 1st Sess. Washington, DC: Government Printing Office.

U.S. House of Representatives. (1980). *Organized crime and hazardous waste disposal: Hearings before the Subcommittee on Oversight and Investigations, Committee on Interstate and Foreign Commerce*, 96th Cong., 2d Sess. Washington, DC: Government Printing Office.

U.S. House of Representatives. (1981a). *Hazardous waste matters: A case study of landfill sites: Hearing before the Subcommittee on Oversight and Investigations, Committee on Energy and Commerce*, 97th Cong., 1st Sess. Washington, DC: Government Printing Office.

U.S. House of Representatives. (1981b). *Organized crime links to the waste disposal industry: Hearing before the Subcommittee on Oversight and Investigations, Committee on Energy and Commerce*, 97th Cong., 1st Sess. Washington, DC: Government Printing Office.

U.S. House of Representatives. (1990). *Sentencing guidelines for organizational defendants: Hearing before the State Sentencing Commission*, 101st Cong., 2d Sess. Washington, DC: Government Printing Office.

U.S. National Advisory Committee on Criminal Justice Standards and Goals. (1976). *Organized crime: Report of the Task Force on Organized Crime*. Washington, DC: Government Printing Office.

U.S. Senate. (1974). *Pesticide oversight: Hearing before Subcommittee on the Environment*, 93rd Cong., 2d Sess. Washington, DC: Government Printing Office.

U.S. Senate, Select Committee on Improper Activities in the Labor or Management Field. (1957). *Investigation of improper activities in the labor or management field*. Washington, DC: Government Printing Office.

U.S. Sentencing Commission. (1990). *Guidelines manual*. Washington, DC: Government Printing Office.

Vago, S. (1994). *Law and society* (4th ed.). Englewood Cliffs, NJ: Prentice Hall.

Vaughn, D. (1982). Toward an understanding of unlawful organizational behavior. *Michigan Law Review, 80,* 1377-1402.

Vaughn, D. (1983). *Controlling unlawful organizational behavior: Social structure and corporate misconduct.* Chicago: University of Chicago Press.

Vogel, D. (1990). Environmental policy in Europe and Japan. In N. J. Vig & M. E. Kraft (Eds.), *Environmental policy in the 1990s: Toward a new agenda* (pp. 266-287). Washington, DC: Congressional Quarterly.

Volk, K. (1977). Criminological problems of white collar crime. In *International summaries* (Vol. 4, pp. 13-21). Rockville, MD: National Criminal Justice References Service.

Weidel, R. A., Mayo, J. R., & Zachara, F. M. (1991). The erosion of mens rea in environmental criminal prosecutions. *Seton Hall University School of Law, 21,* 1100-1124.

Weir, D. (1987). *The Bhopal syndrome.* San Francisco: Sierra Club Books.

Weir, D., & Schapiro, M. (1981). *Circles of poison: Pesticides and people in a hungry world.* San Francisco: Institute for Food Development and Policy.

Weiss, E. B. (Ed.). (1992). *Environmental change and international law: New challenges and dimensions.* Tokyo: United Nations Press.

Whelan, E. (1985). *Toxic terror: The truth about the cancer scare.* Ottawa, IL: Jameson.

Wilcox, F. (1983). *Waiting for an army to die.* New York: Vintage.

Wilson, J. D. (1986). Re-thinking penalties for corporate environmental offenders: A view of the law reform commission of Canada's sentencing in environmental cases. *McGill Law Journal, 30,* 315-332.

Wood, B. D. (1991). Federalism and policy responsiveness: The clean air case. *Journal of Politics, 53*(3), 851-859.

Wright, M., & Imfeld, W. (1991, April). Environmental crimes: Investigative basics. *FBI Law Enforcement Bulletin, 60,* 2-5.

Yeager, P. (1992). *The limits of law: The public regulation of private pollution.* New York: Press Syndicate of the University of Cambridge.

Yochelson, S., & Samenow, S. E. (1976). *The criminal personality.* New York: Jason Aronson.

Zhou, D. (1992). Environmental considerations in the economic development of China. *Arizona Journal of International and Comparative Laws, 9,* 221-225.

Zilinskas, R. A. (1995). Preventing state crimes against the environment during military operations: The 1977 Environmental Modification Treaty. In J. I. Ross (Ed.), *Controlling state crime: An introduction* (pp. 235-281). New York: Garland.

Zou, J., & Zhang, M. (1993). China. In A. Alvazzi del Frate & J. Norberry (Eds.), *Environmental crime, sanctioning strategies and sustainable development* (pp. 275-308). Rome: Canberra.

Zuesse, E. (1981, February). Love Canal: The truth seeps out. *Reason, 12,* 16-33.

Court Cases

Berger v. New York, 388 U.S. 41 (1967).

Dow Chemical Company v. United States, 476 U.S. 227 (1986).

Florida v. Riley, 488 U.S. 445 (1989).

Katz v. United States, 389 U.S. 347 (1967).

Ohio v. Budd Co., 67 Ohio App.2d 23, 425 N.E.2d 935 (1980).

United States v. Britain, 931 F.2d 1413 (10th Cir. 1990).

United States v. Dee, 912 F.2d 741 (4th Cir. 1990).

United States v. Dunn, 480 U.S. 294 (1987).

United States v. Frezzo Brothers, Inc., 602 F.2d 1123 (3rd Cir. 1970).

United States v. International Minerals and Chemical Corporation, 402 U.S. 558 (1971).

United States v. MacDonald and Watson Waste Oil Co., 933 F.2d 35 (1st Cir. 1991).

United States v. Northeastern Pharmaceutical and Chemical Corporation, 810 F.2d 726 (8th Cir. 1986).

United States v. Pacific Hide and Fur Depot, Inc., 532 F.2d 687 (1986).

United States v. Park, 421 U.S. 658 (1975).

United States v. Ward, 676 F.2d 94, 17 ERC 1577, CA4 (1982).

U.S. Department of Energy v. Ohio, 503 U.S. 607 (1992).

Statutes

Atomic Energy Act, 42 U.S.C. § 2011 *et seq.* (1954).

Clean Air Act, 42 U.S.C. § 7401 *et seq.* (1970), amended 1977, 1989, 1990.

Clean Water Act, 33 U.S.C. §§ 1251-1376 (1972), amended 1977, 1978.

Coastal Zone Management Act, 16 U.S.C. §§ 1451-1464 (1972).

Comprehensive Environmental Response, Compensation, and Liability Act, 26 U.S.C. §§ 4611-4682 (1980).

Comprehensive Environmental Response, Compensation, and Liability Act (Superfund), 26 U.S.C. § 9507 *et seq.* (1986).

Criminal Fine Improvements Act, 28 U.S.C. § 604 (1987).

Drug Abuse Prevention, Treatment, and Rehabilitation Act, 21 U.S.C. § 1101 *et seq.* (1972).

Emergency Planning and Community Right-to-Know Act, 42 U.S.C. §§ 11001-11050 (1986).

Endangered Species Act, 16 U.S.C. § 1531 *et seq.* (1973).

Federal Environmental Pesticide Control Act, 7 U.S.C. § 136 *et seq.* (1972).

Federal Insecticide, Fungicide, and Rodenticide Act, 61 U.S.C. § 163 (1947), amended 1972, 1975, 1978, 1980, 1988.

Federal Land Policy and Management Act, 43 U.S.C. § 1701 (1976).

Federal Tort Claims Act, 28 U.S.C. § 1291 *et seq.* (1946).

Federal Water Pollution Control Act, 33 U.S.C. § 1301 *et seq.* (1972).

Harrison Act, 36 Stat. 785, c. 1 (1914).

Insecticide Act, 7 U.S.C. §§ 121-134 (1910).

Marijuana Tax Act, 50 Stat. 551, c. 553 (1937).

Marine Protection, Research, and Sanctuaries Act, 33 U.S.C. § 1401-1445 (1972).

National Environmental Policy Act, 42 U.S.C. §§ 4321-4347 (1969).

National Forest Management Act, 16 U.S.C. §§ 1600-1614 (1976).

Oil Pollution Act, 33 U.S.C. § 2701 *et seq.* (1990).

Pollution Prevention Act, 42 U.S.C. § 13101 (1990).

Public Utility Regulatory Policies Act, 16 U.S.C. § 2601 (1978).

Radiation Exposure Compensation Act, 31 U.S.C. § 3139 *et seq.* (1990).

Refuse Act, 33 U.S.C. § 407 (1899).

Resource Conservation and Recovery Act, 42 U.S.C. § 6901 *et seq.* (1976), amended 1980, 1984.

Resource Recovery Act, 42 U.S.C. § 3251 (1970).

Safe Drinking Water Act, 42 U.S.C. § 300f *et seq.,* 639b; 15 U.S.C. § 1261 *et seq.* (1974).

Sentencing Reform Act, 18 U.S.C. § 3551 (1984).

Surface Mining Control and Reclamation Act, 30 U.S.C. § 1201 (1977).

Toxic Substances Control Act, 15 U.S.C. §§ 2602-2671 (1976).

Index

Africa, 178, 180, 186
Agent Orange, 90-91
    See also Dioxin; Wartime environmental
        damage
Air pollution:
    acid rain, 8, 49
    carbon monoxide emissions, 6
    cost, 8-9
    death and illness from, 7
    emission control devices, 5
    global, 178-179
    greenhouse effect, 23
    other sources, 23
    See also Clean Air Act
Allied Chemical Corporation, 54, 61, 63, 66
    See also Kepone
Antarctica, 178, 183
Arctic, 183
Arizona, 151
Australia, 178, 188-189, 192
Asarco, Inc., 57
Atomic Energy Act of 1954, 97

Basel Convention, 186
    See also Environmental control in other nations
Berger v. New York (1967), 137
Bhopal disaster (India), 58
    See also Union Carbide Corporation
Borjohn Optical Technology, Inc., 154
Brazil, 192

Cairo Guidelines of 1985, 186
    See also Environmental control in other nations
California, 5-6, 40, 48, 51-52, 88, 142-145, 151
Canada, 180, 182-183
Carson, R., 1
Chrysler Corporation, 54

Ciba-Geigy Corporation, 62
China, 178-179, 189-192
Civil sanctions:
    discussion of, 38-39
    weakness of, 23-24
    See also Criminal sanctions
Clean Air Act (1970):
    civil sanctions in, 38
    cost, 8
    criminal sanctions in , 12, 31-32, 34-37, 124
    impact of, 25
    in general, 23
    National Ambient Quality Standards
        (NAAQS), 25
    provisions of, 6, 25, 33-37, 97, 99-100
    violators of, 31-32, 34, 36-37
    workload created by, 109
Clean Water Act (1972):
    criminal sanctions in , 12, 107, 124
    provisions of, 26, 97, 99
    violators in, 157, 160, 174
    weak enforcement of, 99-100
    See also Federal Water Pollution Control Act
        (1972)
Coastal Zone Management Act (1972), 23
Colorado, 88, 93
Comprehensive Environmental Response,
        Compensation, and Liability Act
        (CERCLA):
    criminal sanctions in, 12, 36, 107
    criticism of, 29
    in general, 23
    National Priorities List, 87, 98
    provisions of, 12, 28-29, 36, 98
    Superfund features in, 8, 29, 100, 109
    Reagan's restrictions on, 107-108
Convention on Long-Range Transboundary Air
        Pollution (1979), 186
    See also Environmental control in other nations

Corporate environmental crime, general, 45-59
    as corporate/white-collar crime, 45-46
    by relocated factories, 56-58
    critique of earlier definitions of, 45-46
    dangerous technology transfer as, 57-58
    definition of, 45-46
    developing world as site for, 55-59
    export of hazardous waste as, 55-56
    hazardous waste dumping as, 50-55
    workplace hazards as, 53-55
Corporate environmental crime, explanation, 59-68
    anomie theory, 61
    corporate success as goal, 61-62
    crime-facilitative corporate culture, 63
    Frank, N., 59-60, 67
    integrative approach to, 59-60, 67
    law enforcement, capacity for, 65-67
    Lynch, M., 59-60, 67
    Merton, R., 60-61
    motivation, 60-62
    objective opportunity, 63-64
    opportunity, 62-65
    structural strain, 60-61
    subjective opportunity, 63-64
    summary, 67-68
    techniques of neutralization, 63
Costa Rica, 192
Council on Environmental Quality, 10
Cressey, D., 78-79
Crime definitions:
    drug sales and abuse, example of, 2
    labeling theory, 2
    murder, example of, 2
    social legalist perspective, 2-3
    strict legalist perspective, 2-3
    See also Sutherland, Edwin
Criminal enforcement at the federal level:
    civil enforcement, contrasted with, 124-125
    criminal sanctions, 125
    definition of, 123-124
    first efforts at, 12-13
    interagency cooperation, importance of, 125,
      129
    U.S. Department of Justice (DOJ), role in,
      124-126
    U.S. Environmental Protection Agency (EPA)
      role in, 124-126
    See also Criminal investigation; Criminal
      liability; Evidence, methods of obtaining
Criminal enforcement at the state level, 126-129
    attorney general's role in, 126

contributing factors to increased state role in,
    126
environmental crime task force, 126, 129
state police, role in criminal investigation,
    126-129
See also Criminal investigation; Evidence,
    methods of obtaining; Interagency
    cooperation
Criminal enforcement at the local level, 129-130
    environmental agency-based programs, 130
    police-based programs, 129
    prosecutor-based programs, 129
    See also, Criminal investigation; Evidence,
      methods of obtaining; Interagency
      cooperation
Criminal Fine Improvements Act (1987), 12
Criminal investigation, 130-140
    abnormal activity, as grounds for, 132
    detection of environmental crimes, sources for,
      131-132
    environmental investigation, training for,
      134-136
    indicators of environmental crime, 132-134
    Los Angeles Police Department (LAPD)
      approach to, 134-135
    mysterious moment, as grounds for, 133
    obstacles to, 130
    offensive odor, as grounds for, 133
    proactive investigation, 132-134
    reactive investigation 130-132
    search and seizure, 138-140
    short courses for training, 135-136
    training by regional environmental, 135
    unusual appearance, as grounds for, 133
    See also Evidence, methods of obtaining
Criminal law, 19-22
    civil law, differences with, 21-22
    procedural type, 19-20
    social control function, 20
    social engineering function, 20-21
    substantive type, 19
Criminal liability:
    corporate criminal liability, recent theories of,
      155-156
    corporate officers, liability of, 157
    culpability, objective criteria for, 167-168
    direct criminal liability, 160
    in general, 11, 15, 30, 37
    indirect criminal liability, 160-161
    individual criminal liability, 157-161
    inferred intent, 159
    inferred knowledge, 167

knowing violations, 158-159
limited corporate liability, doctrine of, 154
persons, liability of, 157
responsible corporate officer doctrine, 157-161, 167
state criminal liability, 192
strict liability, 16, 21-22, 43, 156-157, 167
Criminal prosecution at the federal level:
    civil or administrative prosecution, contrast with, 161-162
    modest role, explanation of, 149
    focus of, 148
    growth of, 147-148
    meager accomplishments of, 148-149
    U.S. Department of Justice, role in, 149-150, 162-163
    U.S. Environmental Protection Agency, 149-150, 162-163
    See also Criminal liability; Parallel proceedings; Prosecutorial discretion
Criminal prosecution at the state level, 150-152
    attorney general, responsibilities for, 150-152
    attorney general, variations in role, 151-152
    expanding role of, 150-151
    obstacles to, 151-152
    See also Criminal liability; Parallel proceedings; Prosecutorial discretion
Criminal prosecution at the local level, 152-154
    prosecutorial procedure, 153
    significance of, 152-153
    success, factors contributing to, 153-154
    See also Criminal liability; Parallel proceedings; Prosecutorial discretion
Criminal sanctions:
    civil and administrative sanctions, contrast with, 38-39
    community service, 172
    corporate probation, 171-172
    cost of, 174-175
    criticism of, 44
    definition of, 124, 171
    determinate sentence, 173
    efficient sanction, theory of, 175
    environmental laws with, 30
    federal sentencing guidelines, defects of, 174
    federal sentencing guidelines, impact of, 172-174
    increased emphasis on, 125
    imprisonment, 172
    parole, 173
    probation, 173-174
    Refuse At of 1899, 22

types, 171
Criminalization of environmental law, 1, 10-15, 43-44
Czechoslovakia, 180

Dangerous Ground: The World of Hazardous Waste Crime, 74-77
Deforestation, 94-96
    clear-cutting 94
    phantom trees, 95
    road construction, 95
    timber sales, underestimation of impact of, 95
    tree harvest, overestimation of, 95
    United States Forest Service, role in, 94-96
Dioxin, 90-91
    See also Agent Orange; Wartime environmental damage
Dow Chemical Company, 91
    See also Wartime environmental damage
Dow Chemical Company v. United States (1986), 139-140
Dupont Corporation, 49

Endangered Species Act (1973), 23
Emergency Planning and Community Right-to-Know Act (1986), 98
Environmental control in other nations, 184-191
    acid rain reduction, 186
    air quality, Eastern Europe, 185
    Australia, 188-189
    China, 189-191
    environmental protection, view of developing nations, 187
    environmental protection, view of industrialized nations, 186-187
    European Community, 184-185
    future of, 191-192
    Great Britain, 187-188
    marine protection, 185-186
    waste trading, 186. See also Hazardous waste disposal
Environmental crime:
    definition of, 3, 19
    endangerment, 33-34
    features of, 4
    knowing offenses, 31-32
    negligent violations, 32
    noncompliance with permits, self-reporting, inspection, and fees, 34-37
    types, by offender, 45
    types, under federal sentencing guidelines, 173

See also Corporate environmental crime;
  Governmental environmental crime;
  Organized environmental crime; Personal
  environmental crime
Environmental criminal law at the federal level,
  24-39
  common features of, 38
  criticism of, 43
  definition of, 24
  impact of, 30
  key federal laws, 24-30
  See also Criminal liability; Criminal sanctions;
    Mens rea; Specific laws
Environmental criminal law at the state level:
  discretion, in using, 40
  growth and diversity of, 39-40
  role of the states in, 14-15
  rule of preemption, 40
  states with no criminal sanctions for air
    pollution, 41
  variations in, 41-42
  variations in, influences on, 42
Environmental crisis, global, 177-181
  air pollution. 178-179
  general description of, 177-178
  global warming, 178
Environmental crisis, United States:
  air pollution, 6-7
  economic impact of, 8-9
  extent of, 4-7
  first serious threat, 1-2
  history of, 1-2
  human impact of, 7-8
  national view of, 2
  pollution violations, 5
  public opinion about, -11
  social and psychological impact of, 9
  hazardous waste, 5
Environmental Enforcement Council, 13
Environmental movement:
  and environmental law, development of,
    22-24
  disillusionment in the 80s of, 23-24
  Earth Day, 10
  Sierra Club, 10
  onset and growth, 1, 10-11
European Economic Community, 181
Evidence, methods of obtaining:
  exclusionary rule, 16-17
  grand jury, 138
  search and seizure, 138-140
  search and seizure, alternatives to, 16

surveillance, 136-137
surreptitious monitoring, 137
undercover operations, 138
Exxon Valdez disaster, 50, 155

Federal Bureau of Investigation (FBI):
  general, 12-13
  White Collar Crime Section, 126
Federal Land Policy and Management Act (1976),
  23
Federal Law Enforcement Training Center, 1125,
  128
Federal Pesticide Control Act (1972), 23
Federal Insecticide, Fungicide, and Rodenticide Act
    (FIFRA) (1947):
  criminal sanctions in, 31
  failure to enforce, 100-101
  provisions of, 27-28, 100-101
  violators, 31
Federal Torts Claim Act, (1946), 107
Federal Water Pollution Control Act (1972):
  civil sanctions in, 39
  criminal sanctions in, 31-32, 34-37
  provisions of, 26, 33-37
  violators, 34, 36
Federal weapons production facilities
  Fernald Feed Materials Production Center,
    93-94
  Hanford Nuclear Reservation, 92-93
  Rocky Flats Nuclear Reservation, 92-93
  private contractors, arrangements with,
    91-92
  United States Department of Energy (DOE),
    supervision of, 91-94, 97-98
  See also Governmental environmental crime,
    general; Hazardous waste; Hazardous
    waste disposal; United States Department
    of Energy
Film Recovery Systems, Inc., 54, 154
Finland, 181
Florida, 5, 51
Florida v. Riley (1989), 137

General Electric Company, 49, 51
General Motors Corporation, 48
Germany, 180
Governmental environmental crime, general
  at federal weapons production facilities, 91-94,
    97-98
  at military installations, 98, 102-103

by United States Department of Defense (DOD), 98-99
by United States Department of Energy (DOE), 91-94, 97-98
by United States Environmental Protection Agency (EPA), 99-103
crimes of commission, 85-96
crimes of omission, 85, 96-105
definition of, 83-85
deforestation, 94-96
hazardous waste disposal by the military, 87-88
international law, covered in, 84-85. *See also* International law
nuclear testing by Atomic Energy Commission (AEC), 86-87
social legalist approach, 83-85
strict legalist approach, 83-84
state crime, contrast with, 85
wartime military operations, 89-91
Governmental environmental crime, explanation, 105-111
arbitrary and demanding deadlines, 111
bureaucratic pluralism, 110
Cold War, impact of, 106
comprehensive theory, absence of, 105
defoliation in Viet Nam War, 106-107
depth of conviction, 106
excessive oversight, 110
federal supremacy, doctrine of, 108
fragmented authority, 111
goal attainment, 106
lack of clear and coherent mission, 110-111
legal doctrine, impact of, 107-109
limited resources, 109
overload, 109
shields against litigation, 107
sovereign immunity, doctrine of, 107
unitary executive, theory of, 1107-108
unsupportive legal doctrine, 107-110
weak capacity to enforce the law, 109-111
Great Britain, 186-188, 192

Haiti, 181
Hazardous waste:
at federal weapons production facilities, 92-94
extent of, 5, 50
in Jackson Township, New Jersey, 9
methods of treatment, 50-51
radioactive waste, 92
small quantity generators (SQGs), 5
See also Comprehensive Environmental Response, Compensation, and Liability Act (1980); Evidence, methods of obtaining; Resource Conservation and Recovery Act (1976)
Hazardous waste disposal:
at Cornhusker Ammunition Plant, 99
at Fernald Feed Materials Production Center, 93
at Hanford Nuclear Reservation, 92-93
at Jefferson Proving Ground, 102-103
at Lakehurst Naval Air Engineering Center, 98
at Rocky Flats Nuclear Reservation, 93
by export, 55-56, 186
by Hooker Chemical and Plastics Company, 52-53
by organized crime, 70-77
by the military, 87-88, 97-99
global scope of, 181-182
in the ocean, 87-88
legacy of, 52
Superfund sites, 51
traditional crime, charging as, 39
Hirschi, T., 80-82
Hong Kong, 180
Hooker Chemical and Plastic Company:
case study of, 52-53
denial of responsibility, 63
See also Love Canal disaster; Hazardous waste disposal
Hungary, 179, 192

Illinois, 14
Indiana, 102-103, 150
India, 179, 182, 192
Indonesia, 182
Industrial pollution, 47-50
auto, as source of, 48
Industrial Revolution in England, 47-48
Industrial Revolution in United States, 47-48, 50
new products and materials, as source of, 48
pre-industrial pollution, contrasted with, 47
Intent. *See* Mens rea
Interagency cooperation, 140-145
Alameda model, 142-144
duties of regulatory agencies, 140-141
goals of, 143
importance of, 140-145
key regulatory actors in criminal enforcement, 140
Los Angeles model, 144-145

obstacles to, 142-143
Intercontract Corporation, 56
International law:
    and wartime environmental damage, 89
    basic principles of, 183-185
    brief history, 182-183
    environmental modification techniques, 89
    future of, 192
    growth of, 182-183
    prohibitions against governmental
        environmental crime, 84-85, 89
    shortcomings of, 184
    sources of, 183
    variety of, 183
    See also Governmental environmental crime
Israel, 192

Japan, 180

Katz v. United States (1967), 136-137
Kepone, 54, 61, 63, 66.
    See also Allied Chemical Corporation
Khian Sea incident, 55

Line Air Processing Company, 88
Lome Convention, 186
    See also Environmental control in other nations
London Dumping Convention, 185
    See also International law
Love Canal disaster:
    brief references to, 2, 8, 10-11, 23, 28, 50, 52,
        61, 63, 108-109
    government role in, 103-105
    Niagara Falls, 104
    Niagara County Health Department, 104, 111
    Niagara Falls Board of Education, 103-104, 111
    New York Department of Public Health, 105,
        111
    New York state government, 105

Malaysia, 182, 192
Manchester (England), 48
Maine, 77
Maquiladoros, 56
Marine Pollution Convention of 1973, 185
    See also International law
Marine Protection, Research and Sanctuaries Act
    (1972), 23, 38

Maryland, 77, 81-82, 151
Massachusetts, 88
Mens rea:
    abandonment in Refuse Act of 1899, 30, 166
    absence of, in strict liability, 156-157
    alarm over diminishing status of, 43
    and prosecutorial discretion, 16
    criticism of new standards for, 167
    definition of, 13-14, 154, 166
    erosion of, 13-15, 166
    general intent, 166-167
    knowing, as basis of, 156, 166-167
    knowledge requirement, contrast with, 31-32
    new alternatives to, 15
    specific intent, 166-167
Merton, R., 60-61, 78-79
Mexico, 56, 179, 182-183
Michigan, 49, 52

National Environmental Policy Act (1969), 10
National Forest Management Act (1976), 23, 96
Nebraska, 99
Nevada, 86
New Jersey, 5-7, 9, 40-42, 51, 73-77, 79-81, 88, 98,
    116-120, 151, 172
New York, 6, 40, 49, 52, 72-74
    See also Love Canal disaster
North Carolina, 150

Ohio, 93, 107, 156-157
Ohio v. Budd Co. (1980), 156-157
Oil Pollution Act of 1990, 36
Oklahoma, 160
Oregon, 49
Organized environmental crime, general, 69-77
    and hazardous waste disposal, 70-77
    Chemical Control Corporation of New Jersey
        case, 73-74
    Chester County, Pennsylvania case, 72-73
    continuum, 70, 77
    definition of, 69-70
    group crime, 74-77
    in New Jersey, 77
    infiltration of disposal industry, contributing
        factors, 70-71
    interfirm connections in group crime, 76-77
    Lucchese crime family case, 74
    Ramapo, New York case, 72-73
    small generating firms in group crime, 76
    tactics for infiltration, 71-73

treatment, storage, and disposal facilities
        (TSDs), 75, 77, 79-80
    two-track crime, 75
Organized environmental crime, explanation, 78-82
    anomie, 78
    cultural transmission, 79-80
    differential association, 78-79
    social control, 80-82

Parallel proceedings, 169-171
    definition of, 169
    federal reluctance to use, 171
    justification for, 169
    problems with, 170-171
    See also Criminal liability; Criminal
        prosecution at the federal level
Pennsylvania, 73-74, 77, 151, 181
Personal environmental crime, 1113-120
    avocational crime, 116
    definition of, 113-114
    folk crime, 115-116
    household crime, 114
    mundane crime, 116
    New Jersey, study of, 116-120
    recreational crime, 114-115
    Situ, Y., 116
    types of, 114-115
Pesticides:
    aldrin, 59
    DDT, 58-59
    circle of poison, 59
    leptophos, 59
    pesticide dumping, 58-59, 63
Philippines, 182
Poland, 180
Prosecutorial discretion:
    absence of clear guidelines, 163-164
    and justice, 43
    attitudinal obstacles to prosecution, 168-169
    criteria for decision to prosecute, 164-166
    factors affecting, 162-169
    lack of central review system, 163
    weak culpability, 166-168
    See also Criminal liability; Mens rea; Parallel
        proceedings
    Radiation Exposure Compensation Act (1990),
        87
    Reagan, Ronald, 10, 107-108
    Rebovich, D., 74-77
Public Utility Regulatory Policies Act (1978), 23

Refuse Act (1899):
    abandonment of mens rea, 30
    provisions of, 22, 29
    sanctions in, 22, 29-30
Regional Seas Program, 185
Resource Conservation and Recovery Act (RCRA)
        (1970):
    civil sanctions in, 38
    criminal sanctions in, 4, 12, 25, 31, 33-35
    in general, 23
    hazardous waste dumping, encouragement of, 53
    lax implementation of, 80, 101-102
    provisions of, 4, 11, 24, 33-35, 97, 99, 102
    state role in, 40
    violators, 5, 31, 33-34, 51, 158-159
    workload created by, 109
Rhode Island, 41
Rockwell International Corporation, 51, 53
Russia, 179-181

Safe Drinking Water Act (1974):
    criminal sanctions in, 31
    in general, 23
    provisions of, 27
Search and seizure. *See* Evidence, methods of
        obtaining
Sentencing Reform Act (1984), 12
Silent Spring, 1
Situ, Y., 116-120
South Korea, 182, 192
Special Arms Control Treaty (1977), 89
Stockholm Declaration of 1972, 183
    See also International law
Strict liability. *See* Criminal liability; Mens rea
Surface Mining Control and Reclamation Act
        (1977), 23
Sutherland, E., 3, 45-46, 78-79

Thailand, 182
Toxic Substances Control Act (1976):
    criminal sanctions in, 31, 36-37
    in general, 23
    New Use Rule, 25-26
    provision in, 25, 36-37
    violations, 26-27
    violators, 31, 36
    workload created by, 109
Toxic waste. *See* Hazardous waste
Trial Smelter Arbitration, 182
    See also International law

Union Carbide Corporation, 55, 58
United States Department of Defense (DOD), 98-99
    See also, governmental environmental crime,
        general
United States Department of Energy (DOE), 91-94,
        97-98
    See also Governmental environmental crime,
        general; Federal weapons production
        facilities
United States Department of Energy v. Ohio, 107
United States Department of Justice (DOJ):
    criminal enforcement by, 12-13, 124-126
    criminal prosecution by, 149-150
    Environmental Crime Unit, 12, 125
    Environmental Enforcement Section, 12, 125,
        163
    Parallel proceedings, view of, 171
    See also Criminal enforcement at the federal
        level, Criminal prosecution at the federal
        level
United States Environmental Protection Agency
        (EPA):
    chief purpose of, 99
    crimes of omission by, 99-103
    criminal enforcement by, 12-13, 124-126
    Criminal Enforcement Counsel Division, 125
    Criminal Investigations Division, 125
    criminal prosecution by, 149-150
    failure to enforce laws, 100-102
    lax enforcement against the military, 102-103
    National Enforcement Investigation Center, 149
    Office of Criminal Enforcement, 13, 102, 125
    Office of Solid Waste and Emergency
        Response, 5
    Office of Toxic Substances, 110
    parallel proceedings, view of, 171
    public's view of, 10
    role specified in environmental laws, 24-29
    undermined effectiveness of laws, 102
    weak capacity to enforce law, 109-111
    weak enforcement efforts, 99-100
    See also Criminal enforcement at the federal
        level; Criminal prosecution at the federal
        level; Governmental environmental crime,
        explanation
United States Forest Service, 94-96
    See also Deforestation; Governmental
        environmental crime, general
United States v. Britain (1990), 160
United States v. Dee (1990), 158
United States v. Dunn (1987), 137

United States v. Frezzo Brothers, Inc. (1970), 155,
    174
*United States v. International Minerals and
    Chemical Corporation* (1971), 156
*United States v. MacDonald and Watson Waste Oil
    Company* (1991), 159-160
*United States v. Northeastern Pharmaceutical and
    Chemical Corporation* (1986), 158-159
United States v. Park (1975), 161
USX, Inc., 55

Waste Export Management, Inc., 56
Wartime environmental damage, 89-91
    defoliation, 989
    dioxin, 90-91
    environmental modification techniques,
        prohibition of, 89
    extent of, 89-90
    ground cover, destruction of, 89
    Persian Gulf War, 91
    rainmaking, 89
    Viet Nam War, 89-90
See also Governmental environmental crime,
        general
Water pollution:
    acid rain, 180-181
    chlorination, 7
    global aspects, 179-180
    impact of, 7
    in Jackson Township, New Jersey, 9
    in nonpoint sources, 23
    lead, 7
    public water systems, contamination of, 6
    See also, Clean Water Act (1972); Federal
            Water Pollution Control Act (1972); Safe
            Drinking Water Act (1974)
West Point-Pepperell Company, 63
White-collar crime, 3, 45-46
Wisconsin, 40-41, 150
Workplace pollution:
    cases, 54-55
    cost, 9
    cotton dust, 63
    effects of, 7
    extent of, 53-54
    occupational health and safety laws, violation
        of, 54
    varieties, 54-55
    Velsicol Chemical Company, 63

About
the Authors

Yingyi Situ is Associate Professor of Criminal Justice at Richard Stockton State College of New Jersey. She received her doctorate in criminal justice from Indiana University of Pennsylvania. Her areas of specialization are environmental crime, comparative criminal justice systems, and research methods.

David Emmons is Associate Professor of Criminal Justice at Richard Stockton State College of New Jersey. He received his doctorate in sociology from the University of Chicago. His areas of special interest are criminal justice policy, criminal justice pedagogy, community organization, and violence.